The Occult, Witchcraft & Magic

The Occult, Witchcraft & Magic

AN ILLUSTRATED HISTORY

Christopher Dell

CONTENTS

Introduction

There is no culture on Earth that does not contain within it some form of magic. From the prehistoric shaman whose rituals were intended to ensure success in the hunt to the wizard fantasies of Harry Potter or Tolkien, the idea that there are unseen forces in the world – forces that, through esoteric, occult or arcane knowledge, can be harnessed and used for good or for ill – has proved irresistible.

The word 'occult' comes from the Latin *occultus*, meaning 'hidden'. The underlying assumption is that there is another, unseen world beyond that of day-to-day existence – with magic offering the possibility of connecting these two worlds. The means of connection are many and varied: rituals, charms, amulets, seances, necromancy, esoteric diagrams, symbols, potions, incantations, revelations, special words. And the rewards of successfully connecting with this hidden world are great: we can converse with the dead, win the affections of others, influence the direction of our lives, ward off illness, even understand the greater order of things.

The world of magic can also be the stuff of entertainment and instruction. Folk tales and myths around the globe are suffused with love spells, fantastical creatures, invisible forces, objects with hidden powers and coincidences that defy rational explanation. In ancient Greek mythology, Odysseus battles unearthly monsters and descends into the underworld, while in the Chinese story *The Journey to the West*, the protagonist, a monkey called Sun Wukong, carries a magical iron bar and encounters enchanted houses and landscapes. In *One Thousand and One Nights*, we discover a cave full of magical objects, while the tales of King Arthur revolve around magical swords, enchanted castles, sorcerers and strange spells. And at least since the time of the ancient Egyptians, humankind has enjoyed conjuring and sleights of hand – practices that have survived the advent of science undimmed.

As the lists above suggest, there are many types of magic. Alongside conjuring there is 'primitive' shamanistic magic, marked by its physicality, with incantations and dances performed in specific locations. Then there is the more 'sophisticated', intellectualized and refined Hermetic tradition. There is black magic, aimed at harm, and white magic, aimed at good. There is magic designed to have real-world impact – where sorcerers, witches,

A depiction of a magical ceremony from the 19th century. The caption underneath (not shown) reads: 'Such were the mystic rites, ceremonies and incantations used by the ancient Theurgists to burst asunder the bonds of natural order, and to obtain an awful intercourse with the World of Spirits.'

alchemists, cosmologists, shamans and astrologers use the occult world to effect physical change – and magic as a metaphor for self-growth. An example of the latter can be found in the so-called Western esoteric tradition. Founded in Hermetic and astrological thought, this tradition has itself been appropriated by many different groups and individuals – from Freemasons to alchemists – and has proved itself remarkably flexible and adaptable.

The Roman historian Pliny the Elder, writing in the first century AD, was one of the first to articulate magic's adaptability:

> That [magic] first originated in medicine, no one entertains a doubt … Then … it has added all the resources of religion … Last of all, to complete its universal sway, it has incorporated with itself the astrological art; there being no man who is not desirous to know his future destiny, or who is not ready to believe that this knowledge may with the greatest certainty be obtained, by observing the face of the heavens. The senses of men being thus enthralled by a three-fold bond, the art of magic has attained an influence so mighty, that at the present day even, it holds sway throughout a great part of the world, and rules the kings of kings in the East.

RELIGION AND MAGIC

A strict definition of magic might call it an attempt to shape the various aspects of one's life (environment, fortune, health, etc.) using methods that are not grounded in science, and which, typically, do not appeal to a deity. It is an attempt, in other words, to understand and influence the world through supernatural means, but without recourse to prayer or the intercession of a god. This last distinction is an important one, since it separates magic from religion (even if Pliny, writing in pagan times, saw them as fundamentally linked). And this is salient because, superficially, the behaviour associated with magic can have a religious nature. Ritual lies at the heart of magic, whether in terms of the incantations spoken, the instruments used, or the significance of the date and time of performance. However, while religion is exoteric (intended for the many), magic is esoteric (directed at the few).

Nevertheless, magic often goes hand in hand with religion, and magicians can be found in early Babylonian texts, the Bible, Judaism and Islam. Even in the earliest religions there is confusion around sorcerers – are they artists, scientists, priests, sages or imposters,

ABOVE An Eskimo shaman's mask from south Alaska, designed to transport the wearer to a different plane. OPPOSITE The alchemical traditions use strange, coded imagery and symbolism to pass on magical knowledge. In this picture, supposedly after Nicolas Flamel (see page 186), men seek the alchemical 'white' (mercury) – an allegory of the difficult alchemical process.

Talismans &
Magical Images
made from
The twenty eight Mansions
of
The Moon
&c. &c.

agents of God or of the Devil? The Greeks, Egyptians and Romans – living in a world in which the line between reality and fantasy, divine and mortal, was frequently blurred – embraced magic, whether in the form of conjuring tricks or powerful healing spells. Greek and late Roman mythology (living belief systems in their day) feature both magic and divine power. In ancient Egypt, prayer and magic are often indistinguishable.

Judaism has had a more ambiguous relationship with magic. Being a monotheistic religion, it was difficult for its practitioners to admit that there may be other sources of power in the universe. Yet the mystical side of Judaism has given us Kabbalah, the foundation of much Western magical thinking.

For Christianity and Islam, by contrast, magic was and remains a thing of great suspicion. Generally speaking, Christianity has always attempted to avoid the strange, but the Bible still makes reference to magic, albeit on the fringes. It is clear that while such forms of magic as necromancy – communication with the dead – are seen as possible (and attested to in the Bible), they are ungodly and taboo. Miracles that occur through the intervention of God or a saint are to be welcomed, but magic effected through other channels is to be feared.

One concept that has been used to distinguish magic from religion is that of *ex opere operato*, which translates as 'by virtue of the action'. Essentially, does the practitioner of a ritual expect the outcome to be the result of an intervening force or the power of the ritual itself? If the latter, then it's magic. At the time of the Reformation in Europe, in the mid-sixteenth century, Protestants accused Catholics of believing that the sacraments functioned on an *ex opere operato* basis – in other words, that Catholicism relied on 'magic' words and rituals, rather than the intercession of God.

THE POWER OF LANGUAGE

Given that the authority of most major religions is grounded in a holy text, it is interesting to note that there is also a close association between magic and writing. The word 'grimoire' – used to describe a book of spells – led to our modern word 'grammar', while the Egyptian

OPPOSITE *An 18th-century astrological diagram showing 'Talismans and magical images made from the twenty-eight Mansions of the Moon, etc. etc.'*
ABOVE *Raphael's 16th-century depiction of the vision of the Old Testament prophet Ezekiel, one of the inspirations for Jewish mysticism.*

god of magic, Thoth, was also the god of writing. This association is often found in societies in which the majority were illiterate and knowledge was hidden from the masses.

From the fourteenth century onwards, the possession of books of magic becomes a regular feature of prosecutions. In 1319 the Franciscan friar Bérnard Delicieux was sent to prison for owning a book of necromancy; a century later, no less a figure than Pope Benedict was accused of buying a similar book, in his case from Saracens – arcane knowledge from the exotic East. The inquisitors of the fourteenth century looked back to Acts of the Apostles, in which practitioners of magic in Ephesus (an ancient city on the south-west coast of modern-day Turkey) voluntarily bring their books to be burnt.

In one of history's ironies, however, the Middle Ages in Europe also saw the birth of a new interest in alchemy: the transformation of base materials into valuable ones, in apparent

contradiction of the laws of nature. This (sometimes allegorical) process led to an explosion of interest in the occult from the fifteenth century onwards, blossoming during the Renaissance, and in turn leading to Freemasonry and Rosicrucianism.

It would be difficult to consider any history of magic, particularly in the West, without discussing the *Hermetica*. This powerful group of esoteric writings, the origins of which can be traced back to Egypt between the second and fourth centuries AD, consists of a series of dialogues that almost always feature Hermes Trismegistus, or 'Hermes the Thrice-Great'. The dialogues themselves deal with the nature of divinity and the ordering of the universe, as well as touching on such subjects as alchemy. They are a corpus of 'revealed' knowledge – knowledge that is arcane and hidden from most. At their centre is the *Corpus Hermeticum*, a collection of texts translated into Latin from the Greek by Marsilio Ficino at the end of the fifteenth century.

As mentioned above, the Hermetic tradition feeds directly into the Western esoteric tradition, a collection of different schools of thought. According to the French scholar of Western esotericism Antoine Faivre, this tradition is defined by six key concepts:

✪ Correspondences: the idea that there are sympathetic bonds within the universe, as seen in the notion of macrocosm–microcosm, or the Hermetic saying 'As above, so below';
✪ Living Nature: that all of nature is part of a conscious order, and that everything shares a life force;

ABOVE *A magic carpet from* One Thousand and One Nights.
In Europe, magic was often associated with the 'exotic' Orient.
OPPOSITE *An Indian fortune-teller divines the future of a client.*

Der Handschuech aursvendig.

✪ Imagination and Mediations: that rituals, symbolic images and intermediary spirits can connect different worlds and levels of reality;

✪ Experience of Transmutation: that esoteric practice can transform the individual, principally in the sense of a spiritual transformation;

✪ Practice of Concordance: that all religions, beliefs, etc. stem from a single, original principle, and that understanding this principle will bring the various belief systems into closer alignment;

✪ Transmission: that occult knowledge is transmitted from master to adept, often by means of a process of initiation.

SCIENCE VERSUS MAGIC

In a sense, the history of magic is the history of credulity. In the Age of Enlightenment – coinciding with the seventeenth and eighteenth centuries – the occult branch of magic was challenged by a growing rationalism, and partially replaced by the lighter branch of stage magic, conjuring tricks and sleights of hand, all designed to delight. Magic looked to have been tamed and turned into a parlour amusement.

The influential anthropologist James George Frazer speculated that 'primitive' magic would grow naturally into religion before eventually evolving into science. The relationship between magic and science is a curious one. The ancient Mesopotamians and Egyptians believed that illness could be cured with spells; for them, magic was already both a science and an art. Sir Isaac Newton – no stranger to the occult – was perplexed by the apparent 'action at a distance' that he observed in gravity, assuming it to be in some way magical.

Newton was also fascinated by alchemy, a subject that many of his contemporaries found fascinating too. One such was Athanasius Kircher, a Jesuit priest who delighted in quasi-magical automata and such magical structures as the Temple of Solomon. Much later, the science-fiction writer Arthur C. Clarke would famously observe that 'Any sufficiently advanced technology is indistinguishable from magic.' For the notorious English

OPPOSITE *An image of a hand covered in Kabbalistic signs and sigils, from the 18th century.*
ABOVE *Goya's eerie and unsettling painting of witches in flight, created as the Enlightenment gave way to darker themes in the early 19th century.*

occultist Aleister Crowley, meanwhile, magic was 'the Science of understanding one's self and one's condition' – which brings us to a more contemporary understanding of the occult as being of benefit to the individual's development, rather than having an impact on the physical world. To quote Frazer on the matter, 'magic is always an art, never a science; the very idea of science is lacking in [the sorcerer's] undeveloped mind.'

The end of the Enlightenment also saw the rise of Romantic and Gothic sensibilities that unleashed a new fascination with necromancy, the numinous and the liminal. It also led to people asking where the impulse to do magic might stem from. Both Sigmund Freud and Carl Gustav Jung were interested in magic as a facet of the human psyche. Jung in

particular had a long interest in spirituality, and in 1944 published *Psychology and Alchemy*, which drew a parallel between alchemical symbols and psychoanalytic processes. In *The Red Book*, Jung's posthumously published observations on his own inner life, the Swiss psychologist claims that magic accords with unreason: it is not a rational impulse, but this does not make it unhelpful.

For his part, Freud – an occasional Jung collaborator – saw magical thinking as a form of psychosis, describing how practitioners of magic attempted to project their will on to the world. In his *Introductory Lectures on Psycho-Analysis* (1922), Freud claims that 'Words and magic were in the beginning one and the same thing, and even today words retain much of their magical power.'

THE INNER JOURNEY

Today, magic is frequently described as an 'inner journey', emphasizing psychological transformations over physical ones. The alchemy is one of the mind, a rising through layers of consciousness. Does magic *need* to have a physical impact? One train of thought within magic believes that its power lies not in bringing about external changes, but in effecting internal ones. Modern practitioners are as likely to refer to Jung as they are to the *Hermetica*, while their key tools include hypnosis, trance and scrying (using a crystal ball or other reflective object to tell the future). Magic can also be part of mankind's struggle against mortality, especially in the largely taboo area of necromancy – a practice that the mid-nineteenth-century Fox sisters claimed to be able to perform through their seances.

A fascination with the 'other', outside of 'self', is undoubtedly part of magic's appeal. As with monsters, magic is often seen as being even stronger in distant, little-understood

ABOVE *Sir Isaac Newton, renowned as a scientist, was also a passionate occultist who put together a large library of magic.*
OPPOSITE *'The Tree of the Soul', a diagram exploring how the physical and metaphysical worlds relate to each other.*

Fig. 2.

The TREE of the SOUL.

A. de Para d'Hermès

MAGIE CÉLESTE

CHIROMANCIE

SUCCÈS · GLOIRE

CHANGEMENT · DÉPLACEMENT

ÉCONOMIE · INTÉRIEURE

TRIOMPHE RENOMMÉE
5

TRAVAIL. BONNE CONDUITE

6

VI

IV

INDUSTRIE · COMMERCE

ACCORD · SYMPATHIE

MAIN DE SCIENCE

MAIN DE COMMANDEMENT

3
AFFAIRES

BONNE UNION DES CŒURS
1

CHIROMANCIE ASTROLOGIQUE & PHYSIOLOGIQUE.

MAIN DE GÉNIE

VII

POÈTE & ARTISTE

II

2
AMOUR

VIOLENCE · TRAHISON

III

MAIN DE COMMERCE

MAIN D'INDUSTRIE

MAIN VIOLENTE

JEU NOUVEAU DE BONNE AVENTURE
par les Mains

8
MÉCHANCETÉ

MAIN AIMANTE

I
COURAGE AUDACE

JUSTICE · DOMINATION
AUTORITÉ · DU POUVOIR

MAIN D'INCONSTANCE

V

9
LOI

I

POSITION · RICHESSE

FATALITÉ · DOMINATION
de la chance · ou du hasard

SAGESSE · DIRECTION
de Parents · de Vieillards
ou de gens · d'expérience

12
BIEN-ÊTRE

10
FORCE MAJEURE

11

CHIROMANCIE

places just out of reach. The ancient Greek historian Herodotus described in glorious detail the barbarous peoples who lived in such far-off places, while for Pliny, magic had been invented in Persia – on the very boundaries of the Roman Empire. In the fourteenth century, Crusaders brought occult texts (written in Greek, Egyptian and Hebrew) back to Europe from the Middle East, while it was Ficino's translation of arcane Greek texts into Latin that gave an impetus to Renaissance magic.

The nineteenth century saw a rebirth of occult magic in Europe and North America, manifesting itself in such groups as the Hermetic Order of the Golden Dawn. Looking at pictures of the order's members – who claimed to draw on ancient Egyptian rites – it is clear from their faintly preposterous garb that a large part of the appeal lay in the 'otherness'. Their approach was a combination of Kabbalah, Indian philosophy, Hermetic philosophy, Rosicrucianism, ritual magic from the Middle Ages and Renaissance, and alchemy.

This book takes a chronological approach to the exploration of magic. There are two reasons for this. First, almost all magic tends to look backwards, building on earlier traditions (even if those traditions were sometimes fabrications). In this sense, a chronological approach allows us to see more clearly how these different traditions relate to one another. Secondly, society's attitude to magic has changed significantly over time, often depending on the prevailing religion or philosophy of a particular culture. A chronological approach allows us properly to explore such changes.

However, woven into this chronological approach are various spreads that explore the cross-cultural ideas and trends – for example, alchemy, magical creatures, the influence of magic in literature, and the role of spells and incantations. This allows us to tie together the different strands of magic from around the globe. Completing the book is a series of biographies, interspersed throughout, of some of the key figures in the history of magic.

If James George Frazer – believing as he did that humankind would turn from magic to religion to science – were alive today, he would be disappointed. In an increasingly scientific and demystified world, magic is more popular than ever. A belief in magic seems to be a fundamental aspect of the human condition, and the idea that there are dimly understood forces in the world that, with the right knowledge, can be harnessed for good or evil is a pervasive one. From the earliest prehistoric rituals to the most spectacular contemporary conjuror, the cathartic rituals of Chaos magic or the modern witchcraft of Wicca, magic in all its forms keeps every culture hopeful, fearful and possibly even entertained.

A 'magical' game from 19th-century France, reflecting the growing popular interest in divination and the spiritual, as magic entered the mainstream.

I.
Ancient Magic

The biblical Witch of Endor, seated on an owl throne and surrounded by hellish creatures. She is visited by Saul, who wishes to converse with the dead prophet Samuel.

The earliest known evidence of magical thinking can be found in the cave paintings at such sites as Lascaux in south-west France. The connection between prehistoric cave paintings and magic was first suggested in 1865 by the English anthropologist Sir Edward Tylor, while the French archaeologist Abbé Breuil described the paintings as 'hunting magic', giving power over prey. The locations of these paintings are charged spaces, often difficult to get to, and so the images have been interpreted as providing connections to another, secret world. In this sense, they are signs of early shamanism (see page 245).

The most famous example of shamanistic cave art was discovered at the Trois Frères cave in Ariège, France. There, on the walls of a chamber in the deepest part of the cave, is a remarkable depiction of a 'sorcerer'. A human-like figure frozen in time, he turns to stare at us; his antlers and animalistic gait are unnerving. A similar figure can be found at Lascaux, and it is possible that they represent a kind of shaman in a state of trance.

The first written records of incantations and spells were created many millennia later, in ancient Sumer, one of several civilizations to flourish in Mesopotamia (modern-day Iraq) between the fourth and first millennia BC. The Sumerians developed one of the earliest systems of writing, and from around 2600 BC onwards produced written incantations. It appears that there was 'white' and 'black' magic in ancient Sumer, although the surviving incantations tend to be those approved by the temple. The Sumerian culture informed the Akkadian, Babylonian and Assyrian cultures that overtook it, and Babylonian incantations from 1900 BC onwards are more coherent.

The world of the ancient Babylonians was one filled with spirits and demons, constantly threatening humankind's well-being. In particular, it was believed that demons could cause illness; the female demon known as Lamashtu, for example, targeted pregnant women and babies. Long, complex incantations were deployed against such creatures, appealing to the gods for help, while surviving amulets of Lamashtu suggest that she could be warded off using her own likeness. Lamashtu's worst enemy was another demon, Pazuzu, who is also depicted in numerous apotropaic statuettes (believed to have the power to avert evil or bad luck).

Life in Mesopotamia was also marked by a constant threat of sorcery. One of the best-known anti-sorcery rituals from the period is recorded in the text of the Akkadian *Maqlû*

A painting of a horned shaman, or 'sorcerer', from the Trois Frères cave in France, created around 13,000 BC.

(or 'Burning') series. The other well-known Akkadian text for righting wrongs magically is *Šurpu* (which also translates as 'Burning'). Astrology originated in Mesopotamia, in the second millennium BC, and the ancient Babylonians were intensely superstitious, always on the lookout for omens. Curiously, simply to *witness* an omen – animals appearing in the city, moving statues – could in itself lead to bad luck.

The magical knowledge of the Babylonians – astrology and astronomy included – was passed on to the peoples of Egypt. There, the practice of divination, including the observation of planets, became enshrined in ritual. For the ancient Egyptians, the world was suffused with magic; in fact, it was made by magic. The magical force in question was called *heka*, and all living things had it within them.

In ancient Egypt, magic was conducted by priests, who often wielded a wand made of metal or ivory (over time, however, the practice of magic fell to more professional magicians called *hekau*). As in Mesopotamia, literacy in ancient Egypt was limited to the ruling classes, so for most people written spells were mysterious and unknowable. The spells themselves were cast at dawn, with the rising of the Sun.

One source of information on magic in ancient Egypt is the Westcar Papyrus, which dates from between the twentieth and sixteenth centuries BC. Held today by the Egyptian Museum of Berlin, it tells the story of King Cheops and the magicians, in which a fictitious magician, Dedi, is able to reattach the severed head of an animal. It is unclear, however, whether he is a conjuror – practising sleight of hand – or a genuine magician.

For the ancient Egyptians, knowledge came from Thoth, the god of magic. Thoth was the god not only of magic but also of science, writing and mathematics, and for this reason these disciplines remained closely bound together. Learning attributed to Thoth was distilled into the semi-fictional Book of Thoth, which was supposedly buried under the Nile and protected by a spell.

Egypt was eventually conquered by Alexander the Great, bringing to an end a remarkable civilization. However, the conquest also marked the beginning of a new, syncretic form of thought and religion that would be extremely significant for the future development of magic. In Hellenistic Egypt (fourth to first centuries BC), Thoth

*An ancient Egyptian carved amulet with inscriptions
intended to bring the bearer good luck.*

became conflated with the Greek god Hermes; indeed, the town previously associated with Thoth, Khmun, was renamed Hermopolis Magna. The exceptionally important Hermetic papyri, however – the *Hermetica* among them – date from much later, from the second to fourth centuries AD.

While most of the religions up to this point had been pantheistic, the birth of Judaism marked the ascent of monotheistic thought. This brought with it new challenges for a magical view of the world. One of the earliest mentions of magic in the Bible comes in Exodus 7, where Aaron is pitted against Egyptian magicians (see page 48). Most early mentions of magic in the Bible come in the form of prohibitions, such as those found in Exodus 22:18 ('Thou shalt not suffer a witch to live') and Deuteronomy 18:10–11:

> There shall not be found among you *any one* that maketh his son or his daughter to pass through the fire, *or* that useth divination, *or* an observer of times, or an enchanter, or a witch, or a charmer, or a consulter with familiar spirits, or a wizard, or a necromancer.

In fact, necromancy makes an appearance quite early on in the Bible, in 1 Samuel. Saul, seeking advice on how to defeat the Philistines, calls on God but receives no answer, either through dreams or by means of the Urim and Thummim (see page 50). So he asks his advisors to find him a medium, and they point him towards the Witch of Endor (also known as the Medium of Endor). She then summons up the spirit of the dead Samuel. Here, magic is used as an unorthodox tool, bypassing 'correct' communication with God. The ghost of Samuel berates Saul for disturbing him, and predicts the Israelites' defeat for disobeying God. And so it happens that, the following day, the Israelites are punished for their transgression.

ABOVE *A cippus (or small, low pillar) from ancient Egypt. Said to have magical properties, it depicts Horus controlling scorpions, snakes, an oryx and a lion, and was used to ward off dangerous animals.*
OPPOSITE *Scenes depicting an unknown magical ritual from a Bronze Age rock painting in Tanum, Sweden.*

Sheep's livers were examined in ancient Babylon to read the future. This curious clay representation of a liver covered in magical formulae may have been used as a training device.

MESOPOTAMIAN MAGIC

Covering an area between the rivers Tigris and Euphrates in modern-day Iraq, the ancient region of Mesopotamia was home to the Babylonian, Sumerian, Assyrian and Akkadian cultures. These civilizations also shared much of their mythology, and were the birthplace of astrology and writing.

The earliest incantations found in Mesopotamia deal with curing illness and warding off evil, but by 1500 BC they had expanded to include spells for securing love and winning wars. In a society in which magic and religion were so closely intertwined, it is interesting to ask whether magic was seen to happen through its own power, or through the intervention of the gods. Many incantations end with the refrain, 'The incantation is not mine', giving the power to the gods. Religion and magic were indivisible.

A depiction of a mysterious, magical figure — sometimes called the 'Queen of the Night' — from Babylon. With wings and talons, and flanked by owls, she is clearly a creature with a connection to the supernatural realm.

One of the Maqlû tablets from ancient Mesopotamia, explaining a long and complex anti-witchcraft ritual.

Perhaps the most famous surviving example of Mesopotamian magic is the *Maqlû*, a series of Akkadian anti-witchcraft incantations recorded on nine stone tablets. Performed in the summer months, the incantations involved the destruction of a figurine of the witch, first by burning, then drowning, then crushing. The following is an extract from Tablet V:

My witch and my sorceress is sitting in the
shadow behind a brick pile.
She is sitting there, practising witchcraft
against me, fashioning figurines of me.
I am going to dispatch against you thyme
and sesame,
I will scatter your sorceries, will stuff your
words back into your mouth!

May the witchcraft you performed be aimed
at yourself,
May the figurines you made represent
yourself,
May the water you drew be that of your own
body!
May your spell not close in on me, may your
words not overcome me.

Accusations of witchcraft, however, were rarely made, since they could lead to counter-accusations of witchcraft against the accuser. To test whether a person was a witch, the Babylonians employed a form of trial by water, with witches drowning and the innocent surviving.

*In this 19th-century engraving of a much older scene, a king apparently divines
the future in the presence of Assyrian gods and winged 'genies'.*

29

The Roman god of eternity, Aion, stands in a sphere decorated with zodiac signs, while the bare and leafy trees stand for summer and winter respectively. The four children possibly represent the four seasons.

ASTROLOGY & MAGIC

With the rotation of the stars, and the sense of staring into a distant heaven, it is easy to understand why humans have sought meaning in the skies since prehistoric times. Astrology as a practice arose in Mesopotamia in the early second millennium BC, but soon after can be found in China, Egypt and India, and then later in Greece, Rome and the Middle East.

Astrology, put simply, is the discipline of divining the future from celestial movements. It regards all celestial bodies, including the Earth, as being interconnected and capable of influencing one another.

The most common form of the discipline is 'sun sign' astrology, which looks at which of twelve constellations – Aries, Taurus, Gemini, and so on – the Sun was passing through at a particular time. Together, these constellations form the zodiac, or 'circle of animals'. The other important elements in astrology are the planets. In the classical system, there are seven: the Sun, the Moon, Mercury, Venus, Mars, Jupiter and Saturn.

Planisphere taken from the Temple of Tentyra.

London Published as the Act directs May 5th 1804 by J.Wilkes.

Denon del.   J. Chapman sc.

A 19th-century illustration of the Dendera zodiac, a bas-relief on the ceiling of the Hathor temple at Dendera in Egypt. It is the only complete map of the ancient skies to have survived, and dates from around 50 BC.

In the microcosm–macrocosm theory (see page 151), there is a natural link between the individual and the universe. This notion led to 'medical' astrology, in which the presence of planets in a particular zodiac sign was said to have consequences for one's health. Birth charts would be compared with the current position of the zodiac, while the planets were also seen to be linked to the four humours (blood, yellow bile, black bile, phlegm).

The practical implications of these ideas were that astrologers could determine when surgery should take place, or when a particular procedure was likely to be successful. Some charts, for example, were used to indicate when patients could be bled (a common medical procedure in the pre-modern world).

For many magicians, an understanding of the workings of the celestial bodies was a prerequisite for interacting with them. For the Renaissance scholar Agrippa, writing in *De Occulta Philosophia* (1533), 'magic is so connected … with astrology that anyone who professes magic without astrology accomplishes nothing.'

OPPOSITE *It was believed that each part of the body was influenced by or related to a specific sign of the zodiac.*
ABOVE *While a woman gives birth in the foreground, behind her two astrologers observe the stars and plot a horoscope.*

ABOVE *Combining astronomy with alchemy, the Uraniborg observatory in Denmark was built by the astronomer Tycho Brahe (1546–1601). It was designed according to the magical astrological principles of Marsilio Ficino (see page 190).* OPPOSITE *A Brahmin astrologer sits with charts and texts laid out in front of him.*

So it was that numerous magicians and early scientists – Copernicus, John Dee, Tyco Brahe – were also astrologers, casting horoscopes for the rich and powerful. Typically, horoscopes begin with astrological charts that plot the relative positions of the Sun, planets and zodiac at any given time. On the basis of this information, the astrologer is then able to make predictions about a person's future.

In ancient Greece and Rome, astrologers were known as Chaldeans, after an area of Mesopotamia – Chaldea – renowned for its astrologers and astronomers. There is also evidence of astrology in Egypt early on, and the texts attributed to Hermes Trismegistus show strong astrological influence. In the later years of the Roman Empire, astrologers become more prominent, and by the fifth century AD, one finds something akin to today's form of astrology.

کنگ

maestro che aueua nome can

figura di cano aster trouatore della

arte magicha.

OPPOSITE *A 15th-century depiction of Zoroaster conversing with two devils from the safety of a magic circle.* ABOVE *The 17th-century Clavis Artis manuscript on alchemy was attributed to Zoroaster as a way of establishing a pedigree for arcane knowledge.*

Zoroaster

The founder of the Zoroastrian religion, Zoroaster (also known as Zarathustra), came from ancient Persia, now modern-day Iran. The precise dates of his life are uncertain, but he can be placed between 1000 and 500 BC.

As with King Solomon (see page 52), Zoroaster's importance to the history of magic lies less in what he did than in what he was *believed* to have done. In the hands of the ancient Greeks, Zoroaster began to accumulate exotic detail that transformed him into a powerful sorcerer. The Greeks also believed that Zoroaster was a Chaldean, giving him access to astrological insights. The followers of Zoroaster were known as *magi*, and they too became associated with arcane knowledge – leading eventually to the word 'magic'.

The association between Zoroastrianism and magic was reinforced by Pliny the Elder, writing in AD 77–9. For him, Zoroaster had been the inventor of magic:

> There is no doubt that this art originated in Persia, under Zoroaster … but whether there was only one Zoroaster, or whether in later times there was a second person of that name, is a matter which still remains undecided. Eudoxus, who has endeavoured to show that of all branches of philosophy the magic art is the most illustrious and the most beneficial, informs us that this Zoroaster existed six thousand years before the death of Plato, an assertion in which he is supported by Aristotle.

ANCIENT EGYPTIAN MAGIC

For the ancient Egyptians, everyday life was subject to the dark forces of chaos, and the more they could control these forces, the better. Ritual and magic – the latter known as *heka* – were performed by priests, and were seen as essential to the smooth running of society. *Heka* means 'activation of the soul' (*ka*), in this case the soul of the gods.

Records from the rule of Ramses III (reigned 1187–1156 BC) show how magic was used in people's lives. The Rollin and Lee papyri record the trial of a group of people who had plotted to kill the pharaoh by means of black magic. According to the papyri, they employed not only potions and spells but also a figurine of the pharaoh that they could attack and damage. This was not an isolated case, and harmful magic could also be used against unfriendly states, with effigies of foreign leaders regularly destroyed or burnt.

ABOVE *A papyrus containing magical spells from the Ptolemaic period (332–30 BC).*
OPPOSITE *The Eye of Horus was a powerful symbol in ancient Egypt, used to ward off evil and for protection in the afterlife. This detail is from a painting found in a tomb.*

*Amulets were extremely common
in ancient Egypt. This example,
depicting a Ba-bird, is made of gold,
lapis lazuli and turquoise.*

*The Ebers Papyrus, from around 1500 BC, contains medicinal and
magical formulae, including incantations to see off demons.*

Medicine and magic were practically interchangeable in ancient Egypt, with doctors regularly using spells as part of their patients' treatment. Collections of written spells were highly prized, and were passed down from one family to another. In addition, Egyptians used amulets extensively.

Life in ancient Egypt also ended with magic, and copies of the *Book of the Dead* – which imparts esoteric knowledge of the afterlife – were buried with the wealthy. The book contained spells that could help with the process of judgment before admission into the afterlife.

Anubis and Hunefer, with Osiris and Horus, from a copy of the Book of the Dead. *Such papyri contained the magic necessary to navigate the afterlife.*

An Egyptian amulet with multiple Eyes of Horus.

AMULETS & TALISMANS

Amulets are among the earliest examples of magical thinking, and can be found in all parts of the world. Designed to ward off evil, they are either carried or worn. In his *Natural History* (first century AD), Pliny describes the amulet as an object that protects the bearer from trouble.

Some materials are believed to be inherently magical. The ancient Greeks and Romans, for example, associated certain semi-precious stones with specific gods. The word 'amethyst' – denoting a precious stone composed of a type of quartz – most likely comes from the Greek for 'not drunk', since it was supposed to protect against drunkenness. The Jewish historian Josephus, writing in the first century AD, associated the stones of Aaron's breastplate with the twelve months and the twelve tribes of Israel. Today, birthstones remain popular, related to the signs of the zodiac.

'Toadstones' were believed to
come from the heads of old
toads, and were supposed to be
effective against poisons.

An amulet of the jackal-headed
Duamutef, buried in Ancient
Egyptian canopic jars as the
guardian of the stomach

A LaKaKare charm from
Papua New Guinea, made
from carved coconut and filled
with magical substances. The
strap means it can be carried

This beaded, turtle-shaped amulet
from the Sioux of North America
contains an umbilical cord and was
worn by girls to ward of illness.

A necklace made of glass
beads from Hebron, Palestine,
worn to avert the 'evil eye'.

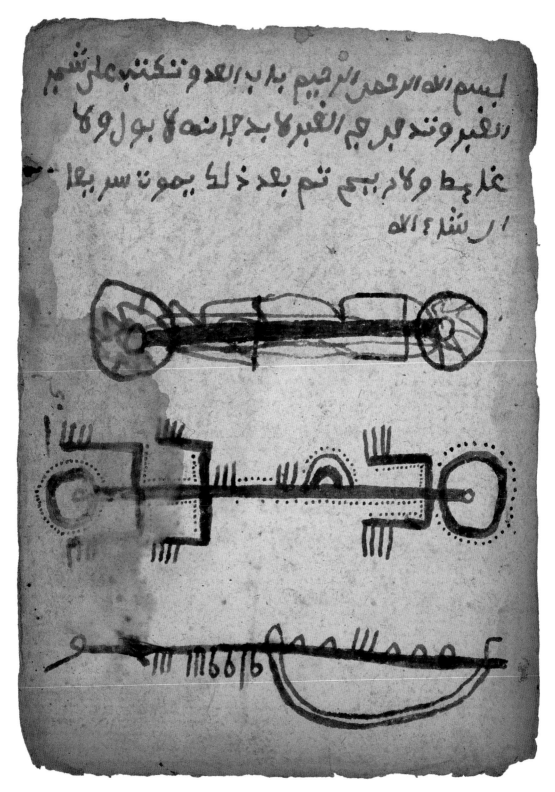

An elaborately drawn 18th-century Sudanese talisman.

ה	וה	וו	פה	י'	
מ	תי	יה	יו'	יה	
ג	עה	פ'	נה	עו	
פ	צו	לה	חי'	מה	
ה	רה	לו	סה	די	

שמירה והגנה למשה דוד בר
אסתר מדבר וממגפה ומאבן
נגף מוע אס

*An amulet written in Hebrew for the protection
of Moses David, son of Esther, from plague.
To the left is its leather case.*

In Judaism, the prohibition on the use of images means that amulets often take a written form. However, even these can be controversial: the medieval Jewish philosopher Maimonides, for example, railed against the 'amulet writers'. Some amulets feature sigils (from the Latin *sigillum*, meaning 'seal') – inscribed or painted symbols seen as having magical powers. Prime examples of this type of amulet can be found in grimoires, such as *The Key of Solomon*.

Whereas amulets are believed to have inherent magical properties, talismans are *given* magical properties by their makers. Examples of talismans include such symbols as the Seal of Solomon, the pentagram and, in its ancient form, the swastika. Typically, the creation of talismans has a strong astrological element, with their power sometimes being dependent on the date and time of their making.

*The wax-tablet Seal of God owned by
the magician John Dee (see page 236).*

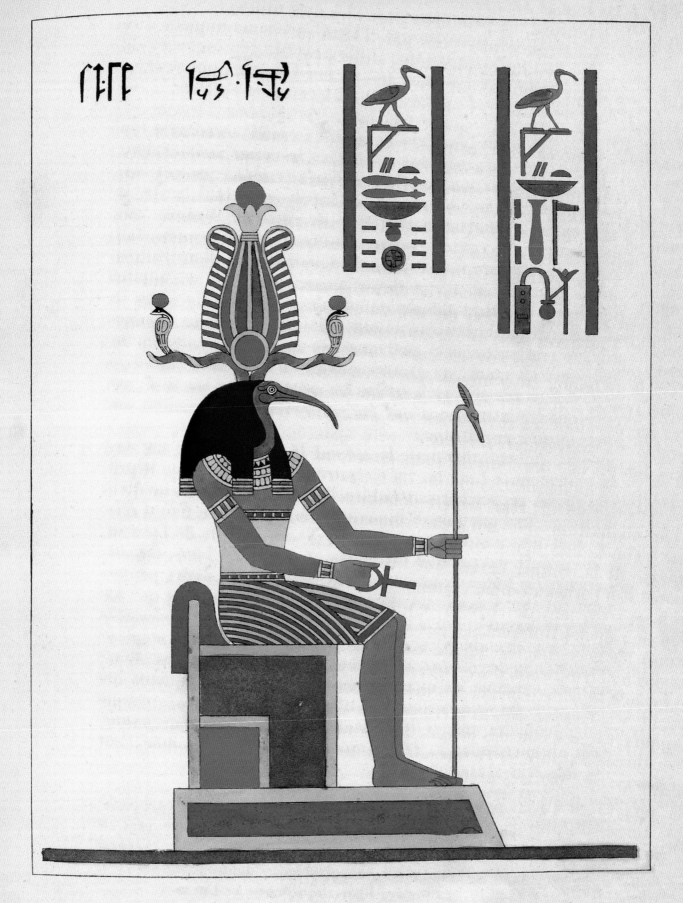

OPPOSITE *The god Thoth in his ibis-headed form.* RIGHT *Thoth in baboon form, as the god of the moon (worn on his head), and in scribe form, as the god of writing.*

Thoth

Usually depicted as a man with the head of an ibis, or as a baboon, the Egyptian god Thoth was originally associated with the moon. However, because moon cycles play a large role in astrology, over time he became associated with magic. Thoth was also the god of wisdom and the dead, and the inventor of writing – the scribe of the gods.

Thoth's later importance in magic stems from the Greek conquest of Egypt by Alexander the Great in 332 BC, and the subsequent conflation of Thoth with the Greek god Hermes (the Greeks were fond of finding local equivalents to their own deities). The Greeks saw Thoth as the god not only of magic but also of astronomy and astrology. Eventually, the association of Thoth with Hermes led to the emergence of a new figure: Hermes Trismegistus (see page 90). The main temple of Thoth was to be found at Hermopolis Magna, formerly the Egyptian city of Khmun.

Attributed to the god is the mysterious Book of Thoth. First mentioned in a fictional story from the Ptolemaic period, it was said to contain spells for talking to animals and seeing the gods. The title has since been applied to many collections of esoteric writings.

Egyptian magic came to the fore again in the nineteenth century, and with it renewed interest in Thoth. Written by Aleister Crowley in the 1940s, *The Book of Thoth* provides instructions on the use of the so-called Thoth deck, a set of Tarot cards co-designed by Crowley and Lady Frieda Harris.

MAGIC IN THE OLD TESTAMENT

Magic appears only irregularly in the Old Testament, with most mentions being prohibitions on witchcraft and sorcery. It is unclear whether or not magic is thought to exist physically, and, if that is the case, what kinds of forces it taps into.

The two best-known magicians in the Bible are the Egyptians Jannes and Jambres. Although they are not mentioned by name in the Old Testament, Jewish tradition describes them as the chief magicians who produce magic in front of Moses and Aaron in Exodus 7:10–12. When Aaron throws down his rod, it becomes a snake through the power of God; Jannes and Jambres then match the trick, but using sleight of hand (whether they are mere conjurors or demonically inspired is uncertain). Aaron's snake then eats theirs.

BELOW AND OPPOSITE *The book of Exodus tells of the stand-off between Aaron and the Egyptian magicians. First they turned their staffs into snakes (below left), then made the rivers flow with blood (below right), then created a plague of frogs (opposite).*

ABOVE AND OPPOSITE *In this dramatic example of necromancy from the Old Testament, Saul consults with the Witch of Endor to conjure Samuel from the dead. In both scenes, Saul falls to the floor in shock.*

In Daniel 2, the Babylonian king Nebuchadnezzar, troubled by dreams, summons 'the magicians, and the astrologers, and the sorcerers, and the Chaldeans'. None can help him, however, and only the divinely inspired Daniel is able to decode the dreams — another victory for God over false idols.

An apparent and unusual reference to magic can be found in 1 Samuel 14:41, where mention is made of two obscure objects, the Urim and Thummim. Said to be stored in Aaron's breastplate, these objects are used in an act of divination, to separate the guilty from the innocent.

ABOVE *Solomon inspects plans for his temple. It was said that the golden statuettes flanking the steps would attack strangers who tried to climb them.*
OPPOSITE *The figure of Solomon remained powerful into the Middle Ages; here, he is depicted in a stained-glass window in Chartres Cathedral, France.*

King Solomon

Solomon, king of ancient Israel from about 970 to 930 BC, is perhaps best known as the son of David. In the Bible he is portrayed as a wise and just ruler – the architect of the First Temple of Jerusalem – but ultimately as a man who turned his back on God, descended into idolatry, and was punished for it. In the centuries that followed, however, a huge collection of stories grew up around Solomon that portrayed the king as a great magician and keeper of arcane knowledge.

Solomon is said to have possessed a magical ring, known as the Seal of Solomon. The motif of the ring was the Star of David, and this image appears regularly in subsequent Western magical symbolism (see page 154). Later tales of the king, from the first century AD onwards, tell of how the ring gave its owner control over animals and the weather.

In the apocryphal Testament of Solomon, the king uses his ring to command demons to build the First Temple. Much later, this temple would become the archetype for all Masonic lodges, while Masonic initiation ceremonies still recreate episodes from the temple's construction. The motif of Solomon's ring is occasionally depicted as a pentagram, a symbol that also became associated with magic in the West. The five-pointed star was seen as a talisman, capable of warding off demons.

Such was Solomon's fame as a magician that two later books of magic bear his name: *The Key of Solomon* (dating from the fourteenth or fifteenth century) and *The Lesser Key of Solomon* (compiled in the seventeenth century). Together, they cover divination, the creation of magical objects, magical operations, and the summoning of demons and angels.

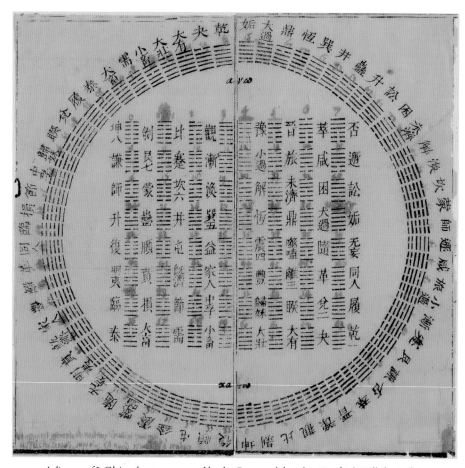

A diagram of I Ching *hexagrams owned by the German philosopher Gottfried Wilhelm Leibniz.*

ANCIENT CHINESE MAGIC

The earliest evidence of magical thinking in China – oracle bones or turtle shells used for divination – date from the second millennium BC. The question requiring an answer would be written on the bone or shell; this would then be anointed with blood before being heated. The subsequent cracking would provide the answer.

Central to Chinese divination was the *I Ching* (*Book of Changes*), probably dating from before 800 BC. Employing cleromancy – the apparently random casting of lots, which was believed to reveal the will of the gods – it is made up of sixty-four hexagrams with broken or unbroken lines. Each hexagram links to a text explaining what is likely to come next.

The *Baopuzi* – one of the key works of Taoism, written by the Jin dynasty scholar Ge Hong (AD 223–343) – discusses such esoteric subjects as alchemy, immortality, elixirs and protective seals. One such seal, the Yellow Spirit Leap seal, could be used to keep bears and wolves at bay. According to Ge Hong, the seal had to be stamped into the ground, in the four cardinal directions, a hundred paces from one's abode.

A portrait of Ge Hong. An adept of Tao,
Ge Hong was believed to possess the secret
to making the pills of immortality.

This ox scapula (shoulder blade)
from the late 2nd millennium BC is an
example of an 'oracle bone'. The diviner
would interpret the cracks in the bone
caused by heating.

Chinese shamans divining the future with a board used for liu po, an ancient Chinese board game.

MAGIC WANDS & STAFFS

The twentieth-century Czech occultist Franz Bardon called the wand 'the most important aid in ritual magic'. The earliest examples can be found in ancient Egypt, where typically they were made of curved ivory and engraved with symbols. Later we find the *barsom* or *baresman* – a tied bundle of sticks – used by Zoroastrian *magi*, in part for divination.

The first literary reference to a wand comes in Homer's *Odyssey*, in which such an object is used by the witch Circe to turn Odysseus' men into animals. More recent literary references include those in C. S. Lewis's Narnia stories, and in J. K. Rowling's Harry Potter series.

Like the wand, the staff can be found in the cultures of both West and East. In that most magical of Chinese epics, the sixteenth-century *Journey to the West*, the Monkey King carries a magical staff that can grow or shrink in size.

LEFT *A Persian warrior carrying a* barsom, *a type of wand composed of bound sticks.* OPPOSITE *In this scene from* Journey to the West, *the Monkey King uses his staff or sceptre to fight the magical Moon Rabbit.*

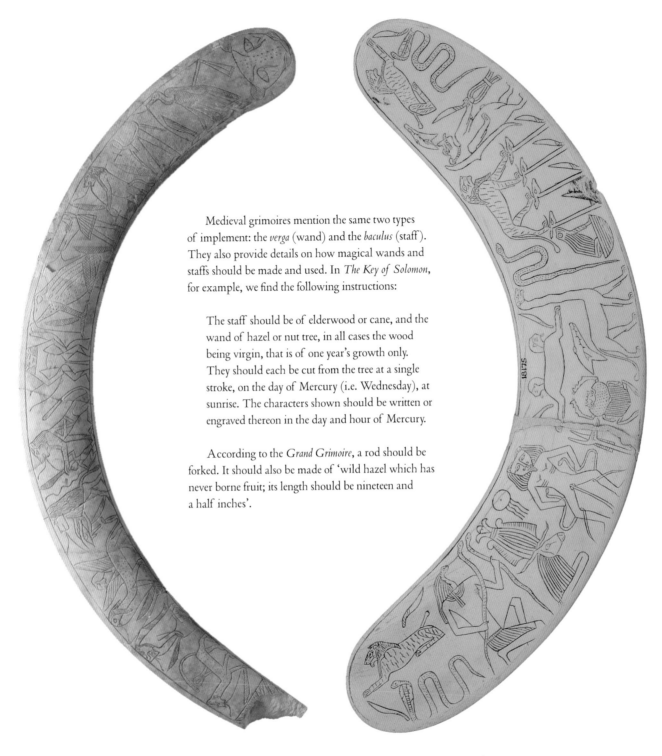

Medieval grimoires mention the same two types of implement: the *verga* (wand) and the *baculus* (staff). They also provide details on how magical wands and staffs should be made and used. In *The Key of Solomon*, for example, we find the following instructions:

> The staff should be of elderwood or cane, and the wand of hazel or nut tree, in all cases the wood being virgin, that is of one year's growth only. They should each be cut from the tree at a single stroke, on the day of Mercury (i.e. Wednesday), at sunrise. The characters shown should be written or engraved thereon in the day and hour of Mercury.

According to the *Grand Grimoire*, a rod should be forked. It should also be made of 'wild hazel which has never borne fruit; its length should be nineteen and a half inches'.

OPPOSITE *Circe brandishes a large wand while offering a cup to Odysseus (pictured in the mirror), in a scene from Homer's* Odyssey. *Circe uses her wand to turn Odysseus' men into animals.*
ABOVE *Two apotropaic wands from ancient Egypt, each carved with such deities as Taweret and Bes, as well as uraeuses (sacred serpents) and mythical creatures. Some figures carry knives to dispel evil spirits. The wand on the right was designed to protect a mother and child.*

II.

Greek & Roman Magic

The witch Circe sits with a book of spells beside her. The animals had previously been Odysseus' men, before she transformed them.

When looking at the cultures of ancient Greece and Rome, it is difficult to determine where religion and mythology end and magic begins. Classical myths tend to be overtly magical, much more so, for example, than the stories of the Old Testament. Through divine intervention, things of this world change form and take on supernatural qualities. The Roman poet Ovid, in his *Metamorphoses*, beautifully captures this world – one in constant magical flux.

In ancient Greece, the concept of magic stemmed largely from Egypt, Mesopotamia and the cultures of the eastern Mediterranean; indeed, the Greek word *magikos* comes from *magos*, a follower of Zoroaster. Like the Romans who came after them, the Greeks took delight in the exotic and the arcane. Pythagoras, for instance, was said to have visited the Orphic, Chaldean and Egyptian mystery schools, absorbing and synthesizing their occult knowledge. For him, numbers were fundamental to creation, an emanation of the divine. Later, such beliefs would give rise to the occult field of numerology.

The distinction between magic and religion in ancient Greece is not clear-cut. Some modern theories suggest that magic was something done privately, whereas religion was practised in public. However, the fact that the patron of magic, Hecate (see page 70), was also a goddess suggests that within the religious tradition there was still room for sorcery.

Magic in ancient Greece did not replace prayer to the gods, but was seen as complementary to it. Plato, in *The Republic*, describes how 'mendicant prophets go to rich men's doors and persuade them they have a power committed to them by the gods of making an atonement for a man's own or his ancestor's sins by sacrifices or charms, with rejoicings and feasts; and they promise to harm an enemy, whether just or unjust, at a small cost; with magic arts and incantations binding heaven, as they say, to execute their will.' This suggests a connection to religion, but also that there was a degree of charlatanism in magical practice.

Plato's words also suggest that magic could be used in day-to-day life. Indeed, ancient Greeks were known for employing *agoge* spells – spells that caused their target to behave in a particular way, potentially against their will. Sometimes, such spells were malicious in nature, deployed against enemies, but they could also take the form of love spells. In Theocritus' play *Pharmakeutriai* (The Witches; third century BC), the main protagonist,

ABOVE *Aegeus consulting the oracle at Delphi, painted on a kylix (an ancient Greek cup).*
OPPOSITE *To win the love of Scylla, the sea-god Glaucus asked for the help of the witch Circe. However, Circe, herself in love with Glaucus, turned Scylla into a monster – as depicted here.*

Samantha, decides to win back the affections of an athlete. She does so with the help of a variety of magical ingredients – barley, bay, bran, wax, lizard – and a magical wheel, bullroarer and gong. Her incantations are addressed to Hecate.

When Alexander the Great conquered a large part of the Near East in the fourth century BC, he set in motion a process known as Hellenization. Nowhere was its impact felt as strongly as in Egypt. Greek philosophy merged with Egyptian mysticism with heady results, including in particular the birth of the Hermetic tradition (see page 90). In the third century AD, the Greek Neoplatonists, led by Plotinus, began to explore the concept of theurgy, the control of gods or spirits through magic.

The Romans inherited much of their religion from Greece; they also shared many of their attitudes to magic. Like the Greeks, they had their own form of 'low' magic, also often employed to curse enemies. In his first *Satire*, the poet Horace (65–8 BC) tells of even more sinister deeds: the witch Canidia digs up human remains in order to use them in magical potions. And in *Pharsalia*, an epic poem by Lucan (AD 39–65), the character of Erictho lives in a tomb, collecting body parts and bringing corpses back to life.

Perhaps it was stories like these – even if they were exaggerations – that led the Roman Empire to take a fairly hard line against magic. According to the historian Suetonius, in 13 BC the emperor Augustus ordered 2,000 magical scrolls to be burnt, while in AD 16 astrologers and magicians were expelled from Rome. In the reign of Tiberius, forty-five male magicians and eighty-five female magicians were executed.

There was, however, a lighter side. Written in the mid-second century AD, Apuleius' *Golden Ass* is a wonderful example of the use of magic in stories. The hero of the tale, Lucius, wants to become a wizard, but accidentally

LEFT *Roman religion was happy to absorb 'exotic' elements from far-flung parts of the empire. This curious hand was used in the worship of Sabazios, a god from ancient Thrace.*
ABOVE *Ideas around religion, mythology and magic migrated easily between the Greek and Roman empires. This illustration shows the different names for the goddess Isis.*

turns himself into an ass. The only way he can return to his previous form is by eating a rose (a flower that is often associated with magic).

By the late fourth century AD, the Roman Empire had adopted Christianity, which brought with it a new attitude to the occult. As a monotheistic religion, Christianity was less immediately threatened by magic: it simply did not accept that magic and God could coexist. Nevertheless, stories about magicians can be found in the New Testament and the Apocrypha. One particularly interesting character is St Cyprian of Antioch, an occult magician who communed with demons before converting to Christianity (and who was subsequently martyred in AD 304). Later, he became famous for *The Great Book of Saint Cyprian*, a book of black magic that almost certainly had little to do with the original saint.

For the ancient Greeks and Romans, Egypt was an exotic place, full of magic. Here, the moon goddess Io is welcomed into Egypt by Isis.

ABOVE *Homer and a doctor are visited by Hermes (right), who brings them the magical herb known as moly. This herb was used by Odysseus to ensure that he did not fall under Circe's spell.*
OPPOSITE *Greek mythology is fundamentally magical, with a vast array of impossible creatures. The half-human, half-horse centaur is a well-known example.*

MAGIC IN ANCIENT GREECE

While ancient Greece is famous for being the birthplace of democracy and mathematics, not everything was entirely rational. During the fourth century BC, there was also a booming trade in magic. As Plato describes it in *Euthydemus*, 'The sorcerer's art is the charming of snakes and tarantulas and scorpions and other beasts and diseases.'

A popular form of magic was the curse etched into a lead tablet, which was then folded and pierced with a nail, and sometimes buried with the dead. Such curses seem to have been used against rival businessmen and athletes, to win the affections of a potential lover, or to ensure success in legal proceedings.

One particularly curious group of magical phrases is today known as the Ephesia Grammata. These words, which even ancient Greeks struggled to decode, have been found inscribed on a variety of objects, including the statue of Artemis in her temple at Ephesus. They seem to have had magical powers as an incantation, but only if pronounced perfectly.

ABOVE *According to Ovid, when the peasants of Lycia attempted to prevent the Greek goddess
Leto from drinking from their well, she turned them into frogs.* OPPOSITE *Magical creatures
abound in Greek mythology. Jason, in his quest for the Golden Fleece, encounters the fierce Colchian
dragon. In some versions, he uses Medea's magic to put it to sleep; in this depiction,
he is devoured by the dragon, but rescued by Athena's drugs.*

The religion of the ancient Greeks, rooted as it was in mythology, is inherently magical. While it might be expected that the gods have supernatural powers, one finds a full spectrum of hybrid and impossible creatures, nymphs and demi-gods, and witches. In Greek mythology, magic is able to operate independently of religion; in fact, the gods themselves are occasionally subject to magical spells.

Oracles were important in ancient Greece, the most famous among them being the Pythia at Delphi. Through oracles, it was believed, humans could consult with the gods. Delphi had been the home of Python, the Earth-dragon, until his death at the hands of Apollo. The site was considered to be the centre of the Earth, and therefore charged with magic and significance.

ABOVE *William Blake's depiction of the witch-goddess Hecate, shown here as a triple entity.*
OPPOSITE *A Roman copy of the Hecate statue by the Greek sculptor Alkamenes. It faces in three directions, with two of the figures clutching a pomegranate, while the third held a torch.*

Hecate

Described by the classical poet Sappho as 'Queen of Night', Hecate was the principal Greek goddess of magic, as well as the goddess of crossroads and the dark phase of the moon. She was the daughter of Perses and Asteria.

Ordinary Greeks worshipped Hecate as a household goddess, with shrines dedicated to her placed at doorways, in the hope of keeping away the spirits of the dead. Once a month, in order to placate Hecate and the restless dead in her care, Greeks celebrated the Deipnon, a meal laid out at a crossroads on a night with no moon.

Often, Hecate is depicted as a triple-faced entity, looking in three directions – in part because statues of her were placed at three-way crossroads. Sometimes, she is also depicted as a dog, an animal that was regularly sacrificed in her honour.

Hecate's equivalent in the Roman pantheon was the goddess Trivia, the goddess of crossroads, ghosts and witchcraft. The name 'Trivia' means 'three roads' – another reference to crossroads, at which sacrifices in her honour would take place. Interestingly, in *The Golden Ass*, Apuleius associates Hecate with the Egyptian goddess Isis.

In recent times, Hecate has become a key figure in neopaganism, and it is worth noting that crossroads continue to have a close association with magic, especially in voodoo and Brazilian magic.

SPELLS, INCANTATIONS
& MAGIC WORDS

All magic relies on language in one form or another. Which is to say, ritual by itself is rarely enough to effect change; rather, it needs to be accompanied by an incantation or spell. Writing in *The Magus* (1801), the English occultist Francis Barrett explained that 'the virtue of man's words are so great, that, when pronounced with a fervent constancy of the mind, they are able to subvert Nature, to cause earthquakes, storms, and tempests … Almost all charms are impotent without words, because words are the speech of the speaker, and the image of the thing signified or spoken of.'

One of the most famous magical words is 'abracadabra'. Thought to be Aramaic in origin, it has been translated as 'I create as I speak'. It is first mentioned in a book from the third century AD, in which it is recommended as an incantation against malaria.

OPPOSITE *A witch casts her spells over a bubbling cauldron resting on a tripod. Magical ephemera fill the room.* ABOVE *Magic relies on both rituals and spells. This diagram shows how to create a circle to raise the spirit of Oberon, king of the fairies.*

A dramatic depiction of an incantation for raising the dead or conjuring a ghost.

In Japanese culture, one finds the concept of *kotodama*, or 'word spirit' – the idea that mystical powers reside in words and names. A famous example of magical words in the West is the Roman Sator Square (a word square containing a palindrome in Latin), the earliest example of which was found in the ruins of Pompeii.

In the Middle Ages, incantations and spells were collected in grimoires. These books of practical magic were kept secret, and their contents closely guarded. In some cases they contain a mixture of Hebrew, Latin, local languages and those that have been entirely invented (as was the case with John Dee's 'angelic' language known as Enochian; see page 236). Often, they also employ substitution ciphers, such as the Theban alphabet (see page 192).

S	A	T	O	R
A	R	E	P	O
T	E	N	E	T
O	P	E	R	A
R	O	T	A	S

The Roman Sator Square.

According to legend, the 12th-century Japanese warrior-turned-architect Kiyomori promised to restore the temples of Miyjima before sunset. Needing more time, he used an incantation to prevent the sun from setting.

ABOVE *Circe clutches her wand, looking at the animals that were formerly Odysseus' men.*
OPPOSITE *This painting of Circe shows a scene from Ovid's* Metamorphoses. *A jealous Circe pours a magic potion into the water that her rival in love, Scylla, is about to bathe in.*

Circe

Circe is a Greek goddess of magic, sometimes also called a witch. The daughter of the sun-god Helios, she was the sister of Aeëtes (responsible for guarding the Golden Fleece) and Pasiphaë (the mother of the Minotaur). Some accounts describe her as a daughter of Hecate. The first written reference to Circe appears in Homer's epic poem *The Odyssey* (composed, it is thought, in the eighth century BC).

According to Greek mythology, Circe lives on the island of Aeaea, in a house in a clearing in a wood – a trope common to depictions of witches. When she meets Odysseus and his men, she attempts to drug them. Odysseus protects himself with a herb, but his men are turned into animals by Circe's magical staff. Circe is also able to enchant wild animals, making them docile.

After turning Odysseus' men back to their original forms, Circe instructs Odysseus on how to get to the underworld, so that he may consult the dead prophet Tiresias on his future. Circe's knowledge of the underworld proves invaluable to Odysseus.

In his *Metamorphoses*, a retelling of Greek and Roman myths, the Roman poet Ovid describes an earlier episode in Circe's life. Spurned by the sea-god Glaucus, she uses foul herbs and Hecate's spells to turn her love-rival, Scylla, into a vicious sea-monster.

Circe's niece Medea was also a sorceress, appearing in the legend of Jason and the Argonauts. There, she shows Jason how to kill the monstrous Python; later, however, she kills her own children in a fit of jealousy.

In a painting based on a tale by the Roman poet Horace, the witch Sagana and her companion Canidia cast a love spell using a magical figurine.

MAGIC IN ANCIENT ROME

The Romans, like the Greeks before them, were partial to cursing rivals. In common with Greek practice, the curses themselves often took the form of inscriptions on lead tablets. Known as *defixiones*, these curse tablets typically call on the gods to 'bind' their victim.

An insight into how curse tablets were used can be found in the *Annals*, a history of the Roman Empire from AD 14 to 68 by the Roman historian Tacitus. The general Germanicus, fearing he had been poisoned, ordered a search of the building he was in. Among the items discovered were 'the remains of human bodies, spells, curses, leaden tablets engraved with the name "Germanicus", charred and blood-smeared ashes, and others of the implements of witchcraft by which it is believed the living soul can be devoted to the powers of the grave'.

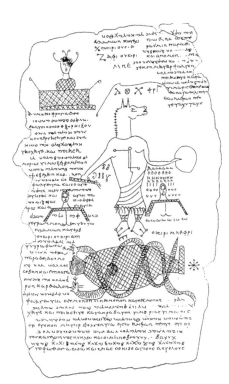

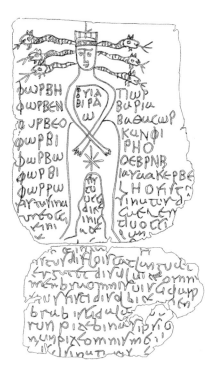

TOP, LEFT *A drawing after a Roman* defixio, *or curse tablet. The figure bound by two snakes represents the victim of the 'binding' action, a rival jockey.* TOP, RIGHT *A drawing of a curse tablet. Part of the text reads: 'Crush, kill Fistus the senator … May Fistus dilute, languish, sink and may all his limbs dissolve.'* ABOVE *A Roman* defixio *discovered in London.*

In this depiction of a theatrical scene, discovered in Pompeii,
two women pay a call on a witch (third from left).

The Roman attitude towards the *ars magica* was somewhat ambivalent. While haruspicy (divination by examining the entrails of sacrificial animals) and augury (divination by the flight of birds) were practised as part of the workings of the state, the *Lex Cornelia de sicariis et veneficis* (82 BC) outlawed the use of magic. Under this law, the punishment for practising magic was crucifixion or being thrown to beasts, while magicians, it decreed, should be burnt. Those caught with magical books should be deported to an island.

From the second century BC to the first century AD, various laws were passed banning astrology and divination; in 139 and 33 BC, astrologers and magicians were officially cast out of Rome. Anti-magic laws grew stronger over time, so that by the fourth century AD just about every form of theoretical and practical magic had been proscribed.

*A fresco from the House of the Dioscuri in Pompeii showing a traveller
visiting a magician (seated, with unusual headdress).*

CUPS & BALLS

Conjuring tricks using sleight of hand can be traced back to at least ancient Rome, while some have suggested that they originated in Egypt or China in the second millennium BC.

The oldest and most widely performed trick seems to be the 'cups and balls' routine, in which a magician – typically using three cups and three balls – makes the balls apparently pass through the cups, employing sleight of hand and misdirection. In ancient Rome the trick was known as *acetabula et calculi*. Alciphron of Athens, writing in late antiquity, describes the trick performed with 'three small dishes' and 'some little white round pebbles'. The philosopher was left 'almost speechless'.

Similar tricks can be found in China ('The Immortal Sowing Beans') and India. The first explanation of cups and balls was published in Reginald Scot's *Discoverie of Witchcraft* (1584).

ABOVE *Hieronymus Bosch's famous painting of the cups and balls trick performed by a street magician. One onlooker cranes forward, dumbfounded, and fails to notice what is happening to his purse.* OPPOSITE *This engraving shows how the cups and balls trick works. In reality, however, the trick is constantly evolving.*

Pl. 1.

Tours de Gibeciere.

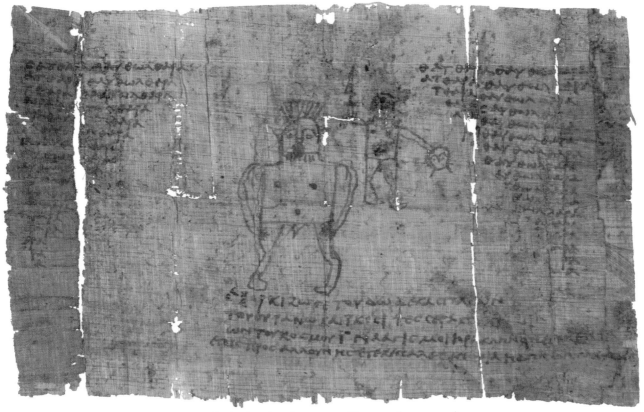

OPPOSITE *Dating from the 3rd century AD, this papyrus features a number of magical texts, including a love spell and spells to summon and send away a god. It also describes how to see spirits in the shining surface of a dish of oil.* ABOVE *A 4th-century papyrus containing a love spell intended to bind Herakles to Allous: 'I adjure you by the twelve elements of heaven and the twenty-four elements of the world, that you attract Herakles … to me, to Allous … immediately, immediately; quickly, quickly.' The figure on the left is the Egyptian god Bes.*

GREEK MAGICAL PAPYRI

The Greek Magical Papyri, a collection of papyri from Graeco-Roman Egypt, is one of the earliest known collections of spells, incantations and alchemical texts. The papyri date from between the second century BC and the fifth century AD, and are written in Demotic, Coptic and Greek. They contain elements of Roman, Greek, Jewish and Egyptian religion and mythology (several invoke Hecate), and were brought together in the early nineteenth century by Jean d'Anastasi, a member of the court in Alexandria. Little is known about their actual discovery, but they may have come from the tomb of a magician in Thebes.

One of the best-known texts in the collection is the Mithras Liturgy, in which initiates learn the secret of immortality. However, the papyri also include spells for dealing with the more mundane aspects of life, such as bedbugs and poor memory. One invisibility spell calls for a ball of dung rolled by a beetle, an owl's eye and the oil of a young olive, which is then smeared over the body. An incantation to Helios makes the spell effective.

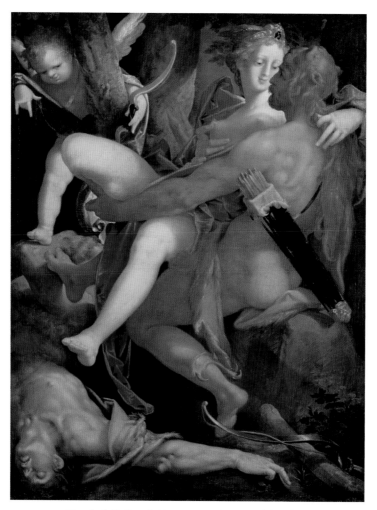

ABOVE *Heracles holds his wife Deianira over the corpse of the defeated centaur Nessus. Years later, Deianira would soak Heracles' robes in a potion made with Nessus' blood, since it was supposed to have magical properties that would ensure his fidelity. Instead, it poisons and kills her husband.* OPPOSITE *A naked witch casts a love spell; the object of her affections seems to be standing at her door.*

LOVE MAGIC

Finding and keeping the perfect partner is a universal human concern – especially when the feelings of attraction are not reciprocated. It is no great surprise, therefore, to discover the presence of love spells throughout history.

Love magic was popular in both ancient Greece and ancient Rome. In the former, two types of love spells were employed: one to incite passion (*eros*), and the other to incite friendship and fidelity (*philia*). Some love spells can be shockingly unsentimental, such as this one from the Greek Magical Papyri: 'remain in her heart and burn her guts, her breast, her liver, her breath, her bones, her marrow, until she comes to me.'

ABOVE *This elaborate love seal from*
The Key of Solomon *contains a quote*
from Genesis: 'This is now bones of my
bones, flesh of my flesh … And they shall
become one flesh' (2:23–4).
RIGHT *This kneeling figurine from the*
4th century AD, pierced with pins, was found
in a vessel alongside a binding love
spell written on a lead tablet.

OPPOSITE *Unwilling to be separated,*
Iseult, an Irish princess, and Tristan,
a Cornish knight, decide to kill themselves.
However, the poison is switched for
a love potion. They fall even more in
love, and run away together.

Mythology brims with tales of infidelity.
In the Greek tradition, Deianira, a wife of the
hero Heracles, is told how to mix a love potion
that will ensure her husband's faithfulness;
however, it contains a poison that eventually
kills him. In the story of Tristan and Iseult –
a tale made popular in the medieval period –
a love potion causes the knight and princess
to enter into a dangerous relationship. It too
ends badly.

In *Zekerboni*, a seventeenth-century grimoire
attributed to the alleged Satanist Pierre Mora,
there is a recipe for a love potion, or philtre,
using such ingredients as a swallow's womb,
a dove's heart – and the caster's own blood.
(Getting the object of one's affections actually
to drink the resulting solution is another matter
altogether.) *The Key of Solomon* includes a seal
designed to win love, employing a quote from
Genesis: 'And they shall become one flesh'.

Hermes Trismegistus

Considering how central Hermes Trismegistus is to the history of magic and alchemy, we know surprisingly little about him. This is mainly because he is mythical. His origins can be traced back to the Egyptian god Thoth, the god of magic and writing, as well as the guide to the underworld. When the Greeks, under Alexander the Great, conquered Egypt in 332 BC, they saw in Thoth the equivalent of their god Hermes, who was also the god of magic and writing. And so a new cult was born, centred on the town sacred to Thoth, Khmun, which henceforth became known as Hermopolis Magna.

Over time, the legend of Hermes Trismegistus acquired additional colour. In the second century BC, the Jewish writer Artapanu, in his account of the life of Moses, drew a parallel between Moses and Thoth. The Roman writer and statesman Cicero, meanwhile, invented a backstory that had Hermes killing the hundred-eyed Argus before fleeing to Egypt, where he taught the Egyptians writing and law – with the Egyptians calling him Thoth.

OPPOSITE AND ABOVE *Hermes Trismegistus is typically depicted wearing 'exotic' clothing. In the engraving above, he holds an armillary sphere, and appears alongside the Sun and the Moon.*

The first concrete references to Hermes Trismegistus are to be found in the Greek Magical Papyri. In one such reference he is called 'Hermes the Elder, chief of all magicians'; in another he is referred to as 'thrice-great', since in ancient Egypt the superlative was constructed by repeating a word three times. Yet another reference, this one taken from a spell, underlines his unique powers: 'Come to me, lord Hermes, many-named one, who knows / the things hidden beneath heaven and earth.'

Central to our understanding of Hermes Trismegistus are the *Hermetica*, particularly the seventeen or so texts that make up the *Corpus Hermeticum* (see page 12). The first text in the corpus, 'Poimandres', describes the spheres of the seven classical planets. Each of the planets corresponds to an aspect of the human soul – Mercury to intelligence, Venus to love and lust, and so on. Indeed, this microcosm–macrocosm concept runs throughout the entire *Hermetica*, being most evident in the Emerald Tablet (see page 228).

ABOVE AND OPPOSITE *Two depictions of the mystical vision of Ezekiel, showing the multi-winged angels, the four animals and the burning wheels. The vision, which is at the centre of the Merkabah tradition of Jewish mysticism, is difficult to interpret.*

JEWISH MYSTICISM
& KABBALAH

One of the earliest forms of Jewish mysticism, practised from AD 100 to 1000, is called Merkabah. Attempting to recreate Ezekiel's vision of God's throne, and Isaiah's vision of God's glory, practitioners sought to experience a mystical ascent through angelic realms. The adept had to know the names of the angels, so that he could gain entry to successive gates. Angels also appear in the mystical tradition known as Hekhalot, in which they are summoned for a greater understanding of the nature of God.

A key work of Jewish mysticism is the *Sefer Yetzirah* (Book of Creation). The text describes how God created the universe by combining the twenty-two letters of the Hebrew alphabet with the ten numerals representing the *sefirot* (emanations from God), thereby giving words quasi-magical power. The letters are broken down into groups: the seven 'double' letters correspond to the seven classical planets and seven days of the week, while twelve 'simple' letters correspond to the signs of the zodiac.

ABOVE *Moses descends from Mount Sinai with the Ten Commandments, given to him by God.* OPPOSITE *A Jewish Kabbalist holds the Sefirotic Tree, or Tree of Life, while he meditates. The central diagram in Kabbalah, the tree shows the ten sefirot, or emanations from God, and how they relate to one another.*

The best-known system of Jewish esoteric thought is Kabbalah, an attempt to explain the relationship between the infinite and divine on the one hand, and the temporal and finite on the other. Originally an oral tradition, it was later communicated in ciphers – thereby making it an occult science.

As in the case of many magical and mystical traditions, Kabbalah began with a 'discovered' book, in this instance the Zohar (meaning 'splendour' or 'radiance'). Its exact authorship remains open to debate: was it written in the second century AD by Shimon bar Yochai – as claimed by the book's 'finder', the thirteenth-century Spanish rabbi Moses de León – or was it in fact authored by Moses de León himself? Some have suggested that it represents the 'oral Torah', a counterpart to the first five books of the Bible supposedly written by Moses – arcane knowledge transmitted to Moses at the same time as he received the Ten Commandments.

PORTAE LVCIS

Hęc est porta Tetragrámaton iusti intrabūt p̄ eam.

זֶה הַשַּׁעַר לַיְהוָֹה צַדִּיקִים יָבֹאוּ בוֹ

OPPOSITE *The Golem of Prague bangs on the door of a synagogue.*
A golem may be brought to life by writing one of the names of God on a piece
of paper and placing it in the golem's mouth. ABOVE *Inscribed with spells —*
in this case in Aramaic — incantation bowls were typically placed
upside down around the home, in order to trap demons inside. This
example was discovered in the Mesopotamian city of Seleucia.

While traditional Kabbalah is used to find the inner meaning of the Hebrew Bible, the branch known as 'practical Kabbalah' is most often associated with magic – specifically, the active shaping of reality through interaction with the divine. Necromancy, because the Torah largely forbids it, remained a marginal practice.

The Talmud – the primary source of Jewish law and legend – is clear that Jews practised magic in late antiquity, typically against demons. Evidence for this includes the incantation bowls from the fourth to sixth centuries AD found in Mesopotamia, with inscriptions in Aramaic or Syriac (the former produced by Jews, the latter by Christians). Many of the inscriptions call on specific angels.

One of the best-known examples of the use of magic in Judaism is the creation of a golem: a clay or mud figure in human form that is animated with divine words. The first practical description of a golem occurs in the twelfth century, although the most famous example, from Prague, dates from the sixteenth.

ABOVE *Elymas the Sorcerer appears in* Acts of the Apostles.
As punishment for his magic, he is turned temporarily blind by God.
OPPOSITE *A story in* The Golden Legend, *illustrated here by a follower of*
Hieronymus Bosch, tells of an encounter between James the Greater (approaching
in the background) and a magician called Hermogenes (seated on the throne).
James has demons bind Hermogenes and bring the magician to him.

MAGIC IN EARLY CHRISTIANITY

The New Testament contains a few examples of magicians who convert to Christianity – the best-known among them being Simon Magus, who had 'bewitched the people of Samaria'. Paul, in his Epistle to the Galatians, condemns magic as a 'work of the flesh', while the Didache (an instructional Christian treatise from the middle of the first century) states clearly 'thou shalt not deal in magic, thou shalt do no sorcery'. The apocryphal stories that followed, through to the lives of the saints in Jacobus de Voragine's medieval bestseller *The Golden Legend*, were even richer in magic.

In the early Christian era, condemnations of other religions as being magical were common (the same accusations were levelled at Jesus and his followers by contemporaries). Nevertheless, Coptic texts from the second century show that early Christianity still contained strong magical elements, including invocations to the Holy Trinity as part of spells. Clearly, there was a balance between indigenous folk magic and the new religion.

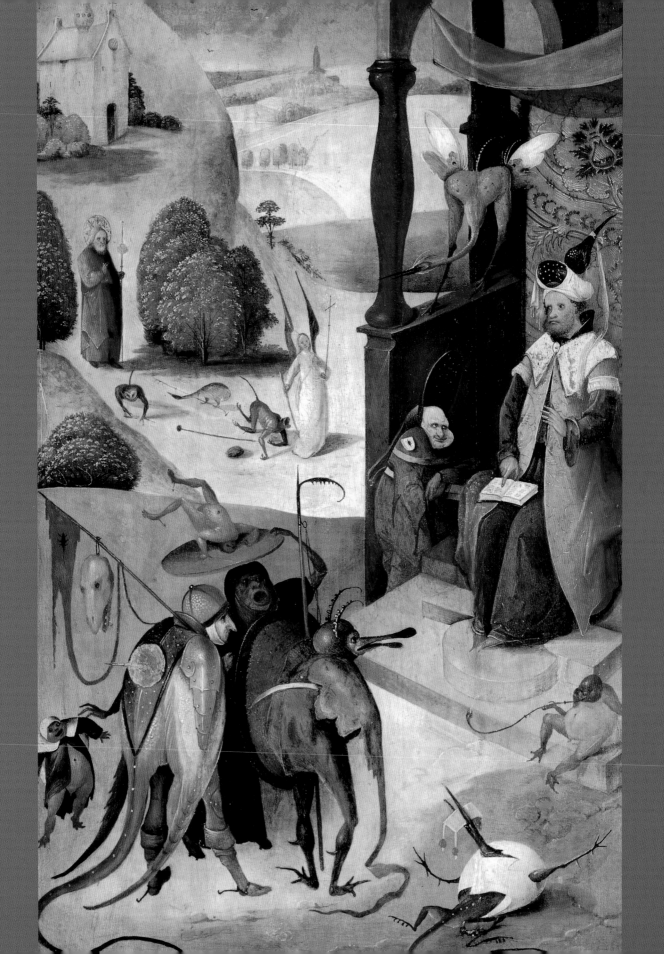

OPPOSITE *Hermogenes eventually renounces his magic and converts
to Christianity. Here, we see his baptism, his magical books abandoned in the foreground.*
ABOVE *Simon Magus, the biblical magician who converted to Christianity, later relapsed
into magic. According to the apocryphal Acts of Peter, he eventually fell to his death
while attempting to levitate above the Roman Forum.*

III.

Northern Magic

An imaginary recreation of a Druidic festival at Stonehenge, one of Britain's most magically charged sites.

While the occult sciences flourished in the warm climates of the Mediterranean and Near East, in the distant north of Europe something else was happening. There, the Celts, and later the Germanic peoples of Scandinavia, were developing their own brand of magic and ritual, one typically close to nature and rooted in the hostile landscape.

One of the earliest monuments to this kind of magical thinking was Stonehenge, in the south-west of England. Built between the third and first millennium BC, it has been associated with sun worship, healing and Druidical rituals. But who were the Druids? The mainstays of religion and ritual in Iron Age Britain and France, they are known mostly through the attempts of Romans and Greeks to understand their culture. The earliest description of a Druid comes from Julius Caesar's accounts of the conquest of the British Isles. However, the Romans then proceeded to stamp out Druidism – the emperor Tiberius (ruled AD 14–37) outlawed Druids, soothsayers and healers – and after the second century AD Druids disappear from the Roman historical record altogether.

There are also no contemporary images of Druids; those familiar to us today are the result of historical reconstruction. Even the familiar association between Druids and mistletoe is based on only a single passage in Pliny: 'The Druids – that is what [the Celts] call their magicians – hold nothing more sacred than the mistletoe.' From Pliny we also know that mistletoe was to be gathered on the sixth day of the moon, and that it had to be cut with a golden sickle. While the Roman's account was itself second-hand, it seems certain that Druidical magic was rooted in nature and the landscape.

The epic stories of the Celtic peoples living in the British Isles and Gaul teem with magical animals, witches and sorcerers, curses and charms. Over time, of course, Christianity also began to have an influence. Early accounts of the spread of Christianity tell how the Druids resisted, using their magical powers. In St Adamnan's *Life of St Columba* – the saint who converted Scotland to Christianity in the sixth century AD – there is a description of the collapse of Druidism. Curiously, the Pictish Druids in this account are referred to as 'magi'. It is also interesting to note that in Irish translations of the Bible, Simon Magus appears as Simon Druí – equating Druid with magician. In later Welsh epics, such as the Book of Taliesin, Druids appear as seers and prophets, able to see into the future.

The Irish and Welsh Celtic traditions are particularly rich in magic, with the Welsh tradition giving birth to the legends of King Arthur. The Irish tradition is perhaps the

The wizard Merlin building Stonehenge. According to some early versions of the Arthurian legends, Merlin uses magic and the help of an African giant to transport the stones to Salisbury Plain, Stonehenge's location in southern England.

t bien retrait et bn role
ne par force a la menom
e purrent fait prendre vn tom

Trahez vous dit merlin en ius
a par fortene fepes plus
forure engine et amou

Siegfried, one of the heroes of Germanic mythology, was made invincible by being
bathed in dragon's blood. Only one part of his body was left unprotected by the magic:
a spot between his shoulder blades, where the warrior Hagen now aims his spear.

most complete in terms of surviving literature, with three key cycles of stories, while in
Brythonic mythology (relating to Brittany, Wales and Cornwall) the key work is the
Mabinogion, a collection of prose tales from the eleventh to thirteenth centuries that are
full of magic and magical objects. In Irish mythology we find the four magical treasures
of the Tuatha Dé Danann, an ancient race of gods: a spear that never misses, a sword
that always kills, a cauldron that always satisfies, and a stone that roars when the rightful
king rests his feet on it. Likewise, in Welsh mythology we find the Thirteen Treasures of
the Island of Britain, including a chariot that will take a man anywhere, a hamper that
replenishes itself, and the magical mantel of Arthur that renders the wearer invisible.

To the east and north of the British Isles another religion and world view was flourishing. In the Germanic and Nordic countries, the pagan Germanic–Norse religion held sway – the religion of Thor and Odin, of Loki and Freya. The Nordic, Germanic and Anglo-Saxon mythologies, which are closely related to one another, are all fundamentally magical, and this magic stretches between the realm of the gods and the realm of humankind.

Because the inhabitants of the Germanic and Nordic regions left no written accounts of themselves, we are forced to rely on the archaeological record and on the accounts of others. Indeed, the earliest records we have of the magic of these peoples come once again from the Romans, specifically Tacitus. Writing in the first century AD, the historian describes the Northerners' use of divination and augury, remarking that they also interpret the neighing of white horses.

The Romans identified the principal god of the Germanic and Nordic tribes as Mercury; the tribes themselves, however, knew him as Odin or Woden. Odin, like Mercury (Hermes for the Greeks), is effectively a god of magic, capable of changing shape and of talking to the dead. As we know from the stories and poems written down in Iceland in the thirteenth century –

known today as the *Prose Edda* and *Poetic Edda* respectively – Odin sacrificed himself to bring the runes to humankind. In the ninth-century Merseburg Incantations, two magic spells written in Old High German, he is called on for his powers of healing. And in 'The Lay of Loddfafnir', from the *Poetic Edda*, Odin claims: 'If up in a tree I see a corpse hanging high, the mighty runes I write and colour, make the man come down to talk with me.' The runes, it was believed, could actually bring a man back to life.

The title page of a manuscript copy of the Prose Edda, *featuring such figures from Norse mythology as Odin, Heimdallr and Sleipnir.*

OPPOSITE AND ABOVE *Celtic and Nordic mythology share a preoccupation with magical objects. Opposite is a depiction of the creation of the Sampo, a mysterious magical object that dominates Finnish mythology; above, men fight over the magic pigskin of Tuis, King of Greece.*

CELTIC MAGIC

The Celts are one of the most mysterious peoples in history, not least because we know about them only through third-party accounts and, early on at least, they left no written records behind. While the Celts covered most of western Europe before the Roman conquest, today their languages survive only in north-west France, Ireland and Wales.

The Celts were animistic, believing that the land was full of spirits; indeed, according to the world view of the Celts, every living thing had a spirit. Druids were a mainstay of Celtic society, but others also engaged in magic. Bards were held in particularly high esteem, and told magical stories of gods and strange creatures. One famous bard, Taliesin – active in the sixth century AD – had the ability to prophesy the future. In Ireland at about the same time we find the *file*, a form of seer-poet who was also capable of seeing into the future.

ABOVE *One of the stories in the* Mabinogion *tells of a battle between the red and the white dragons. This depiction of the battle includes the figure of King Arthur, looking on.* OPPOSITE *Celtic legends are full of heroes and sorcerers. Here, they appear in the dreams of the famous bard Oisín.*

Occasionally, bards would be at the centre of the story. According to legend, the greatest bard of Ireland was Oisín, the son of a woman who had been turned into a deer by a Druid. Oisín is visited by a fairy, Niamh, who takes him to Tír na nÓg, the land of youth. After three years there, Oisín decides to return to Ireland, which he does on the back of a magical horse called Embarr. Arriving home, he discovers that he has in fact been gone for 300 years.

Magic runs throughout Celtic mythology. One of the best-known books of Celtic legends, the *Mabinogion*, tells of such sorceresses as Ceridwen, who brews a potion for a year and a day to give her hideously ugly son wisdom.

This 16th-century woodcut illustrates various forms of divination, including pyromancy (interpretation of fire), hydromancy (interpretation of water), liver divination, palmistry and necromancy.

DIVINATION

Divination is the art of seeing into the future using supernatural means. It is the oldest form of magic, as well as the most widely practised. Although it takes many different forms, it can be broadly divided into two categories: cleromancy (the casting of lots) and omen interpretation. The origin of the word 'divination' means 'to be divinely inspired' – for the will of a god or demon to be expressed through an apparently random occurrence.

A bewildering array of techniques is employed in divination. Rhabdomancy, for example, is divination with a wand or staff (such as dowsing), while bibliomancy involves flicking through a book and choosing a passage at random. In gyromancy a person is placed inside a circle formed of letters and made to spin until they are dizzy. A message then emerges from where on the circle they stumble or fall over.

*A leaf of a divinatory almanac from pre-Columbian Mexico, part of which depicts
the four stages of a woman's life. In the 17th century this codex belonged to Archbishop
Laud, who also collected works by the magician John Dee.*

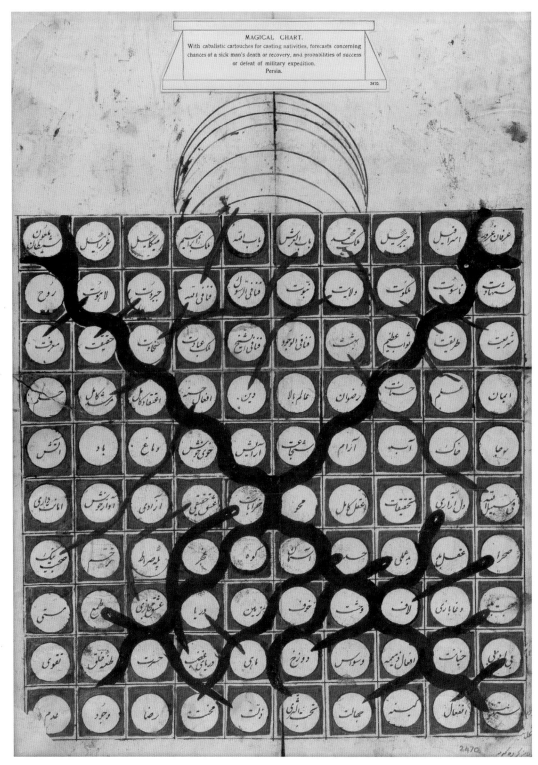

*This mid-19th-century Persian chart was used to divine whether people would
live or die, or whether there would be military success.*

Users of this divination bowl, which features both Islamic and Jewish iconography, may have interpreted the reflection of light on its sides. Other divination methods include casting stones or studying the entrails of a sacrificed animal and interpreting the patterns made.

Divination can be found in unexpected places. In the Acts of the Apostles, lots were cast to determine which of two men should replace Judas Iscariot as the twelfth disciple: 'And they cast lots for them, and the lot fell on Matthias, and he was numbered with the eleven apostles' (Acts 1:26). Belomancy – divination by use of arrows, either by firing them or by drawing them from a quiver – is also referred to in the Bible: 'For the king of Babylon stands at the parting of the way, at the head of the two ways, to use divination; he shakes the arrows, he consults the household idols, he looks at the liver' (Ezekiel 21:21).

Lithomancy is the interpretation of gems and stones, while nephomancy is the interpretation of clouds. Finally, and perhaps most sinister of all, necromancy is communication with the dead in order to predict the future.

The Druids, or the Conversion of the Britons to Christianity.

ABOVE AND OPPOSITE *Among the Druids' rituals was the cutting of mistletoe – regarded as sacred by the Druids – with a golden sickle on the sixth day of the Moon (opposite). The scene above shows this ritual being interrupted by the arrival of Christians, who eventually suppressed the Druidical tradition.*

DRUIDS

Among the Celtic peoples of Gaul, Britain, Ireland and possibly elsewhere during the Iron Age, a Druid was a member of the educated, professional class. They are most commonly referred to as religious leaders, although their numbers also included poets and doctors.

Very little is known about the ancient Druids. They left no written accounts of themselves, and the only evidence for their existence is a few descriptions left by Greek, Roman and various other authors and artists, as well as stories created by later medieval writers.

OPPOSITE AND ABOVE *Very little is known about the original Druids; all we have are fanciful reinterpretations, such as the one opposite. And while some have assumed that it was an exclusively male caste, others have challenged this assumption.*

While archaeological evidence has been uncovered pertaining to the religious practices of the Iron Age, no surviving artefact has been conclusively associated with the Druids of ancient times. Nevertheless, various themes emerge in a number of the Graeco-Roman accounts of the Druids, including that they performed animal and even human sacrifice, believed in a form of reincarnation, and held a high position in Gaulish society. Next to nothing is known for certain about their cultic practice, except for the ritual of oak and mistletoe, as described by Pliny the Elder. In this ritual, after harvesting mistletoe from an oak tree, the Druid would sacrifice two white bulls. They would then make a potion with the mistletoe that was believed to be an antidote to all poisons.

MAGICAL PLACES

Magic is often associated with liminal times and places, particularly crossroads – most obviously in the cult of Hecate. Magic is also frequently associated with dense areas of woodland, with the enchanted forest – a dark, impenetrable space full of magic – being a commonplace in folk stories around the world. Julius Caesar claimed that the Hercynian Forest, an ancient and dense woodland that covered much of southern Germany, was home to unicorns, while in Norse mythology the enchanted Járnviðr is where monsters are born.

Magic is also linked with the centre of the world. For the ancient Greeks this was considered to be at Delphi, the place where the monstrous Python had been killed. Marked by an omphalos, a conical stone representing the 'navel' of the Earth, it also gave rise to the Delphic oracle.

PYTHIA

OPPOSITE *The adventures of Ivan Tsarevich — one of the central figures of Russian folklore — take him to many magical places. In his search for the Firebird and the Horse with a Golden Mane, however, everything hinges on a crossroads, where a critical decision has to be made.*
ABOVE *The Pythia, as the oracle at Delphi was known, being consulted by the people. She was said to deliver her prophecies on the spot where the monstrous Python was killed — hence her name.*

*Stonehenge seems to have been a sacred place even before the present monument was built.
Today, it is seen as a locus for magic, and is especially popular at solstice time.*

Most magical traditions believe that some places are more suitable than others for carrying out magic. Aleister Crowley, wanting to perform the Abramelin ritual, bought an appropriately oriented house in an attempt to ensure the ritual's success (see page 361).

The pyramids of Egypt have long been seen as having magical properties, in part because of their apparent connection to the stars and their geometric underpinnings. The Great Pyramid at Giza, for example, is astrologically aligned with the constellation of Orion.

Scholomance, said to be located deep in the Transylvanian Alps, in what is now central Romania, was believed to be the Devil's own school for black magic. According to legend, every tenth scholar there was kept by the Devil as payment.

Magical places are often deep underground. This 'initiation well', used in magical rites, was excavated at the Quinta da Regaleira estate in Sintra, Portugal.

NORSE & GERMANIC MAGIC

In Norse culture, magic is largely concerned with the business of understanding and shaping destiny. One particularly important character in this regard was the *völva*, meaning 'carrier of a magic staff'. These female seers regarded themselves as servants of the goddess Freya.

There are in fact three types of magic in Norse culture. Ritual magic was called *seiðr*, and was mostly practised by women. It was also associated with the god Odin, and some have speculated that it was shamanic in nature. *Galdr* refers to magic involving runes and incantations; according to legend, it could sink ships and bring about storms. The third type of magic, *trolldómr*, is closest in nature to witchcraft. In the saga of Grettir, the protagonist's mother warns: 'Be wary of sorcery; few things are mightier than black magic.' Over time, with the Christianization of the Nordic countries from the eighth to the twelfth century, these traditions were lost.

Odin leans on his spear while addressing a völva *in 'Völuspá', the first poem in the* Poetic Edda. *Several real-life* völva *graves have been found, containing what appear to be wands.*

Huld is a mythical völva or seiðkona — a woman who practised seiðr *(ritual magic).*
She is mentioned in the Ynglinga saga, *the* Sturlunga saga
and a late-medieval Icelandic tale.

OPPOSITE *This Viking locket contains the remains of a snake.
Such amulets were believed to have magical properties.*
ABOVE *The Norse gods feasted on Apples of Immortality and
Youth, which were looked after by the goddess Idunn.*

Magic is a key component of Norse mythology, with dwarfs, dragons, cursed gold and magical weapons coming together to create a world in which nothing is what it seems. The dwarfs, led by the master magician Hreidmar, were skilled in producing magical objects: Thor's magical hammer, Mjölnir; the spear of Odin; a self-replicating ring called Draupnir.

The most famous of these objects, however, was the cursed ring known as Andvaranaut. Capable of making gold, the ring was guarded by the dwarf Fafnir, who turned himself into a dragon for the purpose. Later, Fafnir was killed by Sigurd, who, after drinking the dragon's blood, was able to understand the speech of birds.

MAGICAL OBJECTS

Perhaps the most common magical object is the ring. In Greek mythology, the Lydian king Gyges possessed a ring that made the wearer invisible; rings with similar qualities can be found in the *Mabinogion* and Tolkien's *Lord of the Rings*. King Solomon was said to have owned a ring that gave him power over the weather and animals; Aladdin, meanwhile, could use his magical ring to summon a djinn, or spirit. In the Anglo-Saxon period, people wore rings bearing magical runic inscriptions.

Magical clothing is also common. The Greek goddess Athena had a cap of invisibility, while the Harry Potter stories by J. K. Rowling feature a cloak of invisibility – one of three magical objects called the Deathly Hallows.

According to Greek mythology, the magical ring of the Lydian king Gyges was found by a shepherd in a bronze horse. The shepherd used the ring to infiltrate the royal household, murder Gyges, and become king of Lydia himself.

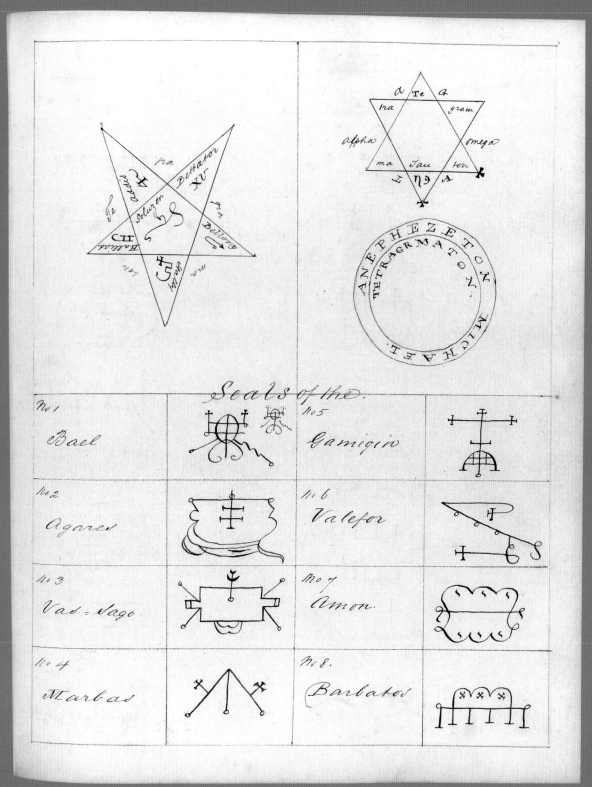

Designs for a variety of magical objects. At top left is a pentagonal figure to be made of gold or silver, and to be worn on the heart. The six-pointed star at top right should be made using calfskin parchment and shown to an invoked spirit, who will be compelled to obey the owner. Beneath that is an image of Solomon's magical ring, with the seals of specific spirits in the bottom half of the page.

*Arthur draws the magical sword Excalibur from its stone, showing him
to be the rightful heir to the throne. In other versions of the Arthurian legend, the
sword is given to Arthur by the Lady of the Lake.*

Sun Wukong, the Monkey King, carrying his magical iron staff, which weighed some 8 tonnes. Each of his hairs could turn into a clone of the monkey.

Magical weapons are a mainstay of mythology. In Japanese folklore the wielder of the sword Kusanagi-no-Tsurugi can control the winds, while Thor's hammer, Mjölnir, always returns to him when he throws it. In the Chinese epic *The Journey to the West*, the protagonist, the Monkey King, carries a magical iron staff called Ruyi Jingu Bang that can be made to shrink or grow on command.

In Welsh mythology, it is said that the sword Dyrnwyn, one of the Thirteen Treasures of the Island of Britain, will burn the hands of an unworthy man. In the mythology of Persia, the sword Shamshir-e Zomorrodnegār – originally owned by King Solomon – offers protection against magic.

Apparently dedicated to Odin, this bracteate (a plate of thinly beaten precious metal) contains the runes for 'alu', a word that had amuletic qualities.

CHARMS, RUNES & SIGILS

The mysterious runes of the Norsemen have long been associated with magic. Found on stones dating from between the fourth and twelfth centuries, they often spell out magical formulas. According to Norse mythology, the runes revealed themselves to Odin after he had sacrificed himself on the tree of Yggdrasil.

In the *Poetic Edda*, the Valkyrie Sigrdrífa (also known as Brynhildr) puts 'gladness runes'

into the drinking horn of Sigurd, in order to create a memory-draught. She instructs Sigurd on the magical properties of runes, showing him, for example, how to carve 'victory runes' into the hilt, grip and inlay of his sword.

It is possible that runes were also used for divination. The Roman historian Tacitus describes a divination ritual involving 'symbols' carved into pieces of wood, but this evidence is inconclusive.

In this scene from the Poetic Edda, Sigrdrífa brings a drinking horn to Sigurd.
He does not know that it contains magical runes.

Swedish rune stones can be difficult to decipher. While the runes were believed to have magical properties, the stones themselves are often used as grave markers.

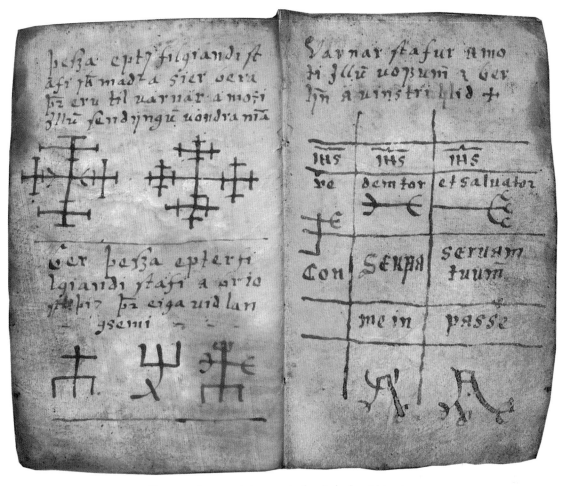

Two pages from a magical manuscript from Iceland, containing staves.

In Iceland, where magical beliefs endured for longer than in other Nordic countries, one finds a wide range of sigils. Also known as staves, these magical symbols were designed to perform a wide range of functions, from warding off enemies and ensuring success in court to curing sickness. In one of the more infamous examples of Icelandic witchcraft, a stave embossed on a pair of so-called necropants – trousers made from the skin of a dead man – guaranteed the wearer great wealth. This somewhat macabre practice was carried out as recently as the seventeenth century.

Anglo-Saxon metrical charms, meanwhile, are aimed at magically influencing situations through incantations. Well-known examples include the 'Nine Herbs Charm' and 'For a Swarm of Bees'. The former is an antidote to poisoning, where the number nine has special significance. The Anglo-Saxon *Lacnunga*, a collection of medical texts and prayers, includes charms to protect against dwarfs.

ABOVE *Some stories tell that Merlin was the son of an incubus and a nun, while others add that baptism at birth converted his knowledge into godly wisdom and prophecy.*
OPPOSITE *In the end, once he had taught the Lady of the Lake everything he knew, Merlin was undone by his own magic – as depicted here by Edward Burne-Jones.*

Merlin

The wizard Merlin is a central figure in the story of King Arthur and his knights. His origins are only semi-mythical, beginning in Welsh legend as the prophet Myrddin. Myrddin's prophecies were first popularized by Geoffrey of Monmouth in around 1130, in the *Prophetiae Merlini*. A little later, in his *Historia Regum Britanniae*, Geoffrey introduced the figure of Merlin – now a powerful wizard – into the court of King Arthur.

Geoffrey's account of Merlin injected some interesting elements into the story, including that the wizard was responsible for building Stonehenge. The third book on Merlin by Geoffrey, *Vita Merlini*, also introduces the figure of Morgan le Fay (see page 142), a powerful sorceress adversary.

Later accounts add yet more colourful detail – for example, that Merlin's father was an incubus (a male demon believed to have sex with sleeping women), from whom Merlin inherited his supernatural powers, or that he had the ability to shape-shift, taking on the form of animals or other humans. In the account by the medieval French poet Robert de Boron, Merlin is responsible for designing and creating the famous Round Table.

Merlin's role as a prophet continued, with the wizard foreseeing many of the conflicts in the quest for the Holy Grail. His end came when he himself fell under the spell of the Lady of the Lake, the ruler of Avalon. Once she had learnt all his magic, she sealed him in a tree (or, in some stories, a cave).

de samit qi portoit sor ses espaules. a pir
de dras estoit forrez dun blanc samit.
Quant il la vestu et appareillie se li dit ne

et mon besaiol le roi pescheor et li do
de par moi qe je li mi recon au plus to
qe ge porre et qe ge en aurai loisir.

OPPOSITE *A miniature from a 14th-century manuscript shows Sir Galahad arriving at Arthur's court, led by a hermit. The rest of the knights are already seated at the famous Round Table.* ABOVE *An Arthurian mosaic in Otranto, Italy. King Arthur is pictured with the man-eating cat known as Cath Palug.*

THE ARTHURIAN LEGENDS

The story of King Arthur and his knights of the Round Table has become one of the world's best-known magical cycles. According to legend, the central figure, King Arthur, was a fifth- or sixth-century ruler of the British Isles, defending them against Saxon invaders. He first appears in Welsh stories, where he is pitted against such supernatural enemies as giants, witches, dragons and monstrous cats.

However, it was not until the 1130s, when Geoffrey of Monmouth wrote his *Historia Regum Britanniae*, that the tales of Arthur and his court became truly popular. Geoffrey's history cements some of the tales' key magical elements: the sword Excalibur, Arthur's magical conception at Tintagel (where his father, Uther Pendragon, uses Merlin's magic to secure the wife of an enemy) and the king's final rest – or is it hibernation? – at magical Avalon.

An injured King Arthur is taken to the enchanted island of Avalon. Accompanying the king on this, his final journey is Morgan le Fay (see page 142).

The legend quickly accumulated further magical detail. The figure of Lancelot and the story's association with the Holy Grail – said to bring eternal life – were added in the twelfth century by the French poet Chrétien de Troyes. The thirteenth century saw the addition of the sword in the stone, set there by Merlin so that only the true king, Arthur, could extract it. Other magical elements clustered around the core story, introducing such figures as Tristan and Iseult, as well as such well-known features as the Round Table. The legend took its final form in the fifteenth century, with Thomas Malory's *Le Morte d'Arthur*.

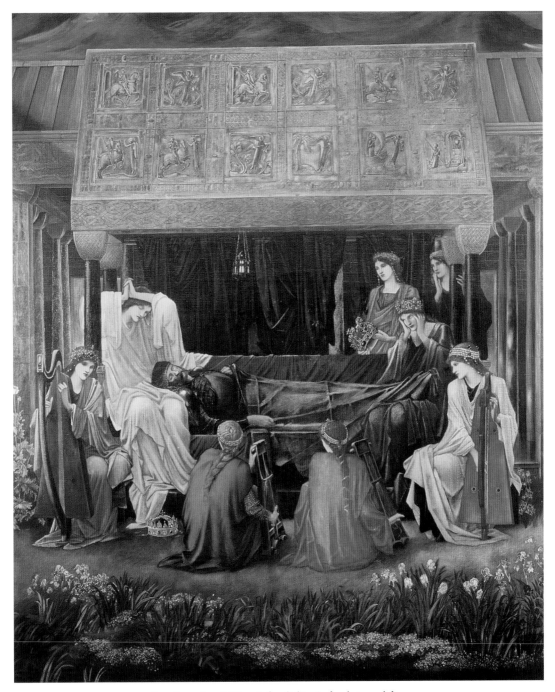

*According to legend, King Arthur died in Avalon, but some believe
that he will return to lead his people when needed.*

Morgan throws Excalibur's sheath into the lake, to the infuriation of Arthur. Some sources claim that she was the king's sister or half-sister.

HOW. MORGAN. LE
FAY. GAVE. A. SHIELD
TO. SIR. TRISTRAM.

Morgan gives a shield to Tristram, the Cornish knight who was also known as Tristan.

Morgan le Fay

The word 'fay' means 'sorceress', and is related to the word 'fairy' (*fae* in Old French). In early accounts, Morgan le Fay is depicted as a healer, an inhabitant – or ruler – of the enchanted island of Avalon.

Beginning as an apprentice to Merlin, Morgan later becomes the enemy of Arthur. The legend of King Arthur and his knights places Morgan as Guinevere's handmaiden, cast out from Camelot and motivated by revenge. Her many attempts to kill Arthur and his wife using magic are foiled.

Descriptions of Morgan's family relationships vary from story to story. According to some, she had eight sisters, all magicians capable of shape-shifting; in others, she is actually Arthur's sister; in others still she is the sister of the Lady of the Lake. Some describe her as the mother of Oberon, the king of the fairies (the father was supposedly Julius Caesar).

Over time, the stories become darker. Morgan is identified as someone who lives 'in defiance of God' and summons dragons. Her home is given as the Vale of No Return, an enchanted realm where her lovers are held prisoner, and she is said to own a magical book of prophecies that is fatal to anyone who reads certain of its passages.

In more recent times, Morgan has become symbolic of the powerful feminine practitioner of magic, as well as a popular figure in contemporary fiction. It is this constant reinvention that has made her so enchanting.

Morgan le Fay the sorceress, performing a magic ritual.

IV.
Medieval Magic

The concept of the witches' sabbath as we now understand it arose in the late Middle Ages.

The medieval period in Europe marked the return of a more sophisticated approach to magic. This approach reflected not only an increasingly refined 'Christian' occult tradition, but also a growing awareness of the earlier Hermetic, Kabbalistic and alchemical traditions – as well as of the work of the Greek philosophers, which had been largely lost in the preceding centuries. Where did these lost ideas re-emerge from? Alchemy in particular was highly dependent on Arabic works, which were a mixture of translations of earlier classical texts and original thinking from the Middle East. For example, the important alchemical and medical treatises by the Persian polymath Rhazes, as well as such works as the *Kitab al-Kimya* (*The Book of the Composition of Alchemy*) by the Arab chemist Geber (see page 228 for both Geber and Rhazes), were translated into Latin in the twelfth century. Such works became mainstays of alchemical thought throughout the medieval period and into the Renaissance. Similarly, the text of the Emerald Tablet, attributed to Hermes Trismegistus, was first translated into Latin from Arabic in the twelfth century.

Another key text translated from Arabic is the *Secretum Secretorum* (The Secret of Secrets). First published in Latin in 1120, in a translation commissioned by the Portuguese queen, it covers the subjects of astrology, alchemy, magic, gems, numbers and science. A thirteenth-century version includes another translation of the Emerald Tablet. The text of the tablet claims that it was translated into Arabic from Greek – and much of *Secretum Secretorum* takes the form of letters supposedly exchanged by Aristotle and Alexander the Great. However, no original in Greek has ever been found. This claim may well have been an attempt to lend pedigree to ideas that were actually syntheses of earlier Hellenistic thinking and Arabic scientific thought.

The medieval period saw a widespread fascination with alchemy, but the steps were often shrouded in secrecy and obscure imagery. This watercolour represents the state of putrefaction (see page 224).

The 13th-century philosopher and friar Roger Bacon became a passionate devotee of alchemy, conducting many experiments – here in a vaulted cloister.

The *Secretum Secretorum* had an enormous influence on thought in the Middle Ages, and some scholars have suggested that it was one of the most-read texts of the time. One person who was profoundly influenced by it was the English philosopher and Franciscan friar Roger Bacon (1214/20–1292). Bacon, who is seen as one of the pioneers of the scientific method, also had a reputation as a sorcerer of sorts, and it is believed that he made a 'brazen head' that could tell the future.

One of Bacon's contemporaries was the German friar Albertus Magnus (*c.* 1200–1280), who took a particular interest in astrology. This led to conflict with other Church authorities, specifically at the University of Paris. There, the zealous Bishop Tempier had condemned 219 practices – including astrology, witchcraft, necromancy and geomancy – that he felt were incompatible with Christian thought.

One of the biggest concerns during the so-called Paris Condemnations was that by correlating outcomes with celestial forces, mankind was effectively relieved of free will. Indeed, the debate highlighted some significant contradictions. On the one hand, many of the tales of saints' lives seemed to be entirely magical. Saints' relics, which were believed to have miraculous properties, became increasingly popular, helped by such compilations of the lives of saints as the thirteenth-century *Golden Legend*. In effect, these relics had become amulets – a situation that, a couple of centuries later, would help give rise to the Reformation. On the other hand, what should the official Christian attitude be towards the increasingly popular and accepted Hermetic works?

By way of a solution, the Church learnt to tolerate astrology while coming down hard on such practices as necromancy. William of Auvergne, writing in the early thirteenth century, tried to distinguish 'natural magic' from evil magic. For him, the former operated according to 'natural virtues' – the innate powers of herbs, planets, stones. By contrast, he roundly condemned divination with demonic help, as well as magical operations that employed images or symbols, what he called 'image magic'. Moreover, he explicitly condemned the work of Hermes Trismegistus.

Such attempts to draw a distinction between 'good' and 'bad' magic did not, however, entirely stem the flow of occult works based on ancient knowledge. Medieval authors brought together spells and rituals in compilations that are known today as grimoires. Ironically, some of this interest in occult traditions was stimulated by the Crusades, especially the Fourth Crusade (1202–04), which led to the sack of Constantinople and the return to Western Europe of many classical manuscripts. Others who journeyed to the Middle East on the Crusades were also under suspicion; famously, the Knights Templar were persecuted for their alleged arcane rituals and demonic dealings. Interestingly, in the early Middle Ages, accusations of witchcraft were more likely to be made against men than against women.

The early thirteenth century also saw the birth of Kabbalah as we know it today, beginning with the 'discovery' of the Zohar – the chief text of Kabbalah – by the Spanish rabbi Moses de León. Spain at that time was still partially governed by Islamic rulers; it also had a large Jewish population, many of whom spoke Arabic. The Zohar spread quickly throughout Europe, and would have considerable influence on later occult and magical thinking in the West.

This early 19th-century mural at Rila Monastery, Bulgaria, reflects late-medieval thinking. One of the inscriptions reads: 'Magicians and healers are servants of the devil. That's why the devil rejoices greatly, jumps around, and dances in front of people who come to them … Those who abandon God, the laws, and the church, and go to the healers, are servants not of God, but of the Devil.'

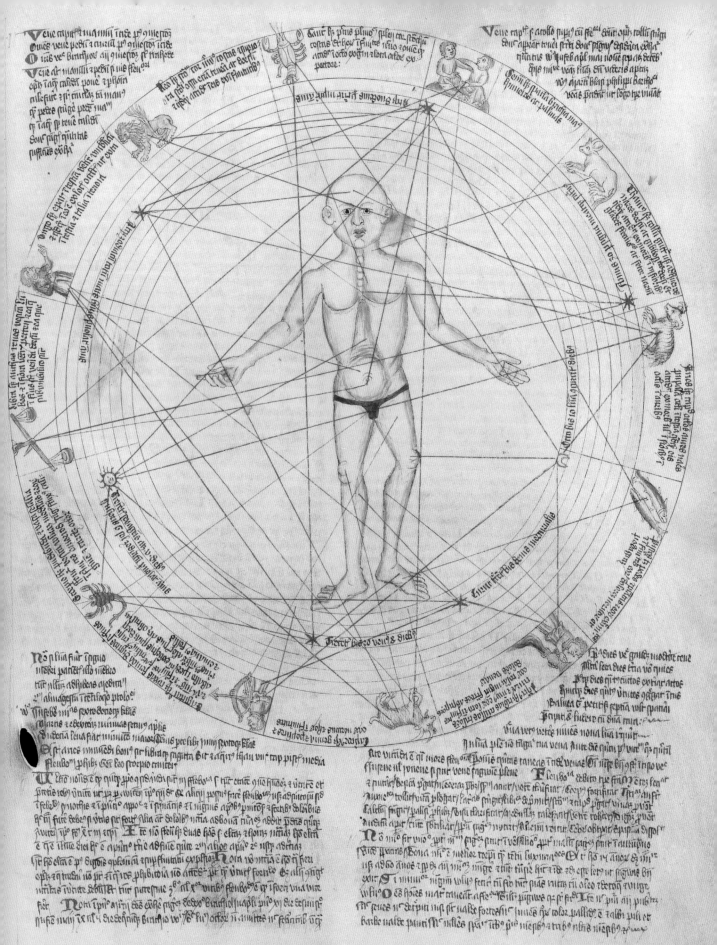

OPPOSITE *This blood-letting chart clearly explains the relationship between the individual and the cosmos, showing the influence of the zodiac and the planets on humans.* ABOVE *The rose window at Lausanne Cathedral in Switzerland is a masterpiece of medieval thought, illustrating the eight winds, the four seasons, the twelve months, the four elements, the zodiac, the four rivers of Paradise, and allegories of Creation. It is a definitive statement of the medieval universe.*

MICROCOSM & MACROCOSM

'As above, so below' is the fundamental tenet of Hermeticism. It is also the rational basis for much of the magic that seeks to influence human affairs through interaction with a higher plane. The idea of an interrelated microcosm (man) and macrocosm (universe) goes back to the concept of the 'Great Chain of Being', derived from Plato and fully developed by the Neoplatonists of the third to the sixth century AD. Simply put,

the Great Chain concept states that everything is interconnected, from God on high down to inanimate objects, with humankind somewhere in the middle.

This interconnectedness is essential to the intellectual underpinning of much magic, since if man is a smaller-scale replica of, or somehow linked to, the universe, then there should be naturally repeating patterns and sympathies between the two.

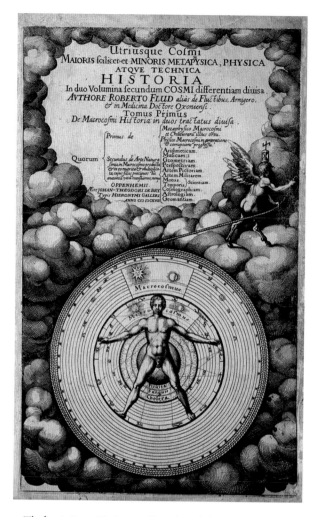

ABOVE *The frontispiece to* Utriusque Cosmi … *(1617–21) by Robert Fludd (see page 291), showing humankind's relationship to the macrocosm. At the top of the illustration, a rope extends from God to Earth.* OPPOSITE *The Middle Ages explained the movements of the planets with a series of rotating spheres, moved by angels. In magical thought, the angels could be contacted and influenced to have an impact on the physical world.*

Well established by the twelfth century – and, of course, reinforcing the hierarchical structure of society at the time – the concept of humankind having a fixed place in the universe was challenged in the Renaissance, when such figures as the Italian nobleman and philosopher Giovanni Pico della Mirandola (see page 196) suggested that humans might elevate themselves above the angels.

Humankind's connection with a divine order endured, however, in the Renaissance concept of the Vitruvian Man. In the sixteenth century Sir Walter Raleigh went even further, likening the hair on a human's head to grass, and the blood in their veins to rivers. It was also reflected in the astrological idea that different parts of the body relate to signs of the zodiac, and that the four humours relate to the four elements.

lautres per mi lairis · las tot tot coluna cuntars
lautres las combo p contens

Dels xii sygnes edela natura deaseus.
Per natura cors amen
Ello cel per son garnimen
in signes. e·vii. planetas
t estellas lizeno enetas
Dels diz signes sapiar quascus

Lus cercles diz zodiacus
ocel entorn en ntrona
maueyra tecorona
t es plantar el se mremen
tabluy fay somouemen

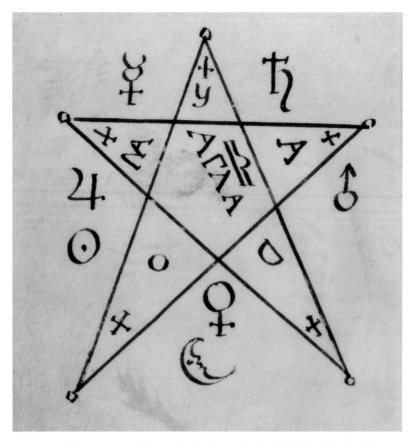

ABOVE *The pentagram seal shown above is often associated with the Devil, but its origins lie with King Solomon. This particular example comes from the* Cyprianus, *or* Black Book *(see page 297).* OPPOSITE *The pentagram is also associated with the human form – an occult version of Leonardo's Vitruvian Man. The illustration at the top shows the correspondences between the stars and the human body.*

MAGICAL SHAPES & SYMBOLS

Symbols and shapes are central to the practise of magic, but in many cases their meanings come from Greek philosophy (although sometimes via the *Hermetica*). Thus, squares can relate to the four directions (north, south, east, west) or the four humours of the Greek world view, while geometry more widely may be used to relate the microcosm to the macrocosm.

The pentagram is familiar to many as an occult symbol, and is often associated with Satan. In fact, the idea that a pentagram pointing upwards is good, while one pointing downwards is evil, is a nineteenth-century invention attributed to Éliphas Lévi (see page 346). Many have traced the pentagram's use to King Solomon, while in Germany it has served as an apotropaic symbol, called the *Drudenfuss*.

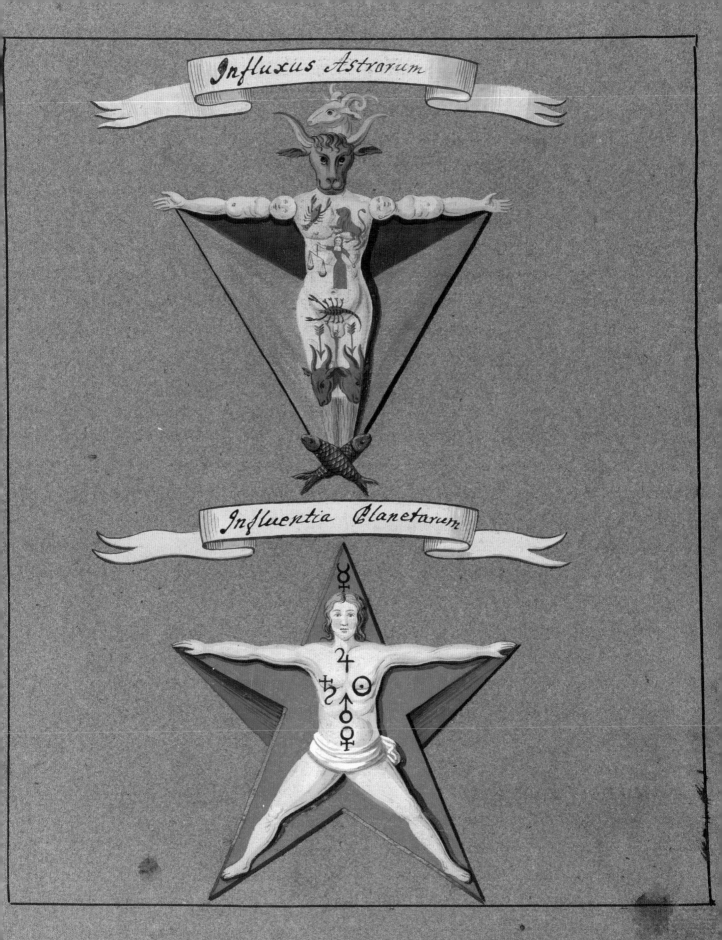

Fig 1

ORNO THOU CRIS HOPHE

Spirit

Fig 2

Fig 3

Alpha et Omega Tronos Sana

Magister.

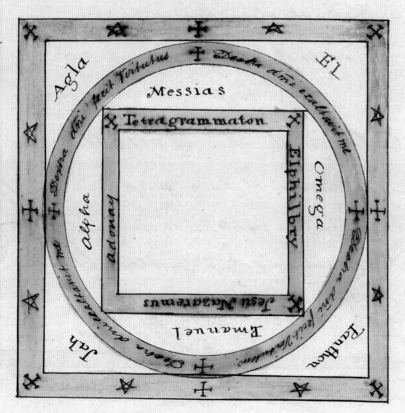

Fig. 4

Agla

EL

Messias

Dextra dmi fecit virtutus · Dextra dmi exaltavit me

Tetragrammaton

Gloria dmi fecit Virtutem

alpha

Adonay

Elphilbry

Omega

Jesu Nazaremus

Emanuel

Gloria dmi exaltavit me

Tamhon

Jah

OPPOSITE AND ABOVE *Circles are important magical shapes. Shown opposite are a series of symbols for invoking the spirits Birto, Agares, Bealpharos and Vassago. The text explains: 'Figure 1 is for the Spirit to appear in; Figure 3 is for the Master, and the figure of the nivern. Figure 2 must be made between them, the circles ought to be made at least 3 feet apart. Figure 4 is a circle for the Master and his Companions to land in when invoking the Spirit Bealpharos.' Above is an ouroboros, a symbol of eternity used frequently in magic.*

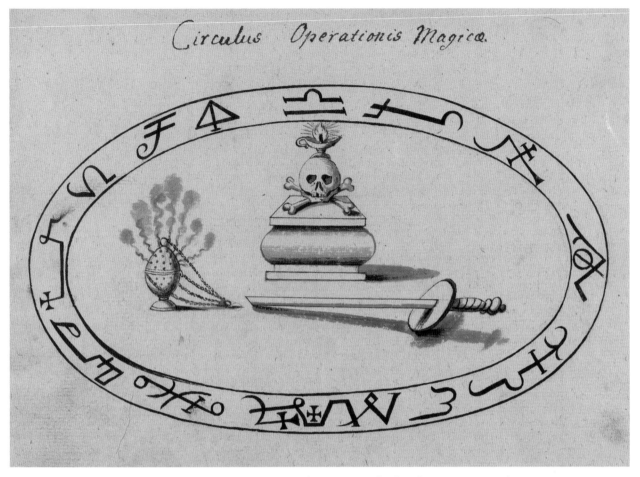

Circulus Operationis Magicæ.

OPPOSITE AND ABOVE *To summon a spirit, the magician must first draw the protective magic circle. Opposite, a magician – pictured with torch, sword and broomstick – seems to be taking part in an act of black magic that requires the hair of a hanged man. Above, the circle contains Kabbalistic symbols.*

The circle appears regularly in both alchemy and practical magic. In alchemy, we find the ouroboros (a snake or dragon swallowing its tail), the symbol of eternity. In practical magic, a circle is drawn around the magician before summoning demons or the dead, so as to offer protection from evil.

Typically, the circle will contain magical symbols and characters.

Witches are often shown congregating in circles, and contemporary practitioners of Wicca use the form regularly. From the circle that is cast, the practitioner is able to build a 'cone of power' through incantation and dance.

Magicians also take great delight in using deliberately obscure symbols. In some cases, they are derived from alchemical or astrological symbols; in others, however, they are pure invention, more related to automatic writing or the embodiment of power in their creation.

Other magical symbols that gain their power in this way include the remarkable Icelandic staves. Perhaps the best known of these is the Helm of Awe, a symbol that grants its wearer protection. Other staves are used for protecting crops, becoming successful or warding off illness. As with the *vévé* drawings found in voodoo (see page 256), the staves' power lies in the creation of the symbols themselves.

TOP *The Helm of Awe, a powerful Icelandic magical stave that instils fear in others.*
ABOVE, LEFT AND RIGHT *Symbols of the spirits of the air, earth, fire and water.*
OPPOSITE *Instructions for ceremonial magicians on how to create a circle that will enable them to raise 'the Mighty Spirit Egin, King of the North'.*

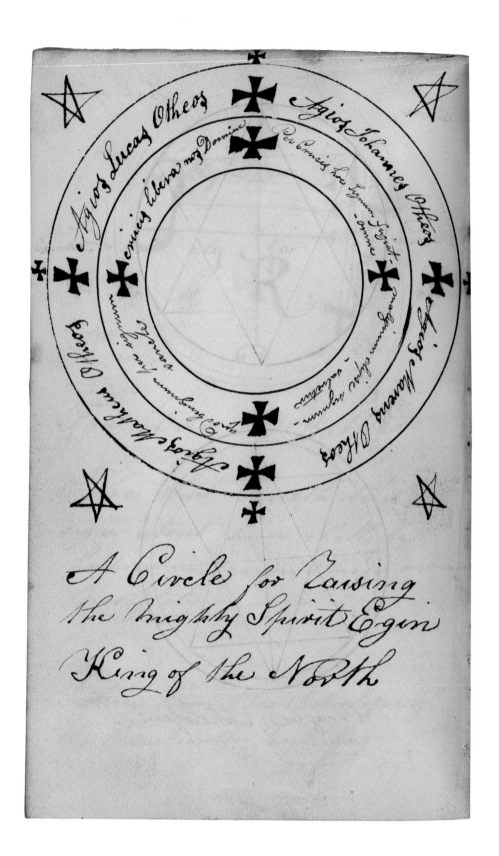

ABOVE *Albertus Magnus lectures to students in Paris.*
OPPOSITE *Albertus expounds his doctrines of physical science in the streets of Paris.*

Albertus Magnus

Albertus Magnus was born in Bavaria in around 1200, and grew to become not only an influential Catholic bishop but also a teacher at the University of Paris. Described as the greatest German theologian and philosopher of his age, he had an enormous influence on the study of Aristotle, and in particular on his student Thomas Aquinas.

Albertus was especially interested in astrology. This he saw as compatible with the Christian world view, since for him the microcosm (man) was inextricably linked to the macrocosm (universe). His *Speculum Astronomiae* (Mirror of Astronomy), written in around 1270, sought to permit astrology in a Christian context. In it, he discusses astrological magic and condemns the (already popular) 'Solomonic' use of seals and talismans, as well as invocations.

After his death, Albertus acquired a reputation as an alchemist and a magician. This was partly due to the German being wrongly identified as the author of certain works. One such work is the *Secreta Alberti* (Secrets of Albert), which contains a number of 'experiments', as well as information on the power of specific stones and plants. While the book may not have been written by Albertus, it displays his interest in the theory of correspondences, and defends the study of magic with an appeal to Aristotle: 'The science of magic is not bad, because thanks to its cognition bad things can be avoided and good things can be pursued.' Part of the legend is that, having perfected production of the philosopher's stone (see page 223), Albertus passed on the secret to Thomas Aquinas.

ABOVE *The demon Belial presents his credentials to King Solomon.*
OPPOSITE *The monstrous 'Lord of Darkness, Dagol', devouring human limbs. Demonology
posited the existence of rafts of demons, each with its own foul characteristics.*

DEMONOLOGY

Demons occupy a strange place within religion and magic, their existence being alternately denied and cited as the cause of misfortune. They play an extremely important role in most occult magic, however, as creatures that can influence the supernatural order, yet without themselves being gods. For this reason, many magicians have sought to contact and control them.

Knowledge of demons was linked to King Solomon in particular, since it was believed that he used them to build his temple. According to the Testament of Solomon (written between the first and fifth centuries AD), he was able to enslave the demons by stamping them with his seal. It is for this reason that Solomonic seals are so prevalent in books on magic: such seals, it was thought, enabled the magician to control supernatural forces.

In the Middle Ages, the key work on the subject was the eleventh-century *De Operatione Daemonum*, by the Byzantine writer, philosopher and politician Michael Psellus. By this point, Christian orthodoxy held that demons *did* exist, but were fallen angels – and should not be contacted.

Seine Rauch A:
Harn von gebraut
und Niesilwurck.
Der fürst der finsternis: Dagol:

LUCIFER,
Empereur.

BELZÉBUT,
Prince.

ASTAROT ,
Grand-duc.

LUCIFUGÉ ,
prem. Ministr.

SATANACHIA ,
grand général.

AGALIAREPT.,
aussi général.

FLEURETY ,
lieutenantgén.

SARGATANAS ,
brigadier.

NEBIROS ,
mar. de camp.

ABOVE *Knowledge of demons – their names, seals, appearances – is central to much magic. These are 'official portraits' of some of the dignitaries of Hell.* OPPOSITE *A startling vision of Hell, with Satan in the centre and tiers of demons punishing sinners.*

Just as angels were arranged in a hierarchy, so too were demons, with Lucifer at the top. A division of labour was introduced whereby each demon had a 'specialism'. While this knowledge may have been interesting to devout Christians, it was far more so to ritual magicians.

Much magic from the Middle Ages onwards focuses on how to summon specific demons by name, in order to make them perform particular tasks. Thus, the sixteenth-century *Pseudomonarchia Daemonum* gives the names of sixty-nine demons, together with the ways in which to summon them. The *Ars Goetia* (the first book of the seventeenth-century grimoire *The Lesser Key of Solomon*) lists seventy-two demons, along with the relevant seal for each. Both works were influenced by the *Liber Officium Spirituum* (The Book of the Office of Spirits).

THE PERSECUTION OF MAGIC

One of the very first anti-magic laws can be found in the Code of Hammurabi, a 'law code' set down in Babylonia in the second millennium BC. The law states that if someone is found to have cast a spell, they must immerse themselves in the holy river to prove their innocence.

Often described as the foundation of ancient Roman law, the Lex XII Tabularum (Law of the Twelve Tables) outlawed magic when it was written in the fifth century BC. In fact, the Roman Empire was a consistent punisher of witchcraft. The Lex Cornelia (82 BC) states that 'Persons who celebrate ... impious or nocturnal rites so as to enchant, bewitch or bind anyone, shall be crucified or thrown to wild beasts ... Magicians themselves shall be burnt alive.' In AD 292 the emperor Diocletian ordered the burning of alchemical books.

In the fourth century AD, St Augustine sought to distinguish magic from miracle, and wrote *On the Divination of Daemons*. However, since only God could suspend the laws of the universe, he also saw little threat from witchcraft.

OPPOSITE *The people of Ephesus, in modern-day Turkey, burn their magic books in front of St Paul.*
RIGHT *The Babylonian Code of Hammurabi, here engraved on a stele, expressly forbade magic.*

ABOVE *The Knights Templar came under suspicion of being heretics and of dabbling in black magic. Many were burnt as punishment.*
OPPOSITE *A Roman soldier oversees the burning of Druids in Anglesey, Wales.*

Things began to change in the thirteenth century, as concerns about heresy increased. Thomas Aquinas argued for the existence of demons, but against magic. In *Summa Theologica* (1265–74), he claims that 'the magic art is both unlawful and futile'. Demons, for him, were capable of facilitating fortune-telling, but did so without going through God.

Thomas was also clear that if 'blending together medicinal herbs, it is not lawful to make use of observances or incantations, other than the divine symbol or the Lord's Prayer'. This meant that, while such groups as the Knights Templar were broken up for high magic and heresy, folk magic went largely unpunished in the early Middle Ages. It was only with the publication of the *Malleus Maleficarum* in 1486 that the widespread persecution of witches began, lasting into the seventeenth century.

LES DRUIDES BRULÉS

dans L'Isle d'Anglesey.

en 64.

Dessiné par Monet   Gravé par David

GRIMOIRES

A grimoire, generally speaking, is a book of spells. More specifically, however, it can also consist of tracts on how to summon demons. The best-known grimoires include *The Sworn Book of Honorius*, *The Munich Manual of Demonic Magic* and the *Grand Grimoire*. The origins of each is at best obscure, although in many cases it is obvious that they share common, yet lost, ancestors.

Supposedly written by Honorius of Thebes, *The Sworn Book of Honorius* is one of the oldest grimoires. The earliest manuscript version dates from the fourteenth century, and was once owned by John Dee (see page 236). However, the first printed copy of the book did not appear until 1629.

The *Picatrix* is another well-known grimoire. Written in Arabic, probably in the eleventh century (although possibly earlier), it includes spells and potions designed to aid the magician, astrological information, and philosophical passages. It had an influence on the Renaissance figures of Marsilio Ficino and Agrippa, and is famous for the wide range of 'unusual' ingredients – excrement, brain, blood – used in its potions.

OPPOSITE *Strange creatures gather round a peculiar-looking harpsichord to sing from grimoires. A witch in bed joins in.* ABOVE *A book of magic spells from Sumatra. The pages are made from tree bark.*

res, et surtout avec ceux qui sont plus doux que les autres;
Si c'est une femme qui doit opérer, qu'elle le porte dans la
poche gauche, ou entre les mammelles; que l'homme écrive
cette figure le jour de Mars : la femme le peut faire grâver
tous les autres jours.

Des Esprits & de leur pouvoir.

L'Esprit supérieur est le Prince qui se nomme Lucifer;
après lui, Belzebut; les inférieurs qui sont sujets à Lucifer,
habitent l'Europe et l'Asie; ceux qui dépendent de Belzebut,
sont dans l'Amérique; Lucifer et Belzebut ont sous eux
deux Chefs qui commandent à leurs Sujets, s'attribuent toute
puissance et ordonnent tout ce qui se fait dans tout le monde:
ils apparoissent à leurs Sujets, en forme d'un Cheval, Serpent
ou Bouc, et à leurs Chefs, en leur forme ordinaire.

Lucifer en Europe et en Asie.

Elestor

Belzebut

Quand tu voudras obtenir quelque chose d'eux, tu dois
premièrement tenir en main leur Caractere, et si tu l'oubliois,
tu

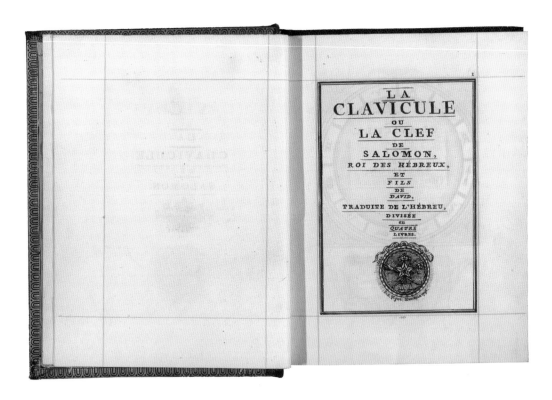

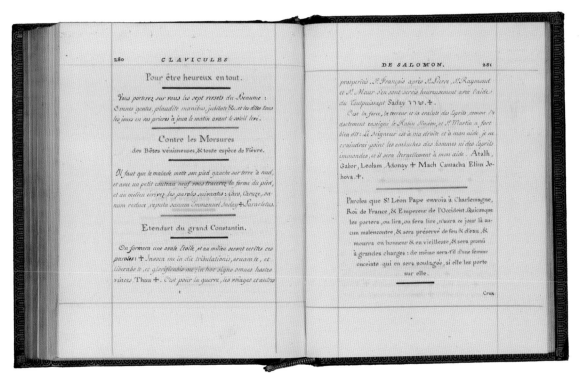

OPPOSITE, ABOVE AND OVERLEAF *A selection of pages from* The Key of Solomon, *including (opposite) a page explaining the hierarchy of demons.*

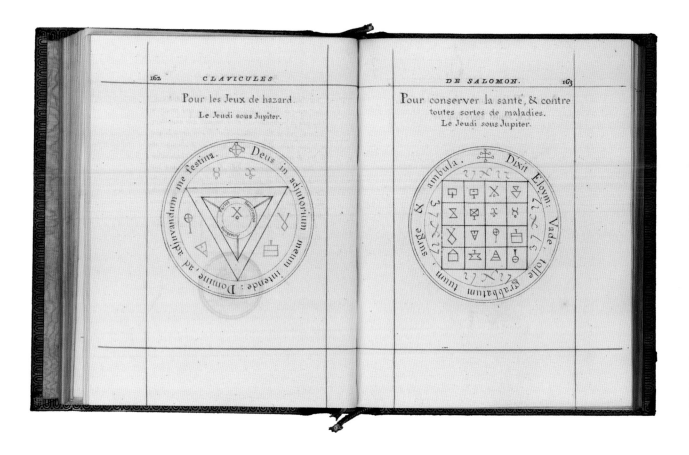

Two very famous grimoires are *The Key of Solomon* and *The Lesser Key of Solomon*. The former appears to be related to a fifteenth-century Greek text, *The Magical Treatise of Solomon*. It contains a variety of spells (how to win love and make oneself invisible, for example), instructions on how to contact and control the dead, and such practical information as what clothing to wear, which instruments to use and so on. The *Lesser Key* dates to the seventeenth century, and contains five books, including the notorious *Ars Goetia*.

Some of the more famous grimoires are seemingly not as old as they claim. *The Book of Abramelin the Mage*, for example, is said to be the autobiography of a Jew named Abraham of Worms, who visited Egypt in the fourteenth century and learnt the magic recorded in its pages. It contains instructions for summoning guardian angels and, in turn, demons – with whose help (guaranteed through word squares) a magician could find buried treasure, ensure love, make themselves invisible and fly. However, the earliest manuscript versions date from the early seventeenth century. Much later, the book would have a significant influence on the Hermetic Order of the Golden Dawn and Aleister Crowley's Thelema (see page 361).

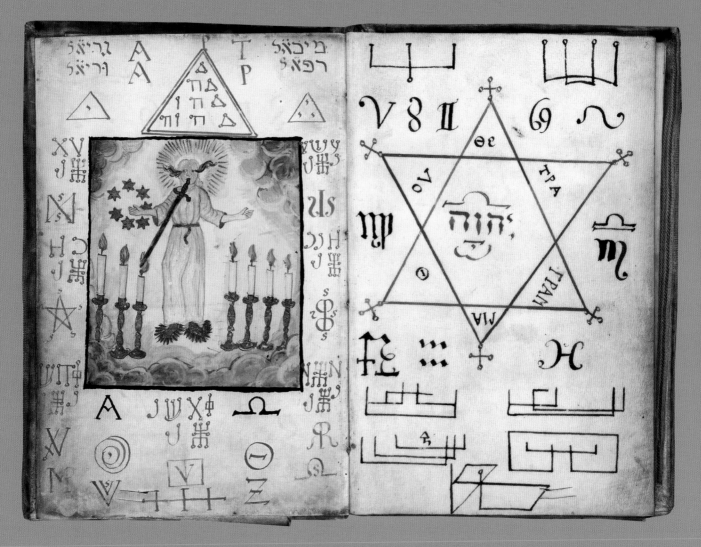

Two pages from an 18th-century Cyprianus. The left-hand page shows the archangel Metatron,
surrounded by alchemical symbols. The right-hand page shows the Seal of Approbata.

MEDICINE & MAGIC

Up until the end of the Middle Ages, it was difficult to tell the difference between medicine and magic. Treatments revolved around herbs, or else tackled a perceived imbalance in the four humours (leading to such practices as blood-letting). Doctors also drew heavily on astrology, as is clear from this extract from Chaucer's *Canterbury Tales* (late fourteenth century):

> With us ther was a DOCTOUR OF PHISIK;
> In al this world ne was ther noon hym lik,
> To speke of phisik and of surgerye,
> For he was grounded in astronomye.
> He kepte his pacient a ful greet deel
> In houres by his magyk natureel.

Later on, the verse mentions that the doctor has read Averroës (the Western name for Ibn Rushd) and Rhazes, both Arabic writers associated with magic and medicine.

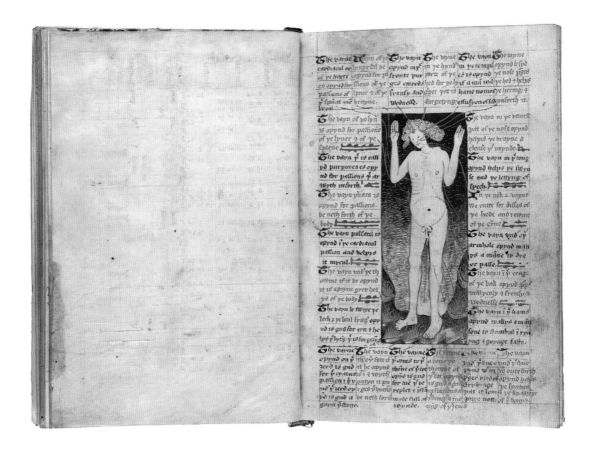

OPPOSITE *A copy of* The Physician's Handbook: English Medical and
Astrological Compendium *(1454).* ABOVE *This allegory shows an apothecary, a physician
and a surgeon made from the tools of their trade. The physician is elevated by his learning – Rhazes,
Avicenna, Arnau de Vilanova – while the apothecary balances the alchemist's alembic on his head.*

MAGICAL PLANTS

Plants and herbs have long been a mainstay of magic, whether used in potions or for ritual. Deadly nightshade was associated with the Greek goddess Circe, while branches of hawthorn were used by Romans to ward off witchcraft – and by Serbs and Croats to kill vampires (in later legend, garlic was used for the same purpose). Mistletoe and oak trees, as we saw earlier, were sacred to the Druids. Some plants used in magic, such as the moly eaten by Odysseus to protect him from Circe's witchcraft, may not even have existed.

OPPOSITE *A Druid holding mistletoe, a plant regarded as sacred in Druidic lore.*
ABOVE, LEFT *It was believed that the mandrake shrieked when plucked, and that the sound could kill a person — or make them go mad. For this reason, the plant was uprooted using either string or a dog.*
ABOVE, RIGHT *Mandrake roots often resemble a human, and were frequently embellished with carving.*

One plant in particular has always been considered especially magical: the mandrake. In part, this is because its roots look uncannily like a human, and in the Middle Ages mandrake-root amulets were common. However, it is also because, when ingested, the root causes hallucinations and delirium.

The association of the mandrake with witchcraft goes back centuries, with its root sometimes used as a poppet (a figure of a human used in sorcery and witchcraft). When Joan of Arc was charged with witchcraft, for example, her accusers claimed that she carried with her a mandrake root.

ABOVE *Plucking mandrake at a distance with the aid of string.*
OPPOSITE *An illustration of mandrake from a medieval Arabic manuscript.*

الحجر من فتات ارض معترمتة ارحم احذقهذا
الفلف من الاحذ مسعته و منفعا و منقطا

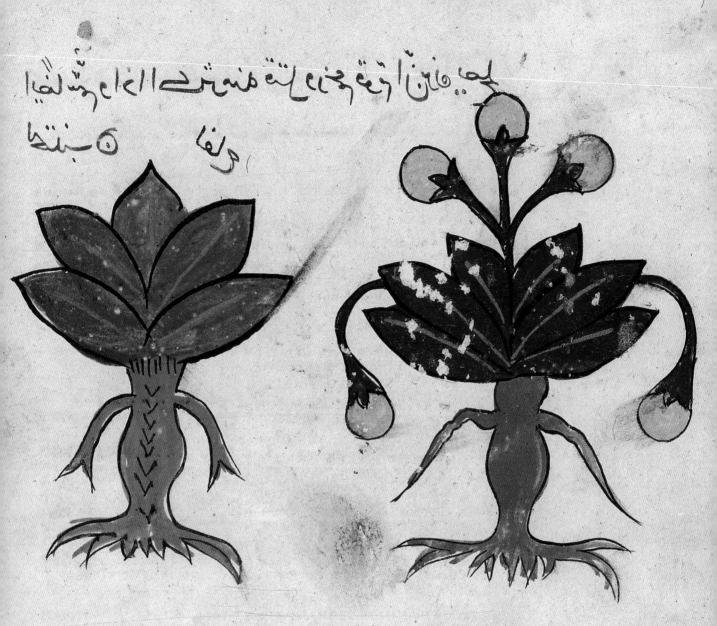

نبتة السلانط هن قلبط احمل قبط خضرا للسانط
من ساعا ورق عبلط ميطه والله من
لهبل حلق حلط احص مص حقنط لها
محض الطم حلط الالوا حلط الفاطلالم

F. Hayman inv.ᵗ et del.   A. Walker sc.

The Druids, or the Conversion of y̆ Britons to Christianity

Druids harvesting mistletoe.

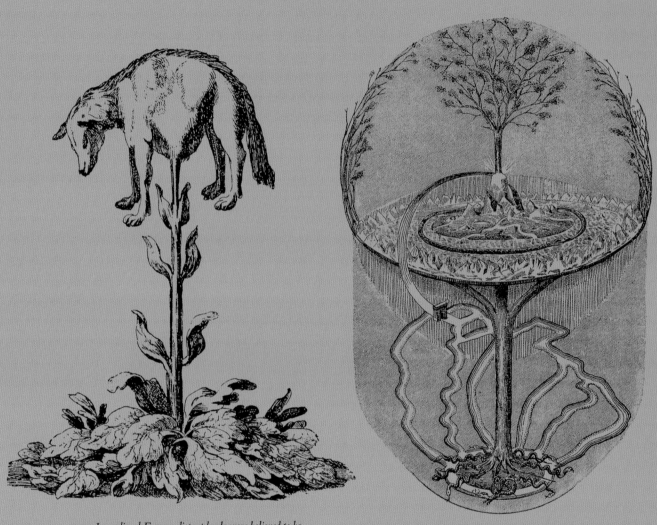

ABOVE *In medieval Europe, distant lands were believed to be*
home to even more miraculous plants. This famous example
is the 'vegetable lamb' of Tartary (Central Asia).
ABOVE, RIGHT *In Norse mythology, the entire world*
was supported by the tree Yggdrasil.

ABOVE *A speculative portrait of Nicolas Flamel.*
OPPOSITE *An illustration of alchemist's equipment, from
a book reputedly written and illuminated by Flamel.*

Nicolas Flamel

In common with some of the other magicians profiled in this book, Nicolas Flamel is famous not for what he did, but rather for what he was alleged to have done. Born in Pontoise, France, in around 1330, he worked as a manuscript dealer and scribe in Paris. He died in 1418, and is buried in the French capital.

It was two centuries after Flamel's death that the stories about him first emerged. In 1612, in a book titled *Le Livre des figures hiéroglyphiques*, a series of claims was made about the Frenchman: first, that he had perfected the art of alchemy, creating the philosopher's stone; and secondly, that with the aid of this legendary substance he had secured not only massive wealth but also immortality for him and his wife. According to the claims, Flamel had become involved in alchemy after acquiring a mysterious book that he could not read. Travelling to Spain to get help with the translation, he encountered a Jewish convert to Christianity who identified the book as being a copy of *The Book of Abramelin the Mage*. Flamel decoded the book, and soon afterwards began perfecting the art of alchemy. Interestingly, while *The Book of Abramelin* itself was supposed to have been written in the fifteenth century, the earliest manuscript dates from around 1608.

The legend of Flamel grew, with alleged sightings of him in the seventeenth century (owing to his immortality), and Isaac Newton discussing him in the margins of his *Theatrum Chemicum*. More recently, he made an appearance as a character in the Harry Potter series (1997–2007), in which he was once again credited with the invention of the philosopher's stone.

V.

Renaissance Magic

The magician John Dee performing an experiment for Queen Elizabeth I.

Stretching from the fourteenth to the sixteenth centuries, the Renaissance is best known for its art, architecture and literature. What is less well known is that it also saw a new fascination with magic and the occult – specifically, the Hermetic tradition and the related areas of alchemy and Kabbalah.

The rise of the Hermetic tradition can be traced to one man: the Italian Marsilio Ficino (1433–1499). Ficino, whose patron was the powerful Florentine Cosimo de' Medici, was fascinated by Plato, and it was while he was working on a translation of Plato from Greek to Latin in 1460 that one of Cosimo's 'text scouts' – someone employed to look for interesting manuscripts – discovered in Macedonia a copy of the *Corpus Hermeticum*. Straight away, Ficino abandoned his work on Plato, and instead began translating the new manuscript into Latin from the Greek. The completed translation was presented to Cosimo in 1463 and published in 1471. For the next century and a half, the Hermetic writings it contained had a marked impact on the intellectual world, provoking the study of alchemy and magic, and influencing the work of Italian philosophers Giordano Bruno and Giovanni Pico della Mirandola.

Ficino's own attitude to magic can be found in the last of his *Three Books on Life* (1489), which includes descriptions of how to harness celestial powers to create amulets and talismans, and make inanimate objects animate. Ficino believed in the 'soul of the world', a spirit that linked all animate and inanimate things. By harnessing this spirit, and the power of the stars, 'magical' change could be effected.

Aside from being a champion of Plato and having a fascination with natural magic, Ficino was a priest. A letter he wrote in 1476 shows that he was well aware of the possible contradiction that this presented: 'People will perhaps laugh at a priest who heeds [astrology]. But I, relying on the authority of the Persians, Egyptians and Chaldeans consider that … Heavenly matters in truth were the sole concern of the Priest.' Members of the establishment were also clearly worried, and in 1489, in front of Pope Innocent VIII, Ficino was accused of practising magic. Only political connections ensured that the accusations were dropped.

OPPOSITE *This group of Florentine intellectuals includes Marsilio Ficino (far left).*
ABOVE *A curious Renaissance depiction of Hermes Trismegistus from Siena Cathedral.*
The book text reads: 'Hermes Mercurius Trismegistus, contemporary of Moses'.

In fact, everywhere in the Renaissance there was confusion over, and a conflation of, the magical and the devout. For example, an intriguing depiction of Hermes Trismegistus in Siena Cathedral, dating from 1488, explicitly identifies him as a contemporary of Moses – and therefore an unexpected but valuable bridge between the pagan and the Christian worlds.

Nevertheless, the Renaissance was an exciting time for intellectuals. Such proto-scientists as Agrippa (1486–1535) and Paracelsus (1493–1541) believed that magic provided them with a shortcut to understanding the meaning of life. Paracelsus, the father of modern medicine, dabbled in astrology and believed that illness was caused by an imbalance between the microcosm and the macrocosm. The study of alchemy, meanwhile, led to modern-style laboratories and the experimental method. For his part, Agrippa gave prominence in his work to the 'Theban alphabet', a magical alphabet of sigils supposedly created by Honorius of Thebes.

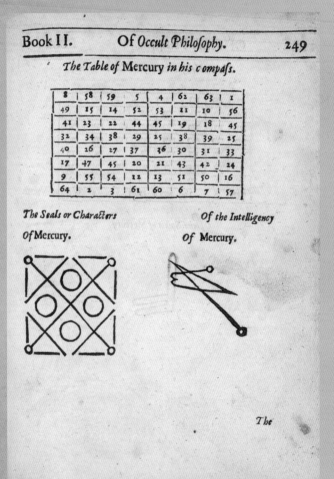

At the same time, new worlds were being opened up as ancient Greek texts were translated into Latin and Italian, and the ruins of Egypt – with all their attendant mystery – were rediscovered. Christopher Columbus's discovery of the New World in 1492 led to an interest in other, non-classical traditions. Some of the artefacts brought back from Mexico by the Spanish conquistador Hernán Cortés had a new life in Europe; the Elizabethan magician John Dee, for example, used an Aztec obsidian mirror for divination.

It has been suggested that the work of Shakespeare – in particular *The Tempest*, written around 1610–11 – reflects this interest in the New World. The key figure in *The Tempest* is the magician Prospero, who draws on the magical abilities of the spirit Ariel. Prospero inhabits an enchanted island, although it remains unclear what is actual magic and what is trickery. At the end of the play, Prospero promises to break and bury his staff and drown his magical book, the sources of his power.

Shakespeare was not the only writer interested in the occult. Christopher Marlowe, in his staging of the Faust story – *Doctor Faustus*, first performed in the late sixteenth century – tells of a German scholar who, tired of the limitations of human knowledge, throws himself into the study of magic, eventually summoning the Devil and making a pact with him. Similar stories can be traced back to the Middle Ages, although one

OPPOSITE *A page from Agrippa's important three-volume study of occult philosophy, first published in 1533.* ABOVE *William Hogarth's painting of a scene from Shakespeare's* Tempest, *with the magician Prospero at the centre, and the monster-like Caliban on the far right.*

of the immediate inspirations for the Faust legend may have been the German alchemist Johann Georg Faust (*c.* 1480 – *c.* 1541).

Edmund Spenser's *The Faerie Queene* – a magical, allegorical poem – was published between 1590 and 1596. Spenser was a friend of the English explorer Sir Walter Raleigh, who also dabbled in the occult. In his *History of the World* (1614), Raleigh expressed his own thoughts on the relationship between magic and witchcraft: 'Now for magic itself … It is true that many men abhor the very name and word *magus*, because of Simon Magus, who being indeed not *magus*, but *goes*, that is, familiar with evil spirits, usurped that title. For magic, conjuring, and witchery are far different arts.'

VERBA SECRE-
TORVM HERMETIS.

VERVM, SINE MENDA-
CIO CERTVM & VERISSI-
MVM, QVOD EST INFERI', EST SI-
CVT QVOD EST SVPERIVS; & QVOD EST SV-
PERIVS, EST SICVT QVOD EST INFERIVS: AD PERPE-
TRANDA MIRACVLA REI VNI', ET SICVT OMNES RES
FVERVNT AB VNO, MEDITATIONE VNIVS; SIC OMNES RES
NATÆ FVERVNT AB HAC VNA RE, ADAPTATIONE. PATER EI'
EST SOL, MATER EIVS LVNA; PORTAVIT ILLVD VENTVS IN VENTRE
SVO; NVTRIX EIVS TERRA EST. PATER OMNIS TELESMI TOTI' MVNDI
EST HIC. VIS EI', INTEGRA EST. SI VERSA FVERIT IN TERRAM, SEPARABIS
TERRAM AB IGNE, SVBTILE à SPISSO, SVAVITER CVM MAGNO INGENIO. ASCEN-
DIT à TERRA IN COELVM, ITERVMQVE DESCENDIT IN TERRAM, & RECIPIT VIM
SVPERIORVM & INFERIORVM. SIC HABEBIS GLORIAM TOTI' MVNDI. IDEO FVGI-
AT à TE OMNIS OBSCVRITAS. HIC EST TOTIVS FORTITVDINIS FORTITVDO FORTIS,
QVIA VINCET OMNEM REM SVBTILEM, OMNEMQVE SOLIDAM PENETRABIT. SIC MVNDVS
CREATVS EST. HINC ERVNT ADAPTATIONES MIRABILES, QVARVM MODVS HIC EST. ITAQVE
VOCATVS SVM HERMES TRISMEGISTVS, HABENS TRES PARTES PHILOSOPHIÆ TOTIVS MVNDI.
COMPLETVM EST QVOD DIXI DE OPERATIONE SOLIS.

Auff Deutsch:

Warhafftig, sonder Liegen gewiß vnd auff das aller warhafftigste, Diß so VNTEN ist, ist gleich dem OBERN;
Vnd diß so OBEN ist, ist gleich dem VNTERN: damit man kan erlangen vnd verrichten Miracula oder wunder-
zeichen EINES EANIGEN DINGES. Vnd gleich wie ALLE DINGE von EINEM DINGE ALLEINE geschaffen,
durch den willen vnd Geboth EINES EINIGEN, der es bedacht; also entspriessen vnd kommen ALLE DINGE von
demselben EINEM DINGE, durch schickung vnd Vereinigung zusammensügung. Die SONNE ist sein VATER, vnd
der MOND ist seine MVTTER; der WINDT hat jn getragen in seinem Bauch: Seine ERNEHRERIN oder Amme
ist die ERDE. Dieser ist der VATER ALLER VOLLKOMMENHEIT dieser gantzen Weldt. SEINE MACHT
IST VOLLKOMMEN, Wann ES ver wandelt wird in ERDE. So soltu das Erdreich vom FEVER scheiden, vnd
das Subtile vom dicken oder groben, gantz Lieblich mit grosser bescheidenheit vnd verstande. Es steiget von der
ERDEN in HIMMEL, vnd vom HIMMEL wieder zur ERDEN, Vnd gewinnet also die Krafft der obern vnd
Vntern. ALSO WIRSTV HABEN ALLE HERRLIGKEIT DER GANTZEN WELT. Derhalben wiche von dir
aller Vnverstandt vnd Vnvermögenheit. Diß ist von aller STERCKE die STERCKESTE STERCKE; Dann es kan
vber winden alle subtiligkeit, vnd durchdringen alle Veste. ALSO IST DIE WELT GESCHAFFEN; Dahero ge-
schehen seltzame Vereinigungen, vnd werden MANCHERLEY WVNDER gewircket; welcher Weg, die selben
zu wircken, dieser ist. Vnd bin darumb genad HERMES TRISMEGISTVS, habende drey theill der WEIS-
HEIT der gantzen Welt. Es ist erfüllet alles was Jch gesagt habe von dem WERCKE der SONNEN.

MERCVRIVS TRISMEGISTVS, in PIMANDRO.

Cùm de RERVM NATVRA cogitare, ac MENTIS aciem ad SVPERNA erigere, sopitis iam corporis sensibus, quemadmodum acci-
dere solet iis, qui ob saturitatem, vel defatigationem, somno gravati sunt: subito mihi visus sum cernere quendam immensa magni-
tudine corporis, qui me nomine vocans, in hunc modum clamaret: Quid est, ò Mercuri, quod & AVDIRE & INTVERI desideras? Quid
est, quod DISCERE, atq; INTELLIGERE cupis? Tùm ego, Quisnam es, inquam? Sum, inquit Ille, PIMANDER, MENS DIVINÆ PO-
TENTIÆ, ac tu vide quid velis, IPSE verò TIBI VBIq; ADERO. Cupio, inqua, RERVM NATVRAM DISCERE, DEVMq; COGNO-
SCERE. Ad hæc Ille: TVA ME MENTE COMPLECTERE, ET EGO TE IN CVNCTIS, QVÆ OPTARIS, ERVDIAM. Cum
hæc dixisset, mutavit formam, et VNIVERSA SVBITO REVELAVIT.
                                                          Sic et cuius DOCTRINÆ
                                                          filio fideli. AMEN.

...rū Triumphaliū illarū, de Humido Radicali aut Primigenio Catholico MVNDI huius, Semineq; Terræ novæ (post Cælorū incendio solutionē, & Elemētorū æstuantiū liquefa-
Apoc. 21.1.) permanente futuræ, in sinu centrali abcondatur, fovetur; passim in orbe Terrarū, tanqua Doctrinæ solidioris de MAGNESIA, LAPIDIS Phil. Vniversalis Subiecto debi-
...is omnib, Impatorie triuphate, faces luculētissi, codicem, veridici, Divinum extructarū; ad Mundi quoq; præsentis, P IGNEM, Sax. præsunt, & Omnia iudicante, Conflagratione, Corr-
...missime fixæ, vere Saturniæ, adiuvantur, ut NEPTVNO, IVNONI atq; VVLCANO, nec minus his ministris a manib, ut vigilatus, ita & laboriosiss. ALCHYMIÆ, Arti Artiū cū Antiquiss.
..., homine aut reperiat Sanctū, aut reddat Sanctū; Mirabilis & Mirifica, tüm ob hæc Omniū visitationi decreto Numinis, Luminis NATVRÆ Sapiētis, petuium consecratariū, P
...riū, Harū VSVM & FRVCTVM, ò Doctrinæ filii fideles, ex Hieroglyphici illarū dogmatis scripto haud fallaci, ME, fideliter admonēte, Philosophia Theosophica, Mēte, Solib-
...osophiæ amator fidelis, & MED. utriusq; DOCT. Arte Spagirica laudib, dignis merito celebrari, Admirationis, Amoris, Honoris & grati Animi ergo, luber ac o vas fecit. Anno a nativ-

HERMETICISM IN THE RENAISSANCE

The volume of Hermetic writings translated by Marsilio Ficino in the early 1460s, the *Corpus Hermeticum*, consisted of a wide range of texts, from collections of spells and rituals to astrological and alchemical treatises. The texts arrived in Florence in Greek, but were believed originally to have been written in Egyptian during the time of the pharaohs. It was not until the early seventeenth century that the scholar Isaac Casaubon proved that the version of Greek used in the texts dated them to somewhere between the second and fourth centuries AD – making them about the same age as the Greek Magical Papyri.

For Ficino and others, however, the *Corpus Hermeticum* provided an authentic, unique insight into truly ancient magic, perhaps even tapping into the occult knowledge of Moses. The work titled 'Poimandres', for example, is a dialogue between God (Poimandres) and Hermes, in which Hermes acquires insights into the workings of the universe. More philosophy than religion, it nevertheless spurred on the study of alchemy, astrology and, most dangerous of all, theurgy.

How could this ancient thinking be reconciled with Renaissance Christian thought? Both Ficino and Giovanni Pico della Mirandola promoted the idea of a *prisca theologica*, a single theology uniting all spiritual traditions. Essentially, Ficino wanted to create a single line of gnostic wisdom going back to the most ancient of times, to Zoroaster and Moses via Plato, Pythagoras and Hermes. This approach also opened the door to such traditions as Kabbalah, and led eventually to Rosicrucianism.

ABOVE AND OPPOSITE
*Two portraits of Giovanni Pico della Mirandola,
showing him at different stages of life.*

Giovanni
Pico della Mirandola

The philosopher Giovanni Pico della Mirandola (1463–1494) was one of the key movers of the Florentine Renaissance. A close friend of Marsilio Ficino, and favourite of Lorenzo de' Medici, he was proficient in Greek, Latin, Hebrew and Arabic. Together with Ficino, Pico was instrumental in introducing Hermeticism to the Renaissance, for defending the practice of magic, and for bringing Kabbalah to a wider European audience.

The highpoint of Pico's career came with the *Oration on the Dignity of Man*. This address, due to be delivered in Rome in 1486 as part of a public debate, has been called the manifesto of the Renaissance. In it, Pico tries to establish humanity's place in the 'great chain of being', but also expresses his hopes that humankind might raise itself above the angels, attaining a mystical union with God. However, the Church intervened and suspended the debate, afterwards censuring some of Pico's theses.

In the *Oration*, Pico states that 'magic has two forms. One consists wholly in the operations and powers of demons, and consequently this appears to me, as God is my witness, an execrable and monstrous thing. The other proves, when thoroughly investigated, to be nothing else but the highest realization of natural philosophy.' Sensing that it would be important to remain on the right side of the Church, Pico added: 'the second, beneficent magic, excites in [man] an admiration for the works of God which flowers naturally into charity, faith and hope.'

IOĀN·PICVS ·MIRANDVLA~

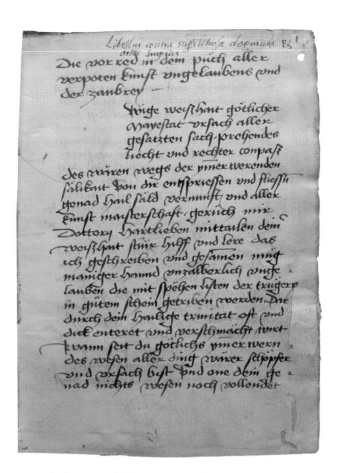

OPPOSITE *A 16th-century depiction of chiromancy, one of Johannes Hartlieb's seven* artes magicae.
ABOVE, LEFT *A wizard equipped with a wand apparently raises the dead using magic.*
ABOVE, RIGHT *A page from Hartlieb's* Book on Forbidden Arts, Superstition
and Sorcery, *in which the Bavarian physician outlines his seven magical arts.*

ARTES MAGICAE

In the fifteenth century, the Church struggled to define what was and was not acceptable in magic. An attempt *was* made at this time, however, by the Bavarian physician Johannes Hartlieb. In his *Book on Forbidden Arts, Superstition and Sorcery* (1456), Hartlieb identifies seven *artes magicae*, or 'magical arts': nigromancy (black magic), geomancy, hydromancy, aeromancy, pyromancy, chiromancy (palmistry) and scapulimancy

(divination using shoulder blades). As can be seen, four of these arts are derived from the classical elements (earth, water, air, fire), reflecting an ancient view of the world.

Hartlieb's *artes magicae* do not include astrology by name, but his book does prohibit ceremonial magic. It also includes the first description of witches' ointment, a hallucinogenic substance that was believed to help witches fly.

ABOVE *William Blake's depiction of Sir Isaac Newton as a divine geometrist, plotting the world with scientific precision. Blake disliked science, seeing it as sterile, but Newton was actively interested in the occult.*
OPPOSITE *The Greek mathematician Pythagoras claimed that 'the world is built on the power of numbers', and is seen as the father of numerology. He also proposed a theory of the 'music of the spheres', which influenced Hermetic thought, especially the relationship between macrocosm and microcosm.*

SCIENCE & MAGIC

While magic relies on supernatural explanations, science aims to find objective explanations of cause and effect. It is for this reason that James George Frazer described magic as 'the bastard sister of science'. They do have some things in common, however, especially in the fields of alchemy, medicine and astronomy. Some of this commonality stems from Pythagoras's observations on the numerical underpinnings of the universe, and numbers can be seen as central to magic.

In the past, science and magic were often confused. Gerbert of Aurillac (946–1003), later Pope Sylvester II, spent time studying in Muslim Cordoba, at that stage one of Europe's principal centres of learning. It was through his studies that the West rediscovered Aristotle, the armillary sphere and the abacus. However, Gerbert's exposure to advanced thinking also made him suspect, and he was accused of having learnt sorcery in Cordoba, as well as having built a 'brazen head' that could predict the future.

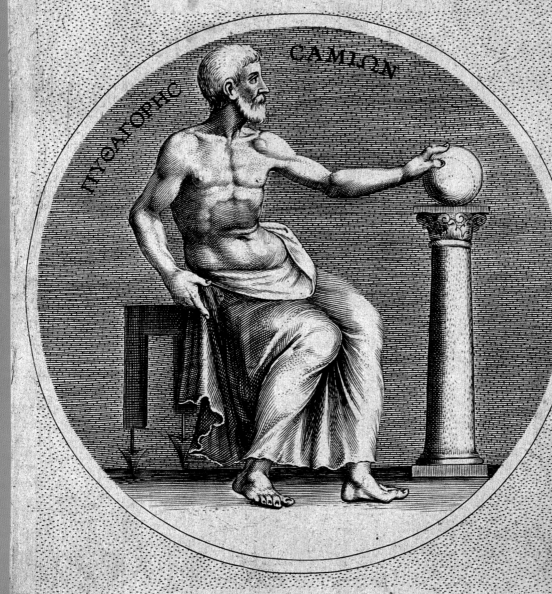

ABOVE *A young Giordano Bruno.*
OPPOSITE *A sculpture in Pietrasanta, Italy,
commemorating Bruno's life.*

Giordano Bruno

Few people in the Renaissance encountered – or courted – quite as much scandal as the mathematician, philosopher and occultist Giordano Bruno (1548–1600). Originally trained as a Dominican friar, he later rejected Christianity outright, claiming to be an Egyptian magus. He was fascinated by the Egyptian god Thoth, and has been identified as a devout Hermeticist, as well as a champion of the pagan past.

Bruno was a contradictory man. On the one hand he argued against the planetary spheres; on the other, however, he believed that demons were material, composed of something lighter than air. He saw magic and 'divine rites' as being key to understanding the soul of the world.

In his treaty *On Magic* (1588), Bruno distinguishes between different kinds of magic, from 'natural magic' (attraction and repulsion in objects, such as magnetism) to 'occult philosophy' (words, chants, symbols) and 'theurgy' (control of spirits). The last of these he condemns, seeing it as dangerous and foolish. For Bruno, creation was connected by a 'universal spirit', so it was logical that an action in one part could produce an effect in another.

Bruno's continued heresy attracted the attention of the Church, and in 1593 he was arrested. At his trial, he was accused of, among other things, 'dealing in magic and divination'. The punishment was death, and in 1600 he was burnt at the stake.

"TREMATE PIU VOI O GIUDICI NEL PROFFERIR LA MIA SENTENZA
CHE NON IO NE L'ASCOLTARLA"

DI GIORDANO BRUNO
CHE LE FOLGORI DEL GENIO DIVINATORE
ALL' EVO SANGUIGNO AVVENTANDO
PRECORSE I VERI ONDE ALBEGGIA
UN DOMANI DI SCIENZA E DI GIUSTIZIA
E DAL ROGO BENEDISSE
- RAPITE AL CIELO DAGLI UOMINI -
LE RESUREZIONI DELLA VITA
VOLLERO CON LE SEMBIANZE EVOCARE
L' APOSTOLATO E IL MARTIRIO

In this scene from Tasso's Jerusalem Delivered, *the sleeping soldier Rinaldo is enchanted by the Saracen sorceress Armida. Later, she carries him off in her flying chariot.*

MAGIC IN RENAISSANCE LITERATURE

The supernatural makes an appearance in much Renaissance literature, contributing to some of the most-read works of the day. This was a time of great epics, such as Ludovico Ariosto's colossal *Orlando Furioso* (1516), which features the wizard Atlante and a sorceress called Alcina.

Torquato Tasso's *Jerusalem Delivered* (1581), an epic poem about the Crusades, also includes a sorceress, Armida. Modelled on the Greek goddess Circe, Armida turns the Christians into animals. Elsewhere in the poem there are magical shields, rings, nymphs and magical plants. Tasso was criticized for including these magical elements — so much so that, towards the end of his life, he rewrote the poem and removed them all (the revised version was not successful). *Jerusalem Delivered* influenced Edmund Spenser's epic magical poem *The Faerie Queen* (1590–96).

Here, the magician Ascalon uses a magic shield to conjure up the heroic feats of Rinaldo's ancestors.

ABOVE, LEFT AND RIGHT *Based on a conflict between Charlemagne and the Saracens, Ariosto's* Orlando Furioso *is rich in magic. On the left, Ruggiero, riding a hippogriff, rescues Angelica by killing a dragon; Angelica herself owned a ring that countered all enchantments. On the right, knights and damsels are held prisoner in Atlantes' magical castle, bound by spells.*
OPPOSITE *Subtle the Alchemist poses as an astrologer, in a scene from Ben Jonson's play* The Alchemist.

The plays of William Shakespeare well reflect the keen Elizabethan interest in magic. Shakespeare's best-known magician is Prospero, who bewitches an entire island in *The Tempest*. At the end of the play, Prospero vows to 'break my staff, / Bury it certain fathoms in the earth', and to drown his magical book 'deeper than did ever plummet sound' (V. i). Even more famous are the three witches from *Macbeth*, who predict the Scottish general's rise and fall. They brew a hideous potion using 'eye of newt, and toe of frog / wool of bat, and tongue of dog' (IV. i), among many other ingredients. Whether they shape fate or merely reflect it is left open to interpretation.

The legend of Faust, who sold his soul to the Devil in return for knowledge and magical powers, first appeared in *Historia von D. Johann Fausten* (1587), a collection of stories about the real-world figure of Johann Georg Faust. This book was quickly translated into English (1592), but the story became even more popular when adapted into a play by Christopher Marlowe (*Doctor Faustus*, 1604). Elsewhere, the subject of alchemy became the object of satire in Ben Jonson's *The Alchemist* (1610).

The ALCHYMIST.

Drug. This and please your Worship,
I am a young beginner & am building
of a new Shop and like your Worship just
at corner of a Street, here is the plot on't.
Act I.   Scene 3.

Graham pinxt.   Grignion sculp.

London. Printed for J. Bell British Library, Strand. April 14. 1791.

OPPOSITE *Holding a staff and standing in a magic circle, the wizard Prospero – the main protagonist in*
The Tempest *– summons the spirit Ariel. Ariel is bound to serve Prospero after the wizard rescues
the spirit from the spell of a witch.* ABOVE *In this scene from* Macbeth, *the Scottish
general and Banquo encounter the Three Witches on a heath.*

ABOVE AND OPPOSITE *The legend of Nostradamus — seen here in depictions from the 18th and 19th centuries — lived on long after the astrologer's death.*

Nostradamus

Born in Provence in 1503, Michel de Nostredame originally studied medicine. The first thirty years of his life were largely unremarkable, but in 1534 his wife and children were killed by plague. He left France and began to travel, including to Italy, where he came into contact with occult sciences. He published his first almanac, containing prophecies, in 1550, after which he produced a new one every year. It was also at this time that he Latinized his name.

Nostradamus's major breakthrough came in 1555, when Catherine de' Medici, the intensely superstitious Italian wife of the French king Henry II, became aware of Nostradamus's work. She was alarmed by the prediction of her husband's death, but also had Nostradamus draw up horoscopes for her children. Nostradamus was far from being a professional astrologer, however, and his contemporaries criticized him for not fully understanding how to cast a horoscope.

The question of exactly how Nostradamus came by his prophecies remains open to debate. Certainly, they can be linked to the desperate times in which he lived, marked by regular outbreaks of plague, continuous war and religious tension. It has been suggested by some that he would induce his revelations by staring into a bowl of water until images emerged – a form of scrying similar to the technique used by John Dee (see page 236).

Others have suggested that Nostradamus used a form of bibliomancy, allowing books to fall open at random – a technique also used at other times with the Bible by those seeking divine advice. What is certain is that he drew heavily on the work of other writers, including the Renaissance friar Girolamo Savonarola and the fourth-century Neoplatonic philosopher Iamblichus, specifically his *Mysteries of the Egyptians, Chaldeans, and Assyrians.*

J'annonce vérité simplement et sans pompe.

Et mon présage vrai nullement ne me trompe.

Michel Nostradamus naquit a St. Remy petite Ville de Provence le 14 du mois de décembre de l'an 1503 à l'heure de midi il était fils de Jacques Nostradamus notaire Royal de cette Ville et de Renée de St. Remy damoiselle, il était petit fils tant paternel que maternel de médecins et mathématiciens célébres il fut reçu docteur en l'université de Montpellier dont il exerça la charge de professeur, ce grand homme a vécu sous les regnes de Louis XII. Francois Ier. Henry II. et Charles IX. dont il fut médecin, il retourna à Salon autre Ville de Provence et y mourut en bon chrétien après avoir été tourmenté par les goutes qui dégénérées en hydropisie, le suffoquérent au bout de huit jours, ayant prédit l'heure et le jour de sa mort qui arriva entre trois et quatre heures du matin le 2 juillet 1566.

A Paris chez Jean Rue St. Jean de Beauvais No. 10.

ABOVE *From the Renaissance onwards, witches have typically been depicted as women. The witch shown here is clearly an agent of dark forces — as personified in the strange creatures surrounding her cauldron.*
OPPOSITE *In this painting by Goya, owls, flying demons, hideous faces, poppets and what appear to be children's body parts in a basket combine to produce an image of terror.*

WITCHCRAFT & ITS PURSUIT

The traditional Western image of the witch dates from the fourteenth or fifteenth century, more or less the time when witches began to be persecuted. Up to that point, witches — male and female — had been key parts of isolated communities across Europe, offering a mixture of healing, medicine, knowledge of herbs, amulets and protection against harmful forces. Today, such individuals might be called 'cunning folk', 'folk healers' or 'white witches'.

It is possible to identify many different traditions of witchcraft, even within Europe. Most can be categorized as 'shamanic', in the sense of someone possessing special powers and using them for the benefit of their community. Examples of the various traditions include the *benandanti* (or 'good walkers') in Italy and the *táltos* in Hungary. Members of both groups fought against 'evil' witches, but also showed such witch-like characteristics as an ability to turn themselves into animals.

OPPOSITE *Albrecht Dürer's study of four witches. Through the open door on the left, we see the muzzle of a demon, while the floor is littered with bones.* ABOVE *By the 16th century, witchcraft was associated with the Devil, the strange and the unearthly. This chaotic scene shows a witch unleashing grotesque and frightening spirits.*

In Europe, belief in witches was discouraged up until the late Middle Ages. Indeed, in 785 the Council of Paderborn, held to debate the Christianization of the Saxons, had outlawed the belief, and into the thirteenth century belief in the existence of witchcraft was seen as a heresy. Even when the Inquisition got underway in about 1232, it focused on eradicating religious unorthodoxy, allowing practitioners of folk magic to go unnoticed.

A significant change in attitude came in 1486 with the publication of the *Malleus Maleficarum* (Hammer of the Witches). Written by two Dominican inquisitors, Heinrich Kramer and Jacob Sprenger, the book associated witches with the Devil; it also made a firm link between witchcraft and women. It was officially condemned by the Catholic Church in 1490, but continued to be used by both Catholics and Protestants for another two centuries.

Matthew Hopkins Witch Finder Generall

My Imps names are

Holt

1 Ilemauzar
2 Pyewackett

Jarmara

Sacke & Sugar

3 Pecke in the Crowne
4 Griezzell Greedigutt

Newes

Vinegar tom

Correctly Copied from an extreme Rare Print in the Collection of J. Bindley Esqr.

Publish'd as the Act directs March 20 1792 by J. Caulfield London

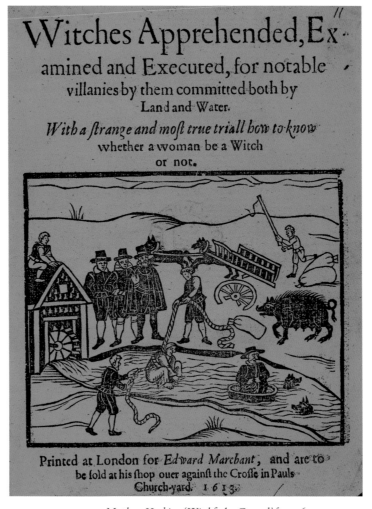

OPPOSITE *Matthew Hopkins, 'Witchfinder General' from 1644
to 1647, is pictured with two witches. They are naming their 'familiars'.*
ABOVE *Those accused of witchcraft were often subjected to trial by water or fire. Here,
a suspected witch is dunked to see whether they will float (guilty) or sink (innocent).*

In this new climate of suspicion, an array of lurid tales and beliefs about witches sprang up. The idea of the witches' sabbath – a nocturnal meeting of practitioners of witchcraft – planted itself in the popular imagination, complete with human sacrifice and declarations of allegiance to the Devil, while accusations of child theft became common. Witches were sometimes accused of harming their victims by sticking needles into wax effigies, a practice not unlike that found in voodoo.

One particularly tenacious belief was that witches were often accompanied by 'familiars' – spirit animals that did their bidding. These animals would drink the witch's blood, talk to them and attack their enemies. It was also widely believed that witches could fly, sometimes on broomsticks.

THE
Discovery of Witchcraft:
PROVING,
That the Compacts and Contracts of WITCHES
with *Devils* and all *Infernal Spirits* or *Familiars*, are but
Erroneous Novelties and Imaginary Conceptions.
Also discovering, How far their Power extendeth in Killing, Tormenting,
Consuming, or Curing the bodies of Men, Women, Children, or Animals,
by Charms, Philtres, Periapts, Pentacles, Curses, and Conjurations.
WHEREIN LIKEWISE
The Unchristian Practices and Inhumane Dealings of
Searchers and *Witch-tryers* upon *Aged, Melancholly,* and *Superstitious*
people, in extorting Confessions by Terrors and Tortures,
and in devising false Marks and Symptoms, are notably Detected.
And the Knavery of *Juglers, Conjurers, Charmers, Soothsayers, Figure-Casters,
Dreamers, Alchymists* and *Philterers;* with many other things
that have long lain hidden, fully Opened and Deciphered.
ALL WHICH
Are very necessary to be known for the undeceiving of *Judges, Justices,*
and *Jurors,* before they pass Sentence upon Poor, Miserable and Ignorant People;
who are frequenly Arraigned, Condemned, and Executed for *Witches* and *Wizzards.*

ABOVE *Reginald Scot's* Discoverie of Witchcraft *(here shown in a later edition) was
instrumental in sharing the secrets of magic, but also in debunking many myths around witchcraft.*
OPPOSITE *Witches are typically shown flying on broomsticks, but in this case the
mode of transport is a garden hoe. She is giving the evil eye.*

In 1521 Pope Leo X issued a papal bull condemning witches to death, and in 1542 Henry VIII of England issued the first anti-witchcraft Act (repealed by his more liberal son, Edward VI, a few years later). The anti-witchcraft Act of 1563 took action 'agaynst Conjuracions Inchauntmentes and Witchecraftes'. The fact is that many of those targeted were poor, single women.

In the midst of this growing persecution there were at least a few voices of reason. One was that of Reginald Scot, who in 1584 published *The Discoverie of Witchcraft*. In this very important book, Scot went to great lengths to understand magic tricks, explaining that much magic was in fact sleight of hand.

Interestingly, in southern Europe the level of persecution was considerably lower. In 1538 the Spanish Inquisition cautioned against believing the *Malleus Maleficarum*, and in the Basque witch trials of 1609–11, in which 7,000 cases were inspected, the Inquisition concluded: 'These claims go beyond all human reason and may even pass the limits permitted by the Devil.'

ABOVE *Catherine Deshayes, here shown in her laboratory, was at the centre of the Affair of the Poisons, a murder scandal in late-17th-century Paris that led to several members of the French aristocracy being charged with poisoning and witchcraft.*
OPPOSITE *A dramatic moment in the Salem witch trials – in this case, the trial of George Jacobs Sr. Jacobs was one of six men who were convicted and hanged during the trials.*

The persecution of witchcraft peaked in the early seventeenth century. In 1604 James I of England claimed that witches were 'loathe to confess without torture'. One of those who took up this challenge was Matthew Hopkins (*c.* 1620–1647), the self-appointed 'Witchfinder General'. Similarly, witch trials and executions took place throughout Scandinavia, Germany, the Baltic states, Switzerland and Hungary.

In France, one of the most famous witch trials was that of Catherine Deshayes, known as 'La Voisin'. Starting out as a fortune-teller, La Voisin later developed theatrical black masses – sometimes involving a naked woman as an altar – officiated by a Catholic priest. She was sought out by members of France's aristocracy, including the mistress of Louis XIV, Madame de Montespan. However, she was eventually arrested, and burnt as a witch.

The last high-profile witch trials were held in Salem, Massachusetts, between 1692 and 1693. Despite the misgivings of some of those involved, and the fact that the prosecutions hinged on the testimony of just two girls, the now infamous Salem witch trials led to the execution of nineteen people.

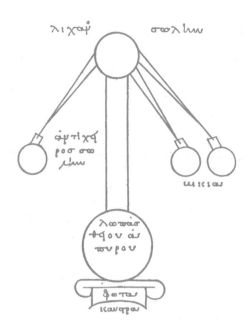

TOP *A drawing of distillation apparatus, taken from a Greek
manuscript of alchemical treatises dating from around the 5th century AD.*
ABOVE *Aristotle pictured with the philosopher's stone. The Greek philosopher believed that
all compounds were made up of the four elements (water, fire, earth, air); the idea that compounds
were not fixed led to the belief in the possibility of the transmutation of substances.*

Mary the Jewess, a celebrated alchemist of the 1st to 2nd centuries AD.
Today, her legacy survives in the term 'bain-marie', a technique that she described.

ALCHEMY

The central premise of alchemy is that base metals, such as copper, tin or zinc, can be transformed into precious ones – typically gold, but also the philosopher's stone (via a process known as the Magnum Opus). Rooted in the material world, alchemy seeks fundamentally supernatural transformations. In a more general sense, however, the alchemical process is about achieving perfection, whether physical or metaphysical, chemical or spiritual. This split between physical and metaphysical worlds – both cloaked in symbolism and metaphor – makes the concept of alchemy initially difficult to understand.

According to Zosimos of Panopolis, an Egyptian alchemist from the fourth century AD, the first true alchemist was Mary the Jewess, who lived at some point between the first and third centuries AD. Zosimos claimed that fallen angels had taught women the secrets of metallurgy. Here, Zosimos was already turning to ancient knowledge – that of the Egyptians on the one hand, and that of the Hebrews on the other. He also gave alchemy a spiritual dimension, seeing the alchemical vessel as a baptismal font.

In physical alchemy, the principal apparatus is the alembic, which is used to distil chemicals. Many different types of alembic are used, depending on the task at hand. Distillation, however, is just one of the techniques employed in alchemy, and the Magnum Opus originally had four stages: *nigredo* (burning until black), *albedo* (purification), *citrinitas* (turning silver into gold) and *rubedo* (the creation of the philosopher's stone). The first stage could be achieved the 'dry way' (by fire, calcination) or the 'wet way' (by putrefaction). A more in-depth version of the Magnum Opus has twelve stages, the last of which is 'projection' – a material that can be mixed with such metals as mercury to create gold.

Success in alchemy was elusive, and no straightforward recipes exist. Indeed, alchemists delight in obscurantism, and in hiding their secrets in hard-to-fathom diagrams – many of which are still not fully understood.

Many alchemists toiled ceaselessly in unsafe conditions to discover a process to turn base materials into more valuable ones.

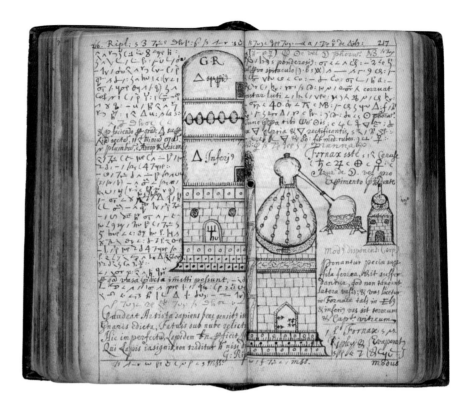

RIGHT *The belief in alchemy lasted well into the scientific age. This description of alchemical apparatus dates from between the 16th and mid-18th centuries.*

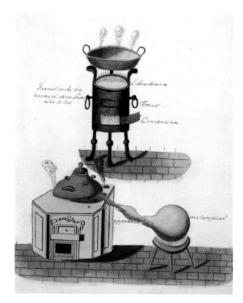

LEFT *A depiction of an alchemical furnace, from a manuscript written by Raymundus Lullius.*
ABOVE *An 18th-century depiction of alchemical apparatus. The equipment required for the distillation processes was also repurposed in the service of more scientific fields.*

perfectionis ostensio

OPPOSITE *An illustration of the second cycle of transformation in alchemy, from the*
Rosarium Philosophorum, *a 16th-century treatise that discusses the alchemical process
from a physical and spiritual angle. The green lion stands for the 'greening' process, and is a solar
symbol; the Sun tree is another solar symbol, while the pelican stands for the 'reddening' process.
In the centre is a hermaphrodite atop a triple-serpent, representing the work of perfection.*
ABOVE *This painting of an alchemist being tempted by Luxuria – the personification
of wealth – reminds us that the spiritual goals of alchemy should outweigh the material ones.*

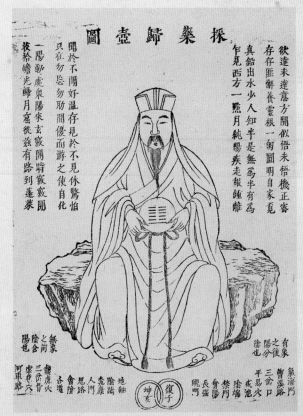

ABOVE, LEFT *A portrait of the Arabic alchemist Jabir ibn Hayyan, known in the West as Geber.*
ABOVE, RIGHT *An illustration from a mid-17th-century Chinese book on internal alchemy.*
OPPOSITE *An imagining of the Persian alchemist Rhazes (Muhammad ibn Zakariya al-Razi)
conducting alchemical experiments in his laboratory in Baghdad.*

Fundamental to alchemy is the Emerald Tablet, supposedly written by Hermes Trismegistus, but found only in Arabic books from the sixth century onwards. The tablet was allegedly discovered in a vault below a statue of Hermes in Tyana (an ancient city in the southern part of modern-day Turkey), where it was held by a corpse on a golden throne.

With the Muslim conquest of Egypt in the seventh century, Egyptian ideas made their way back to the Arabian peninsular. Physical alchemy flourished in Baghdad and Persia. Jabir ibn Hayyan (721–815, known as Geber in the West) developed a theory that all metals contain some sulphur and mercury, building on the Aristotelian belief in the four properties of hotness, coldness, dryness and moistness. In the tenth century, the Persian scientist and alchemist Muhammad ibn Zakariya al-Razi (865–925, known as Rhazes in the West) wrote the *Kitab al-Asrar* (*Liber Secretorum* in Latin), which details the tools of the alchemist.

Alchemy can also be found in China. However, although it is driven by the same goal – the transmutation of matter – as other alchemical traditions, the influence of *I Ching*, Taoism and the *Wu Xing* means that Chinese alchemy has a significant spiritual bias. Metals were thought to be male and female, lunar and solar. The key early work in Chinese alchemy is the *Yellow Court Classic*, which dates from before the fourth century AD.

CHYMICALL CHARACTERS

Notes of Metalls

Saturne, Lead	♄
Iupiter, Tinne	♃
Mars, Iron	♂ 🜜
Sol, the Sun, Gould	☉
Venus, Copper, Brasse	♀
Mercury, Quicksilver	☿
Luna, the Moon, Silver	☾

Notes of Minerall and other Chymicall things

Antimony	♁ ◇ ◇
Arsenick	🜺 🜻
Auripigment	🜽 🜾
Allum	○ 🝭
Aurichalcum	🜦 🜧 🜧
Inke	🜨
Vinegar	🜊
Distilld Vinegar	🜋 🜋
Amalgama	aaa E ## 🝛
Aqua Vitæ	🜈
Aqua fortis, or separatory water	🜅
Aqua Regis or Stigian water	🜆
Alembeck	🝪
Borax	🝁 🝂
Crocus Martis	🜞 🜟
Cinnabar	🜓 🝏
Wax	🝊
Crocus of Copper or burnt Brass	🜣 🜤 🜥 🜦 🜧
Ashes	🝗
Ashes of Harts ease	🝘
Calx	🝓
Caput Mortuum	🝎
Gumme	🝋
Sifted Tiles or Flower of Tiles	□
Lutum sapientiæ	🝔
Marcasite	🜿 🜿 II
Sublimate Mercury	🜐 🜑

Notes of Minerall and other Chymicall things

Mercury of Saturne	🝝
Balneum Mariæ	MB
Magnet	🝮
Oyle	🝆 🝇 🝈
To purifye	🝣
Realgar	🜼 🜽 x
Salt Peter	🜕
Common Salt	🜔 🜖 🜗
Salt Gemme	🜘 🜙
Salt Armoniack	🜹 🜹
Salt of Kali	🜸 🝟
Sulphur	🜍 🜎
Sulphur of Philosphers	🜏
Black Sulphur	🜏
Soape	◇
Spirit	🝐
Spirit of wine	🝑 🝑
To sublime	🝞 🝞
Stratum super Stratum or Lay upon lay	🝜
Tartar	🜿 🝀 🝁
Tutia	🝅
Talck	🝛
A covered pot	🝃
Vitriol	🜖
Glas	🝄
Urine	▣

Notes of the foure Elements

Fire	🜂
Aire	🜁
Water	🜄 ≈
Earth	🜃
Day	🝯
Night	🝰

FINIS.

Alchemical works of art are rich in symbolism; often, they are visually spectacular as well. *Splendor Solis* (The Splendour of the Sun), the earliest version of which dates to the 1530s, is the classic illustrated work on alchemy, explaining the philosophy of the process. Over time, many other illustrated works – often obscure – emerged. One such is the Ripley Scroll. Attributed to the English alchemist George Ripley (*c.* 1415–1490), the scroll describes the various steps of the twelve-stage alchemical process. Less than two dozen copies of the scroll have survived.

In alchemy, the seven classical planets are associated with the seven classical metals – the Sun with gold, the Moon with silver, Mercury with mercury, and so on. The symbols for each of the metals come from astrology. Similarly, each step of the twelve-stage process is associated with one of the twelve signs of the zodiac, which are used as a sort of cryptic shorthand.

OPPOSITE *A guide to the chemical-alchemical symbols in use during the 17th century. Alchemical diagrams, often impenetrable at first, become intelligible simply by knowing how to decode the symbols used.*

RIGHT *Three versions of the Ripley Scroll. Ripley's most famous work was 'The Compound of Alchymy' (1471), a poem that describes 'the right & perfectest meanes to make the Philosophers Stone'. The scroll is an illustration of this poem, going through the various processes required to make the magical substance.*

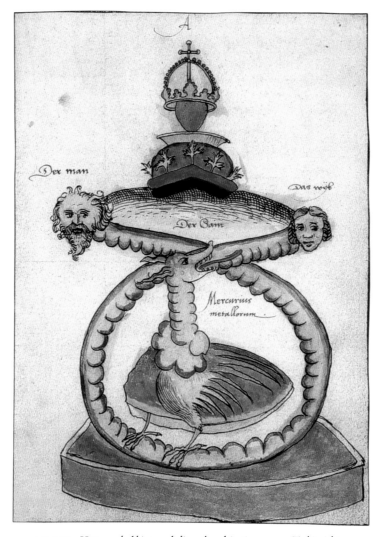

Der man *Das wib* *Der Sam* *Mercurius metallorum.*

OPPOSITE *Here, a naked king symbolizes the calcination process. To his right are three harpies.* ABOVE *A depiction of mercury as a man–woman–serpent composite. Such unifications of opposites are often the ultimate goal of alchemical work.*

Animals are regularly used to represent the different stages of alchemy. Thus, a white swan stands for 'whitening', a green lion for 'greening', and a pelican for 'reddening'. The ouroboros – a dragon or snake devouring its own tail – is a symbol of the never-ending cycle of alchemy. The caduceus – two serpents entwined around a rod – is another symbol for mercury, while the word 'cinnabar' (used to describe a bright-red mineral consisting of mercury sulphide) comes from the Persian for 'dragon's blood'.

Other images are determinedly strange, referring to the combination of opposites: hermaphrodites, male and female, kings and queens. For Michael Maier, writing in the sixteenth century, the true goal of alchemy was the unity of opposites.

*This three-headed monster in an alchemical flask represents the composition
of the philosopher's stone: salt, sulphur and mercury.*

Alchemical imagery often draws on recognizable religious themes. Here, the Magi shelter in a cave on their way to Bethlehem. This represents mercury converted into sulphur, at the moment of its fixation.

ABOVE *The Monas Hieroglyphica, the mysterious symbol that John Dee created for himself.*
OPPOSITE *This eerie image shows what is believed to be Dee and Edward Kelley
communicating with the spirit of a dead woman.*

John Dee

John Dee (1527–1608/9) was one of the
most controversial and fascinating figures in
the court of Elizabeth I. A mathematician,
occultist, astrologer and alchemist, he acted as
an occasional tutor to the queen, also casting
her horoscopes. Prior to Elizabeth's ascent, he
predicted the demise of Queen Mary, leading to
a brief period of imprisonment. However, when
Mary died, Dee was made Royal Astrologer.

In 1564 Dee published *Monas Hieroglyphica*,
a treatise explaining a glyph that he himself had
created. Dee was motivated more than anything
by a desire to understand the inner workings of
the universe. A devout Christian, he also believed
that God's plan could be discerned in numbers.
However, during the last thirty years of his
life, he sought answers more and more through
occult and supernatural means, bypassing the
divine communion in favour of direct contact
with angels and the dead. In particular, Dee
practised scrying. He was disappointed with the
results, but in 1582 met the mysterious Edward

Kelley, who seemed to have a gift for supernatural
communication.

From his home in Mortlake (now a suburb
of south-west London), Dee began with Kelley
a long series of angelic conversations that resulted
in a stream of revelations. The angels spoke to the
men in Enochian, a language supposedly used by
God to communicate with Adam. The angels
promised to teach this language to Dee, so that he
could unlock the secrets of the universe. Many
texts were dictated to him in Enochian, although
later on they also came with a translation in
English. The language is faintly reminiscent
of Hebrew, but much of it is impossible to
understand. Kelley and Dee spent the next six
years touring central Europe, working on their
angelic conferences and alchemy.

When Dee returned to Mortlake, he found his
house vandalized, and his prized library – one of
the most important in England – largely stolen.
He ended his days in relative poverty, not much
closer to understanding the universe's secrets.

VI.
World
of
Magic

A voodoo altar with fetishes in Abomey, Benin.

W hile the Western magical tradition of Egypt, Greece and Rome has been highly influential internationally, there are many other magical traditions around the world, some of which have had an even greater influence. These take many different forms, from the shamanism of Korea and Siberia to the rituals of voodoo or hoodoo practitioners.

'Shamanism' is a term that has attracted a certain amount of controversy in academic circles. While some believe it should be reserved only for the 'true' shamans of Siberia, others – notably the Romanian historian Mircea Eliade, in his well-known book *Shamanism: Archaic Techniques of Ecstasy* (1951) – have seen strong similarities between disparate cultures and applied the term liberally. Eliade believed that these cultures were all 'primitive' in their thinking, acting mostly out of fear and unable to distinguish between symbol and reality.

It is true that the 'magico-shamanic' traditions of North America, Siberia, Africa, Australia and North East Asia share some striking similarities, although no one today would describe them as 'primitive'. In all cases, the figure of the shaman is the society's point of contact with the supernatural. Typically, shamans either are born with the gift or have some sort of near-death experience that bestows it upon them. They are also expected to go into trances on behalf of the wider community, whether to recover lost souls, cure illnesses or win the favour of higher beings.

Frequently, magic is something that is seen as being stronger in cultures that are not our own, and it is fascinating to consider how practices have travelled across cultural boundaries. The Western tradition, for example, is the result of knowledge migration from Greece and Mesopotamia to Egypt, to the Arab world, and then to Western Europe. But this tradition also made a further journey, to Latin America and the Caribbean. There, along with elements of Christian belief, it combined with the magical traditions of the slaves brought by Europeans from Africa, chief among them being the West African *vodun* (see page 252). The result was voodoo. Because the religion is based on the belief that God is distant, and cannot be contacted directly, all petitions in voodoo are directed to spirits called *loa*. The sorcerers of voodoo, known as *bokors*, practice both black and white magic – including, on occasion, the creation of zombies. Today, voodoo is strongest in Haiti, although a branch is also associated with Louisiana.

OPPOSITE *This 19th-century engraving shows a shaman from the Payaguá people, a river tribe of central South America, attempting to turn away a hurricane using a spell.*

ABOVE *A magical flying carpet, piloted by Russian folk hero*
Ivan Tsarevich. With him he carries the caged Firebird.
BELOW *Clients consult an Indian astrologer.*

Similar syncretic religious and magical traditions
emerged in the Spanish colonies of South America,
where witchcraft was greatly feared. Colombia, for
example, saw a witch-hunting craze in the early seventeenth century that resulted in the deaths of many
Afro-Caribbean women. Elsewhere, fear of African
beliefs and folk magic led to persecution, not to mention
many unexplained deaths in custody. Slave-owners,
in particular, were quick to accuse their bondsmen of
using black magic against them. From the nineteenth
century onwards, Brazil, which mixed Moorish, Jewish
and West African cultures, was home to perhaps some
of the most fascinating magical traditions of all, including *candomblé* and *umbanda*.

In Arabian countries, *One Thousand and One Nights*, also known as *Arabian Nights*, is one of the most famous vehicles for magical stories. Compiled in the early Middle Ages, the book contains such fantastical tales as those of Princess Parizade and the Magic Tree, Prince Hussain's magical flying carpet, a magical tent that can grow to fit an army, and of course the magic lamp that contains a genie. With regard to magic carpets, it is interesting to note that King Solomon was also reputed to have owned such an object. Measuring sixty miles in each direction and made of green silk, Solomon's carpet was carried on the winds, over which he had control. Clearly, the king was the originator of many magical traditions.

In the *Arabian Nights* story, Prince Hussain had bought *his* magical carpet in India, a country vast and impenetrable enough to be seen as innately magical. Hinduism has a long history of astrology and divination, but also of alchemy and witchcraft. Indian alchemy — known as *rasayana* — aims at lengthening life and discovering perfection, using mercury, making the body immortal. Interestingly, India became the home, for a short while at the beginning of the twentieth century, of the theosophy movement. Also noteworthy is the fact that Aleister Crowley, among other occultists of the same period, studied and wrote about yoga.

Finally, a rich vein of magic and witchcraft can be found in the Slavic cultures of Eastern Europe and Russia. There, the early god of magic, Veles, is a trickster god, similar to Hermes in Greek mythology. In pre-Christian Russia, the sorcerers known as *volkhvs* were believed to be able to see into the future. Slavic folklore is also steeped in magic, with one of the key figures being the witch-like Baba Yaga. Deformed and unpredictable, she flies around in a pestle, furnishing other protagonists with magical objects, including a towel than can turn into a bridge and a ball that shows the way.

The Russian witch Baba Yaga flying in her pestle.

OPPOSITE *The hypnotic beating of the shaman's drum helps them reach a different level of consciousness, enabling them, in turn, to commune with supernatural spirits. This shaman is from Mongolia.* ABOVE *A shaman or medicine man from Australia. In Aboriginal culture, shamans deal with sickness, and reach the Upper World of the spirits via a magical rope.*

SHAMANISM

Shamanism is a complex set of beliefs and rituals that includes belief in guardian spirits and metamorphosis, and in a world that can be contacted only through ecstatic means, such as trances. As a consequence, shamanism might be considered an early ancestor of both religion and magic, although it is arguably more proactive than religion in trying to determine outcomes.

Shamans induce trances and visions through a variety of means, from drumming, chanting and spinning to psychoactive substances and meditation. Once in a trance, they are said to enter a supernatural dimension in which they are able to interact with spirits – whether malevolent or benevolent – in order to have an impact in the physical world of day-to-day experience.

A Jakutian Priest invoking his deities to cure a sick man.

ABOVE AND OPPOSITE *Shamans bang drums and engage in dance in order to invoke spirits to cure a sick person and rid them of evil.*

The term 'shaman' was originally used to describe a magical person from the Tungusic peoples of Siberia, and a popular theory maintains that the rituals of the first shamans were intended to ensure a successful hunt. Such practices have been seen by anthropologists from Korea to North America, and even perhaps in prehistoric cave paintings.

Related to the Siberian shaman is the medicine man. This figure, responsible for healing using a mixture of supernatural and herbal means, can be found throughout the world. The Yupik tribe of North America, for example, perform elaborate rituals to rid people of bad spirits.

OPPOSITE *Three Navajo men in ceremonial dress — complete with elaborate masks and body-painting — perform the Yeibichai medicine ceremony.* ABOVE *A shaman's rattle made by the Haida people of the Pacific Northwest. It has been carved in the shape of a raven and a killer whale.*

NATIVE AMERICAN MAGIC

Within Native American culture, the fabric of existence is seen as a continuum, with humankind closely linked to and highly dependent on nature. Being able to communicate with nature – specifically, with spirit guides and magical animals – was regarded as vital to survival, not least because earth spirits could be both benign and harmful. In order to commune with the natural world, shamans would use drumming and pipe-smoking to put themselves in a trance.

Witches – in the sense of those who practise harmful magic – can also be found in Native American culture. Some tribes believed that witches had learnt their craft from the Raven, the Native American trickster deity. In Navajo culture, witches (almost always male) acquire their power by breaking a taboo – for example, by murdering a relative. To activate their curses, the witches use the powder of dried-up corpses; the curses themselves can be removed only by a medicine man. Within Navajo tradition, there is also the figure of the skinwalker (*yee naaldlooshii*), a person capable of using magic to turn themselves into any animal they wish.

A medicine man from the Siksiká (Blackfoot) people performing rites over a dying man.

All Native American societies feature a medicine man of one kind or another. These individuals know the sacred formulas, songs and rites, as well as the healing properties of herbs. They wear masks to scare off evil spirits, and in some cases ceremonies can last for days. Their target is not necessarily physical illness alone, but disorder in general.

The Tlingit people of the Pacific Northwest are well known for their shamans. Shamanic powers are generally inherited, together with the principal tools of shamanism, including drums and rattles. Masks are used to commune with specific spirits. In Greenland, Inuit shamans (*angakkuq*) had the power to create monsters called *tupilaqs*. Horrendous composites, occasionally featuring even human body parts, they were made in secret at night, animated with chants, and sent out to exact revenge on enemies.

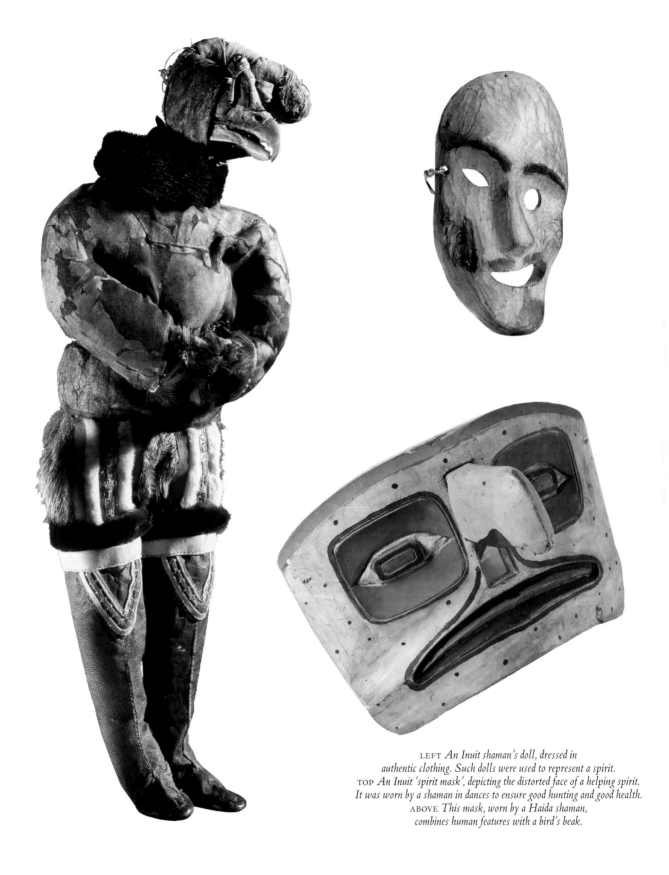

LEFT *An Inuit shaman's doll, dressed in
authentic clothing. Such dolls were used to represent a spirit.*
TOP *An Inuit 'spirit mask', depicting the distorted face of a helping spirit.
It was worn by a shaman in dances to ensure good hunting and good health.*
ABOVE *This mask, worn by a Haida shaman,
combines human features with a bird's beak.*

VOODOO & HOODOO

Today, voodoo is most commonly associated with New Orleans and the Caribbean, but its origins can be traced back to the *vodun* practices of West Africa. In fact, it is possible to identify some differences between Louisiana voodoo and Haitian voodoo. The former, for example, places importance on the gris-gris, originally a West African amulet containing verses from the Koran, but becoming over time any voodoo amulet that could be used to curse another person. 'Voodoo dolls' are most associated with the Louisiana branch of the religion.

Haitian voodoo (sometimes spelt 'vodou') became popular in the late eighteenth century, when it was believed that the Haitians' magic had made them invincible against the French. However, vodou remained outlawed in Haiti for most of the nineteenth century.

BELOW *A voodoo shrine in Togoville. Togo is also home to some of the world's largest fetish markets.*
OPPOSITE *This panel is taken from the shack of a voodoo practitioner in Adjarra, Benin. It advertises the various ailments treated by the practitioner through sorcery and animal sacrifice.*

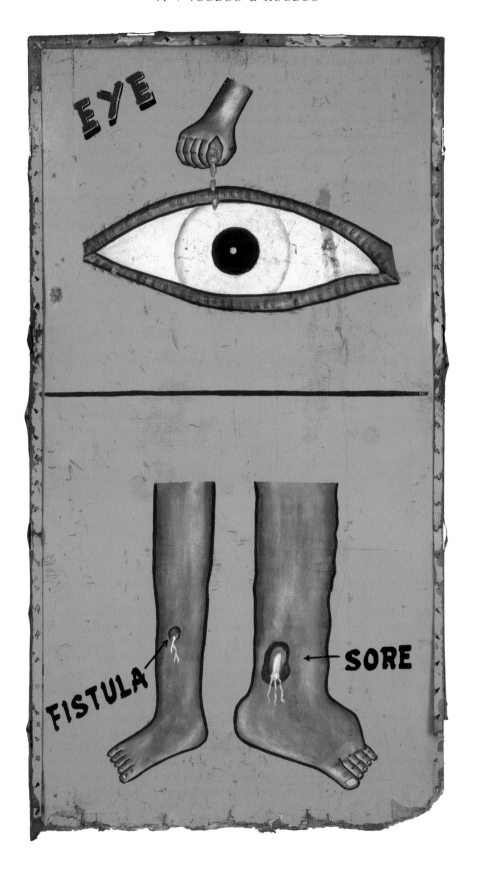

OPPOSITE *A fetish from the Akodessewa Market in Lomé, Togo, believed to be the largest voodoo-fetish market in the world.* ABOVE *A Haitian voodoo altar, bringing together a wide range of symbolic objects and religious imagery. All Haitian voodoo altars feature a cross, which stands not only for the divine but also for the crossroads.*

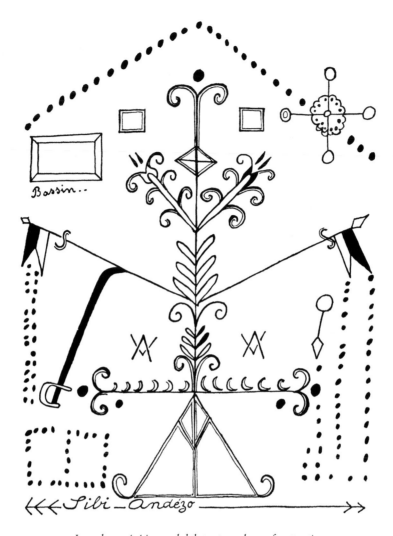

In voodoo, a vévé *is a symbol that acts as a beacon for attracting the* loa, *or spirits. This* vévé *is for the* loa *known as Simbi-yandezi.*

Originating from the Mississippi Delta, hoodoo combines African and Native American beliefs into a single, magical system – one that was supposed to give slaves some control over their lives in otherwise desperate circumstances. God is seen as a magician who conjured up the world in six days of spells, while the Bible is seen as a book of magic, with biblical figures being hoodoo 'doctors'.

Moses in particular is seen as a conjurer. Indeed, the *Sixth and Seventh Books of Moses* – grimoires allegedly written by the Hebrew prophet, but likely dating from the eighteenth or nineteenth century – are part of the hoodoo corpus. Other texts in the corpus include John George Hohman's *Pow-Wows* (1820; see page 299). Talismans are very important in hoodoo, with the most important of them all – guaranteeing protection – being the Bible.

A Cuban follower of the Palo religion draws a magical symbol on the floor of the temple in Santiago de Cuba.
The symbol is central to the act of releasing the spiritual powers linked to the temple's altars. Palo is one of a group
of syncretic religions, voodoo and candomblé *included, that developed among slaves from Congo.*

LATIN AMERICAN MAGIC

In the countries of Latin America – Brazil in particular – one finds fascinating syncretic practices dating back to the early nineteenth century, bringing together Christian, spiritualist, African and animistic traditions. Foremost among them is *macumba*, which in the twentieth century developed into the *quimbanda* and *umbanda* traditions. The magical practices of *quimbanda* are spectacular. Held at crossroads at midnight, the *trabalho* ritual typically involves alcohol, red and black cloths, cigars, and singing.

The *candomblé* religion is also found in Brazil. A combination of the beliefs of the West African Yoruba and Fon peoples, it originated in the sixteenth century. The word *candomblé* means 'dance in honour of the gods', and in the central dance itself, worshippers are possessed by the spirits (*orixás*), offerings are made (animal, vegetable, mineral), and divinations are cast.

OPPOSITE *This mosaic-covered skull represents Tezcatlipoca, or 'Smoking Mirror', the Aztec god of sorcery (among other things). Tezcatlipoca was associated with obsidian mirrors, as used by the Aztecs – and, later, John Dee – for scrying.* ABOVE *A* candomblé *dance ritual, Brazil.*

ABOVE *An owl figurine and various fetishes on an altar in
Bahia, Brazil. The chicken feathers are evidence of a recent sacrifice.*
OPPOSITE *A page from the Dresden Codex, a Mayan book from the 11th or 12th century,
which contains astronomical and astrological information, as well as ritual schedules.*

The indigenous populations of Central and South America – the Olmecs, Aztecs and Mayans, among others – were all strongly superstitious. In the case of the Aztecs, those born on certain days were believed to have magical powers (including the ability to transform themselves into other creatures), while the forearm of a woman who had died in childbirth was considered highly magical. Divination was achieved using corn kernels and beans, or by interpreting the actions of a snake.

The Mayans were also keen practitioners of divination and astrology. Evidence suggests that they practised scrying, and interpreted the flight of birds and the throwing of seeds. The Olmecs believed that magicians could turn themselves into jaguars, while the Quiché Mayan *Popul Vuh* (Book of the Community) tells how the magical incantations of an old man and woman had been instrumental in forming plants, animals and humans.

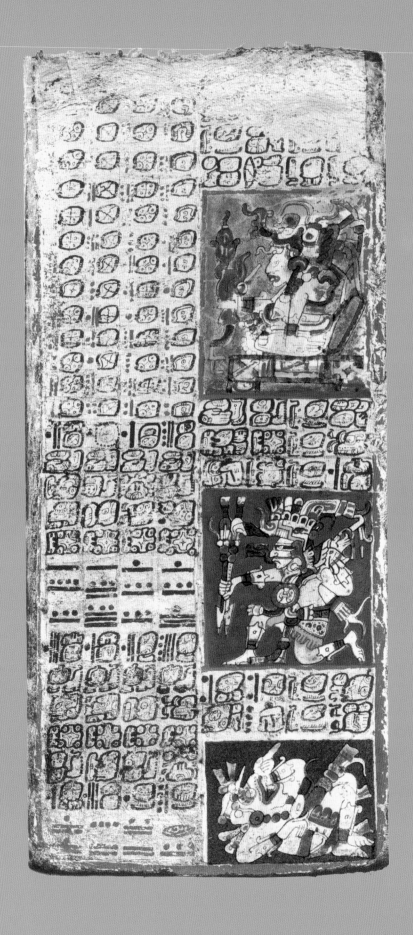

MAGIC IN AFRICA

In Africa, many magical traditions remain strong. In Nigeria, for example, the Ifá divination rituals, which offer insight into the future and the spiritual realm, are still widely practised. The rituals themselves use sacred palm nuts and a divination chain. The chain makes patterns in a bowl filled with dust, and the patterns are interpreted using a substantial body of texts.

So-called black-magic markets can be found throughout Africa, the largest of which – the Marché des Féticheurs – being in Lomé, Togo. As with similar markets found in neighbouring Benin, it sells parts of animals, amulets and fetishes. As we have seen, the local belief system, *vodun*, is related to the voodoo of Haiti and the Caribbean. However, it does not involve the casting of spells, but rather communication with ancestors. More concerned with the active casting of spells and the creation of amulets is the West African juju – often interpreted as 'black magic'.

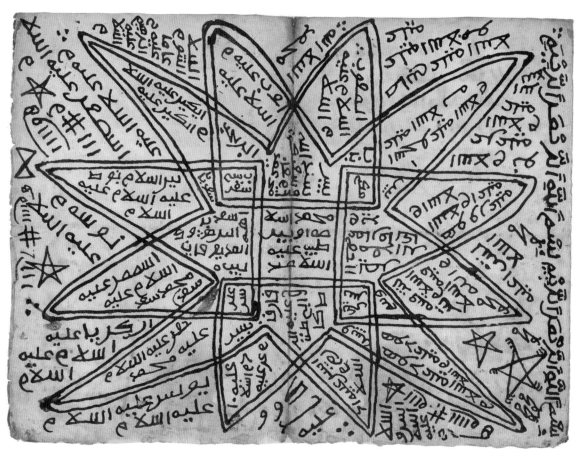

ABOVE *A Sudanese drawn amulet that includes spells against the 'evil eye'. Note the profusion of five-pointed stars.*
OPPOSITE *This drawing from the 19th century, complete with what the rather sensationalist artist believed were signs of human sacrifice, depicts a 'juju house' on the Bight of Biafra.*

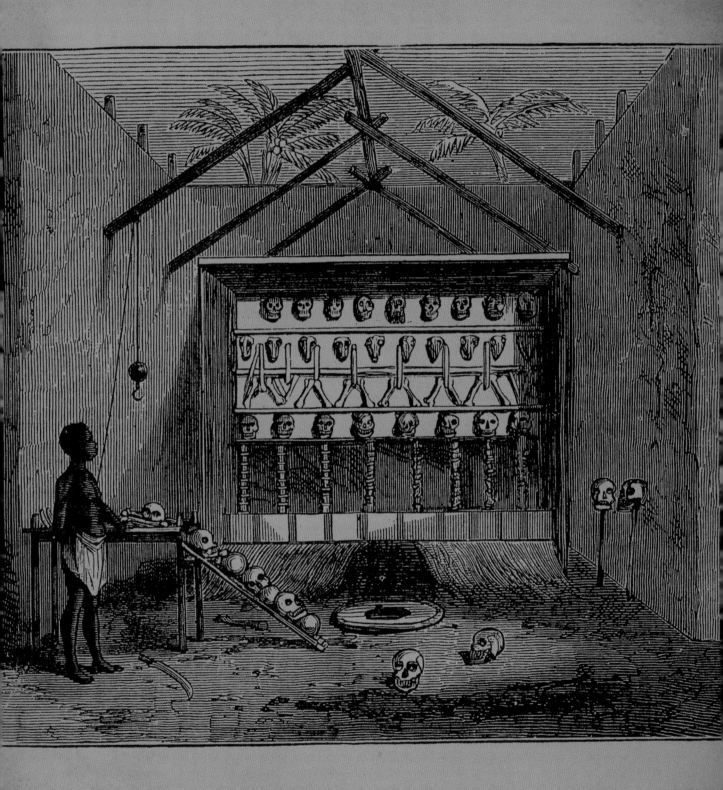

Men dressed as Nigerian Yoruba spirits perform during a voodoo ceremony in Ouidah, Benin. Each spirit represents the reincarnation of a dead member of the Nigerian 'Nagu' clan.

ABOVE *A nkondi figure made by the Kongo people of Central Africa. Such figures, into which nails were hammered, were believed to house spirits that could seek out and do harm to a chosen victim.*
RIGHT *A Senufo fetish figure from the Côte d'Ivoire.*

OPPOSITE *A Swazi medicine man or shaman
performing a 'witch-smelling' ritual.*
ABOVE *A medicine man or shaman of the
Nkose tribe divines the future in a bowl.*

In South Africa, especially among the
Zulu, 'witch smellers' were common up until
the Suppression of Witchcraft Act of 1957.
These specialists, typically women, would hunt
out witches, who would then be killed – or at
least banished.

In Kenya, Kikuyu witch doctors were
believed capable of manipulating others' life
spirits. Indeed, belief in witchcraft remains
widespread in Kenya, with sporadic witch-hunts
resulting in executions. Those capable of
communicating with spirits are called *nganga*;
they are also seen as medicine men and women,
or healers.

For the Zande people of Central Africa,
witchcraft touches every aspect of life, serving
to explain any strange coincidence or misfortune,
no matter how trivial. Powers of witchcraft are
inherited, and are sometimes used by those who
possess them without their knowing it.

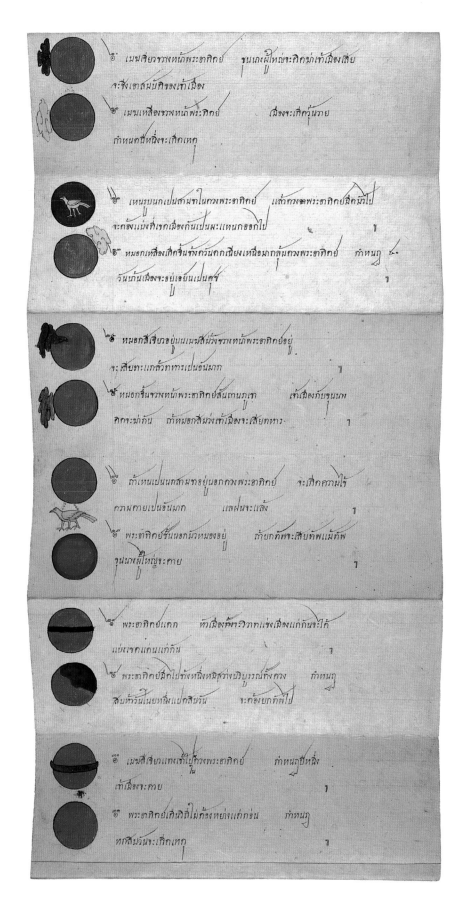

๑ เมฆจริยารวมหน้าทัพพระอาทิตย์   ขุนเภทผู้ใหญ่จะกิดฆ่าเท้าเมืองเสีย
จะจึงเจาสมบัติขอมเท้าเมือง

๒ เมฆเหลืองรวมหน้าพระอาทิตย์   เมืองจะเกิดวุ่นวาย
กำหนดปีหนึ่งจะเกิดเหตุ

๓ เหนรบนกเปนสามทาในกวงพระอาทิตย์   แล้วกลฉฉพระอาทิตย์ยึดมาไป
จะกลงแบ่งที่เรกเมืองกันเปนพะแหนกออกไป   ๑

๔ หมอกเหลืองเกิดขึ้นรับควันอกกเสียเหนือมากลุ่มกวงพระอาทิตย์   กำหนด ๕
วันบ้านเมืองจะอยู่เอนเปนศุข   ๑

๕ หมอกสีเขียวอยู่นเมฆฝีสีผ่วังรวมหน้าพระอาทิตย์อยู่
จะเสียทะแกล้วทหารเปนอันมาก   ๑

๖ หมอกขึ้นรวมหน้าพระอาทิตย์สันถานภูเท   เท้าเมืองกับขุนเภท
กิกะฆ่ากัน   ถ้าหมอกสีม่วงเท้าเมืองจะเสียทหาร   ๑

๗ ภาเหนเปนนกสามทายอยู่นอกกวงพระอาทิตย์   จะเกิดความไร้
ความตายเปนอันมาก   แลฝนจะแล้ง   ๑

๘ พระอาทิตย์ขึ้นนอกมัวหมองอยู่   ถ้ายกทัพจะเสียทัพแม้ทัพ
ขุนเภทผู้ใหญ่จะกาย   ๑

๙ พระอาทิตย์แตก   ทาวเมืองผ้าววิวาทแบ่งเมืองแก่กันจะได้
แบ่งเรกแกนแก่กัน   ๑

๑๐ พระอาทิตย์ฉีกไปทั้งหนึ่งหลังสว่างปิบูรวณทั้งกวง   กำหนด
สิบห้าวันในยหนึ่งแปกสียวัน   จะกลงยกทัพไป

๑๑ เมฆสีเขียวแทงเท้าไปก้วงพระอาทิตย์   กำหนดปีหนึ่ง
เท้าเมืองจะกาย   ๑

๑๒ พระอาทิตย์เกิดผิกสีไม่ก้วเทย่าแก่ก่อน   กำหนด
ทกสิบวันจะเกิดเหตุ   ๑

OPPOSITE *This Thai manuscript on astronomical fortune-telling shows various observed features of the Sun and their interpretation. The penultimate observation – the Sun with a green band – indicates the imminent death of a king.*

RIGHT *A silver Balinese kris, or ceremonial knife, and its wooden sheath. Such knives are believed to contain spirits, and can bring either good or bad luck. The hilt depicts Batara Bayu, god of wind, wealth and well-being.*

MAGIC IN SOUTH EAST ASIA

Thailand, a profoundly Buddhist country, also has a parallel magical tradition. Perhaps the best-known example of Thai black magic is the rather grisly *Kuman Thong*, or 'Golden Little Boy'. Originally, a *Kuman Thong* was made using a dead fetus, often surgically removed from its mother's womb. While chanting an incantation, a witch doctor would roast the fetus before covering the body in gold leaf. The reanimated spirit of the fetus would then do the witch doctor's bidding.

The Philippines, and in particular the island of Siquijor, is also known for its syncretic magical traditions. The *mananambal*, a kind of medicine man or healer, is also able to perform black-magic rituals, including the boiling of a person's possessions in order to inflict harm on them. A type of ritual known as *barang* involves feeding ginger root to a beetle before sending it out to find a named victim. The beetle then enters the victim's body with the purpose of causing harm.

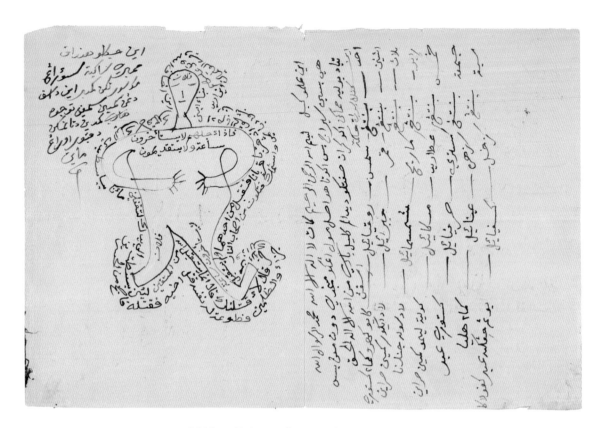

*A Malayan black-magic charm, intended to curse the recipient
with a fatal illness. It is written in the language of djinns.*

*This buffalo rib has been carved by the Karo-
Batak people of Sumatra with magical symbols
to create an amulet against injury by bullets.*

Two Malayan exorcists dressed in elaborate costume.

OPPOSITE *This* kareau *figure from the Nicobar Islands was made by a* menluana, *a healer who communicated with the spirit world. It was left outside the house of a sick person to drive away illness-causing spirits.* ABOVE *The Great Pustaha, a book of magical spells produced by the Batak people. Dating from the 19th century, it is intelligible only to the initiated.*

In Indonesia and Malaysia, the *dukun* is a similar figure to a shaman or sorcerer. Most commonly found in Java and Bali, *dukuns* specialize in herbs and healing. They also function as mediums, and sometimes even as sorcerers, performing exorcisms.

Among the Batak people of northern Sumatra, magical and divination spells, as well as formulas and recipes, were gathered in a *pustaha*, an accordion-style book made from tree-bark cloth. Batak shamans, known as *datu*, also used these books to record charms, while the book itself could be used as an amulet.

In the Trobriand Islands of Papua New Guinea, magical spells are widely owned by older members of tribes, and exchanged – a line at a time – for small gifts. Particularly popular are love spells.

LEFT AND ABOVE *Zhang Guolao,
a* fangshi *and one of the 'Eight
Immortals' of Chinese mythology,
was famous for being able to make
himself invisible. He was also famous
for being able to put his horse into a
small box or bag when it wasn't needed
(see left), adding water when it
was required once more.*

RIGHT *This Japanese figure of a*
sennin — *immortal man or magus —
shows the influence of Chinese thought.*

OPPOSITE *A scene from* The
Sorcerer's Revolt, *a Ming-dynasty
story about three sorcerers who help a
general overthrow the government.
On the right, seated, is the figure of
Hu Yong'er, a sorceress who was
conceived after her mother burned
a magical painting.*

FAR EASTERN MAGIC

Magic has been central to Chinese culture since prehistory. The *fangshi* – meaning sorcerers or magicians, although also translatable as 'gentlemen possessing magical recipes' – were in favour from the third century BC to the fifth century AD, and were specialists in Taoist magic, including *xian* (immortality) techniques and alchemy. Indeed, some have suggested that the Taoist way of life largely originated with the *fangshi*, in a unique combination of philosophy and magic.

The *fangshi* did not find favour in all parts of Chinese society. Gu Yong, for example, a minister from the first century BC, was particularly critical: 'All these occultists … who rather are brimming with claims about the strange and marvellous, about spirits and ghosts … who have mastered the transformation of base metal to gold, who have made uniform the five colours and five stores within their bodies – those occultists cheat people and delude the masses.'

Abe no Seimei (left) was a leading practitioner of onmyōdō *during the Heian period (794–1185). His symbol (above) was the pentagram, as can be seen on the well in the grounds of the Seimei Temple in Kyoto. The water in the well is believed to have magical properties.*

Princess Iwanaga, a figure from Japanese mythology, performs the ritual known as ushi no toki mairi (ox-hour shrine visit), so called because it takes places at the hour of the Ox. Carrying candles on an iron crown, the practitioner – usually a scorned woman – must visit a Shinto shrine every night for seven nights at precisely two o'clock in the morning, to drive nails into a tree and pray for the death of their unfaithful lover.

In Japan, the esoteric cosmology known as *onmyōdō* is based on the Chinese principle of *Wu Xing* ('Five Elements' or 'Five Phases'), which describes how elements interact, and the concept of yin and yang. Introduced to Japan from China in the sixth or seventh century AD, it became a system of divination controlled by the government in the interests of the state.

Known as *onmyōji*, the practitioners of *onmyōdō* were engaged in fortune-telling and the fight against evil spirits. Famous practitioners included Abe no Seimei (AD 921–1005) and Kamo no Yasunori (AD 917–977). The latter revealed his talent at an early age, being able to see demons without formal training. Seimei's emblem was a pentagram (known in Japan as the Seimei-star), which represented the *Wu Xing*. Some said that his mother had been a *kitsune* – a magical, nine-tailed fox.

ABOVE, LEFT *Princess Takiyasha, legendary daughter of an evil magician, invokes toad magic in an attempt to overcome her enemy, the hero Mitsukuni. Following her father's death, Takiyasha met Nikushisen, the spirit of a toad, whose witchcraft enabled her to raise a rebellion. She was ultimately defeated, however, by Mitsukuni's courage.* ABOVE, RIGHT *In Japanese storytelling, shape-shifting is common. Here, an old witch assumes the shape of a giant cat in order to distract young women visiting a local shrine.* OPPOSITE *The 17th-century magician and adventurer Tenjiku Tokubei, riding on a giant toad, makes a magical sign with his fingers.*

Central to Japanese mythology, religion and magic is the concept of *kami* – the gods and spirits that dwell in everything. To connect with these spirits, a person might go through a *miko*, originally a female shaman comparable to the Pythia of ancient Greece, who would go into an ecstatic trance. Interestingly, in the eighth and ninth centuries AD, the government tried to limit the practice of trance and magic to temples, so as to keep it under official control and avoid its abuse.

By the nineteenth century, shamanistic practices in Japan had been largely outlawed. The country's mythology, however, continued to teem with magical creatures and monsters. *Yokai* (supernatural creatures; see also page 284) come in many different forms, from the harmless-looking *kappa* to the *oni* (demons or ogres) and the dangerous *tengu* (goblins). And then there are the *Tsukumogami* – household items that, on reaching their one hundredth birthday, come alive.

TOP *According to legend, Minamoto no Yorimitsu — a 10th-century warrior known as Raiko — was commissioned to rid Japan of bandits. In this triptych, one of the bandits, a magician called Hakamadare Yasuke (on the right, making a magical sign), decides to protect himself by conjuring a huge snake; however, Raiko's black dog attacks the snake, showing Raiko and his men (on the left) that it is not real.* ABOVE *Powerful magicians take part in a competition.* OPPOSITE *A woodcut of Hakamadare Yasuke and his fellow robber-magician Kidōmaru engaging in a competition of tricks. Kidōmaru conjures up a venomous snake, while Hakamadare Yasuke summons an eagle.*

ABOVE *In this print by the Japanese artist Hokusai, a woman wearing an iron crown with three candles summons a supernatural creature as part of a cursing ritual (see also page 277).*
OPPOSITE *Two panels from a screen depicting Korean shamanism.*

While Korea too embraced the Buddhism and Confucianism coming from China, it also had its own, unique tradition of shamanism, one that continues to be practised today. Known as Muism, it is an ancient form of shamanism, similar to the Wu tradition in China, yet co-exists with more modern beliefs. The Korean shaman – typically a woman, but occasionally a man – performs rituals to encourage gods to intervene in human affairs.

When a male shaman performs the rituals, he wears a woman's outfit.

Korean mythology is also populated by magical creatures. The *dokkaebi* are inanimate objects transformed into demons, with magical hats that make them invisible; they also carry clubs that function as magic wands. *Haechi* are creatures that protect against chaos, and have been used by geomancers to cancel out yang energy.

MAGICAL CREATURES

Monsters and magical creatures can be found in every part of the world. Usually the embodiment of a deep-seated fear, they are often the centre of terrifying stories; on occasion, however, they can also be the product of magic. Typically (although by no means always), such creatures are impossible hybrids – mixtures of real animals contorted into unlikely and horrifying new forms.

One of the best-known magical creatures is the unicorn. References to this mythical animal can be found in the writings of the ancient Greeks, who believed that it lived in far-away India. In the Middle Ages, it was thought that the unicorn could be tamed only by a virgin, and that a cup made from the animal's horn was capable of neutralizing poisons. Unicorn horn – actually narwhal tusk – was a highly prized commodity.

White stags were associated in Celtic and Christian lore with miracles and visions; in particular, it was believed that they were messengers from the supernatural realm. In ancient Greek and Roman mythology, the caladrius – a snow-white bird known as the Dhalion in Greek mythology – refuses to look at any ill person who is not going to make a full recovery.

ABOVE *A virgin taming a unicorn. According to legend, unicorns were drawn to a maiden's purity; later, this story was interpreted by Christian writers as an allegory of the Annunciation and the Incarnation of Christ. The unicorn also appears in alchemy as a symbol of the 'White Stone'.*
OPPOSITE *Demons typically take on abominable, impossible forms. Such magical hybrid creatures can be found in every culture, but this particular example appears in a book on magic and demonology.*

So gelingt der Astharoth zu erscheinen.

Oriens. Baimon. Ariton. Gogaleson. Zugula.

Asa

Vezol

Chuz

OPPOSITE *The Japanese* kappa *is a magical, water-dwelling demon. Here, it is pictured wrestling with a human hero.*
ABOVE *The Persian hero Bahram Gur, said to be based on the 5th-century Sasanian Persian king Bahram V, kills a formidable dragon.*

One special type of magical creature is the dragon. Tales of this legendary beast most likely originated in Mesopotamia, but its popularity later spread both westwards and eastwards, to Europe and the Far East. In China and Japan, it became a creature with magical properties, ruling weather and water. In Europe, dragon's blood in the story of Siegfried allows the hero to understand the language of birds; in Greek mythology, dragons or snakes bestow this power on humans by licking their ears. Dragons are also frequently depicted in alchemical works.

Japan has more supernatural creatures than any other nation. Known as *yokai*, many of these creatures have special abilities; the *satori*, for example, is a monkey with mind-reading powers. Another well-known *yokai* is the *kappa*, a frog-like, pond-dwelling creature that has impeccable manners, but which can also attack unexpectedly.

287

VII.
Enlightenment Magic

An occult funeral meal is held in a church.

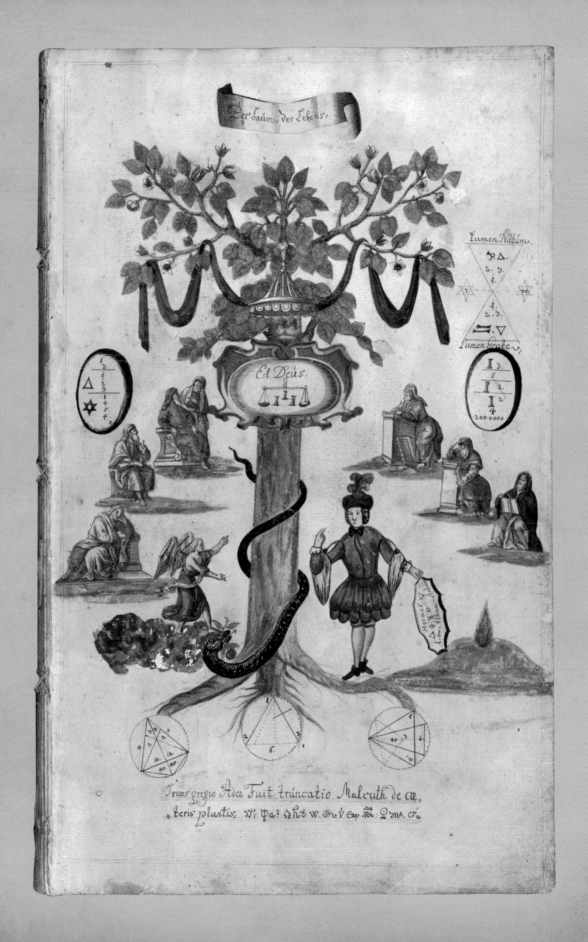

The Renaissance saw the birth of a new curiosity about the world, one based on a revival of interest in classical antiquity. But while it sowed the seeds of scientific thinking, it also remained optimistic that there were shortcuts to acquiring knowledge. From the seventeenth century onwards, scientific advancements gradually eroded the power of religion and superstition — or so the story goes.

In fact, the seventeenth century began with a burst of occultism in the shape of three pamphlets published between 1614 and 1616, purportedly telling the story of Christian Rosenkreuz, head of the secretive Rosicrucian Order. These pamphlets, or manifestos, told how Rosenkreuz had acquired knowledge of the occult while in the Middle East, and that this knowledge could now be passed on to adepts.

One of the defenders of Rosicrucianism, Robert Fludd (1574–1637), was a well-known Kabbalist and astrologer. Early in the 1600s Fludd took part in a notorious (and bad-tempered) exchange with Johannes Kepler on the relative virtues of scientific and Hermetic knowledge. In 1616 he published a tract defending the existence of the Rosicrucian brotherhood. Fludd believed that higher truths were best explained through symbolism, and he and Kepler exchanged pamphlets that discussed the true nature of things — mathematically from Kepler's side, metaphysically from Fludd's. Kepler accused Fludd, not unreasonably, of writing in an 'occult and shadowy manner', of creating 'dense mysteries', and of taking unnecessary delight in 'symbolism'.

In 1612, just a couple of years before the story of Rosenkreuz appeared, the legend of Nicolas Flamel was first published in *Le Livre des figures hiéroglyphiques*. Up to that point, Flamel had been remembered — if at all — as a seller of books. Where the legend came from is unclear, but it was widely accepted until the eighteenth century, when Etienne-François Villain voiced a number of doubts in his *Histoire critique de Nicolas Flamel* (1761).

The seventeenth century was a turbulent time politically and religiously as well. In 1632 Galileo was forced to recant his heliocentric observations about the universe before

OPPOSITE *A German manuscript from around 1735 brims with a mixture of transcendental alchemy, Kabbalistic musings and religious controversies. It ends with thoughts on Biblical prophecies.*
ABOVE *Robert Fludd, the eminent English physician, mathematician, astrologer and Kabbalist.*

the Inquisition, while in England, amid the ravages of the Civil War (1642–9), Matthew Hopkins began his reign of terror as the self-styled 'Witchfinder General'. In France, the witch-hunts of 1643–5 were the largest the country had ever seen; the Netherlands, however, did away with all punishments for witchcraft in 1648. Of course, witch-hunts continued in America for some time afterwards, and the last execution for witchcraft in Europe took place in Poland as late as 1793.

On the opposite side to Hopkins in the English Civil War was Elias Ashmole. Later a founding member of the Royal Society (England's leading scientific institution), Ashmole typified the intellectual conflict of the day, being at once scientific-minded but also fascinated by alchemy. Nevertheless, he was careful to define a magus as 'a Contemplator of Heavenly and divine Sciences … a name (saith Marcellus Ficinus) gratious in the Gospell', and under no circumstances 'a Witch or a Conjurer, but a wise man and a Priest'.

It is believed that Ashmole was a Freemason – in which case he would have been one of the first. Freemasonry built on many of the currents in magical thought, especially the ritual element. By the late eighteenth century, however, it had taken on a structure and officialdom previously unknown to its members. Relying on initiation ceremonies that were quasi-magical in nature, it was embraced by both the aristocracy and the new middle classes (including members of the clergy). Being open to all religions, it also reflected the ideals of the Enlightenment.

It is also interesting to note the huge number of occult manuscripts dating to the eighteenth century. One of these, *La Très Sainte Trinosophie*, was allegedly written by Alessandro Cagliostro (1743–1795). Cagliostro typifies eighteenth-century magicians – on the one hand feted by such societies as the Freemasons, and on the other constantly beleaguered by scandal and easily accused of being a conman. *La Très Sainte Trinosophie* has also been attributed to the Count of St Germain (?1712–1784). Probably hailing from Transylvania, the count claimed to be hundreds of years old, and that he could turn lead into gold. He was embraced by the royal courts of Europe, from France and the United Kingdom to Germany, where he set up an alchemical laboratory.

Antoine Court de Gébelin (1725–1784) was a French student of the occult. His particular contribution to the subject, in his multi-volume *Le Monde primitif, analysé et comparé avec le monde moderne*, was the association of the Tarot with the ancient Egyptian (and likely mythological) Book of Thoth. Another essay in Court de Gébelin's work – by the Comte de Mellet – associated the twenty-two trump cards of the Tarot with the twenty-two letters of the Hebrew alphabet. This association was picked up by Court de Gébelin's contemporary Etteilla (Jean-Baptiste Alliette, 1738–1791), who popularized the use of Tarot for divination. It was also Etteilla who introduced to the interpretation of the cards the four elements and astrology.

THE DEVIL AND Dr. FAUSTUS.

OPPOSITE *Athanasius Kircher was one of the key intellects of the 17th century. This engraving summarizes his efforts to link the Hermetic and Christian traditions.* ABOVE *The story of Doctor Faustus held thrall well into the 19th century, although increasingly it was seen as a fable.*

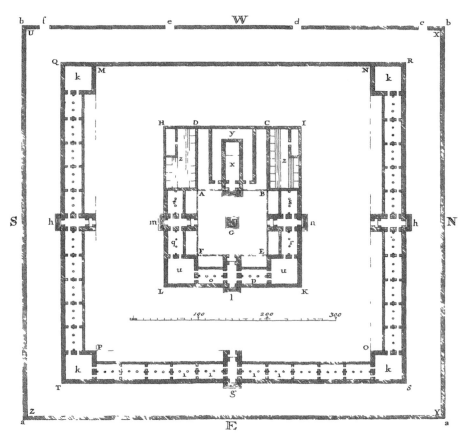

Sir Isaac Newton's reconstruction of the Temple of Solomon. As an example of mystical or symbolic architecture, the temple fascinated many in the 17th century, including the emergent Freemasons.

MAGIC & RATIONALISM

The Age of Enlightenment, which placed rational, scientific thought at the centre of decision-making, did not immediately supplant magic and the occult. Sir Isaac Newton, while being the first to articulate the laws of gravity, was fascinated by the alchemical process and hoped to discover the philosopher's stone. On his death, he left behind not only a library of 169 books on alchemy, but also heavily annotated translations of the original Rosicrucian manifestos (see page 308).

The eighteenth century saw the introduction of more widespread education and, as a result, the birth of a more literate public. This in turn provided an outlet for lurid books on magic; indeed, the century was marked by a profusion of works on the subject, possibly because there was no longer any fear of prosecution from the Church.

The late seventeenth century saw the emergence of a sensationalist and secular press, with articles often accompanied by illustrations. Miracles and magic were reported, and by the late eighteenth century the professional fortune-teller had appeared, making a living through the publication of their work.

CARTAS
ERUDITAS, Y CURIOSAS,

En que, por la mayor parte, se continúa el designio

DEL THEATRO CRITICO
UNIVERSAL,

Impugnando, ó reduciendo á dudosas, varias
opiniones comunes:

ESCRITAS

POR EL MUY ILUSTRE SEÑOR

D. Fr. Benito Geronymo Feyjoó y Montenegro,

Maestro General del Orden de San Benito,
del Consejo de S. M. &c.

TOMO PRIMERO.

NUEVA IMPRESION.

MADRID. M.DCC.LXIX.

Por D. Joachin Ibarra, Impresor de Camara de S. M.

Con las Licencias necesarias.

A costa de la Real Compañia de Impresores, y Libreros.

The frontispiece to Cartas eruditas y curiosas *by the Spanish monk Benito Jerónimo*
Feijóo y Montenegro (1676–1764). Ironically, Feijóo was one of the staunchest advocates of
science and education, horrified by the superstition of ordinary people.

Eerfte Boek fol 87

Jan Luyken inven et fecit.

Poftuur van een Laplander zoo als hy met de Tover-trommel ter aarde legt

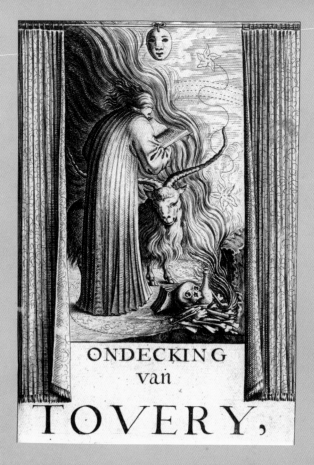

ONDECKING
van
TOVERY,

OPPOSITE *Without access to modern healthcare, most people outside of cities – in this case, in Lapland – relied on folk magic and healing well into the 19th century.* ABOVE *Superstition remained strong during the Enlightenment, and growing literacy led to the spread of such sensationalist books as this Dutch publication,* Ondecking van tovery *(Uncovering of Sorcery).*

FOLK MAGIC IN EUROPE

The intellectual currents of science took much longer to reach everyday life than they did the academies. Well into the nineteenth century, people – especially outside large cities – would still consult 'cunning folk' about illness, improving their luck, retrieving something that had been stolen, or removing the 'evil eye'. This was true throughout Christian Europe, but was particularly prevalent in Scandinavia, Britain and Eastern Europe.

Scandinavian practitioners of witchcraft would consult their copy of the *Cyprianus*, a grimoire also known as the Black Book. In Norway, Mor Sæther (1793–1851) became nationally famous as a healer, but also spent periods of time in prison. Similarly, in England, the Witchcraft Act of 1735 introduced punishments for those dabbling in witchcraft – not as practitioners of black arts, but as confidence tricksters.

*An astrological chart from about 1840 showing a range of possible political
and social events from the future. Among the figures illustrated are King Arthur
and Merlin. Such pamphlets were extremely popular in the 19th century.*

This historic barn in Pennsylvania incorporates hex signs based on the compass rose, a tradition that originated in Europe.

The eighteenth and nineteenth centuries were also marked by a growing interest in horoscopes. Almanacs began to be published, giving a mass public access to predictions about the future. Later, these predictions would be incorporated into newspapers.

Traditional European magic also found its way to the United States. One popular book there was *Pow-Wows; or, Long Lost Friend* (1820), written by the Pennsylvanian-Dutch healer John George Hohman. A collection of magical spells and folk remedies (often with supernatural elements), the book continued to be popular into the twentieth century. So-called pow-wow magic includes hex signs to ward off evil, while its syncretic spells typically appeal to Jesus and Mary.

ABOVE *A bust of Elias Ashmole that underlines his classical credentials.*
OPPOSITE *The title page from Ashmole's* Theatrum Chemicum Britannicum.

Elias Ashmole

Although not a practising magician himself, Elias Ashmole (1617–1692) proved to be an important vessel in the collection and dissemination of magical thinking. In classic seventeenth-century style, this role in no way conflicted with his position as one of the founding members of England's foremost scientific institution, the Royal Society; rather, all of this fell under his interest in antiquarianism.

Ashmole's interest in the occult took on many forms. In his diaries he makes a number of references to being a Freemason – these being among the very first references to the organization anywhere. He was also believed to be a Rosicrucian. During the English Civil War, Ashmole provided pro-Royalist astrological readings, while William Lilly, the foremost astrologer in England in the seventeenth century, provided readings in favour of the Parliamentarians. After the war, the two became close friends.

Also after the war, Ashmole became the alchemical 'son' of the renowned Rosicrucian philosopher William Backhouse. In 1650 Ashmole published *Fasciculus Chemicus*, a translation into English of alchemical works compiled in Latin by Arthur Dee, John Dee's son. Ashmole spent time with Arthur Dee, and had planned to write a biography of his father. Ashmole's most important alchemical publication was *Theatrum Chemicum Britannicum* (1652), a collection of Hermetic-influenced poetry that included work by George Ripley, John Dee and Edward Kelley, among others.

A spectacular automata by the French magician Robert-Houdin,
in which the woman 'teaches' the bird to sing a tune.

AUTOMATA &
PHANTASMAGORIA

St Augustine, in his *City of God* (fifth century AD), discusses how Hermes Trismegistus used magic to animate statues. The original reference to this activity appears in the Hermetic book *To Asclepius*, where Hermes himself claims that man-made images can be transformed and given life through the agency of angels or demons.

This dream of the 'magical' animation of statues became a reality, of sorts, with the development of automata: devices that appear to move independently of any outside force. First documented in the Middle Ages, they became more common in seventeenth-century Europe. Similar devices – known as karakuri puppets – can be found in seventeenth- to nineteenth-century Japan. In nineteenth-century Europe, automata played a part in the stage magic of the French conjuror Robert-Houdin (see page 338).

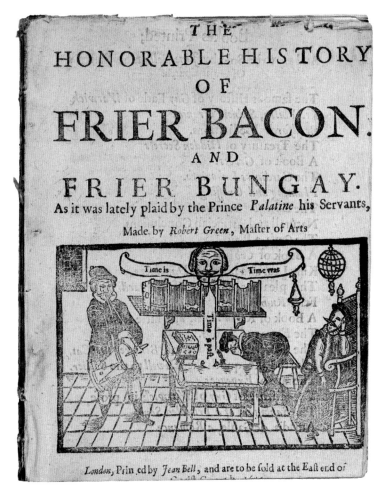

The frontispiece from a copy of a play about Roger Bacon. The illustration includes a depiction of the friar's 'brazen head', an automaton that could tell the future.

ABOVE *A Parisian audience in 1799 is terrified by floating ghosts and demons. These phantasmagoria were created using a 'fantoscope', a type of magic lantern patented by the Belgian physicist and stage magician Étienne-Gaspard Roberts, known as Robertson.* OPPOSITE *Another demonstration of Robertson's fantoscope.*

Phantasmagoria are grisly or eerie illuminations that give the impression of being real. Projections made with a magic lantern date back to the seventeenth century and the work of the German polymath Athanasius Kircher (although others have also been credited with the invention of the magic lantern). They became especially popular, however, in the late eighteenth century.

Johann Georg Schröpfer (1730–1774), a German occultist and Freemason, ran a coffee shop in Leipzig where he held seances for entertainment. As part of the show, he projected images of ghosts on to clouds of smoke using a magic lantern. Eventually, he was driven mad by his own projections, and committed suicide after promising to resurrect himself (he didn't). The effect of his shows on the public was spectacular, and at the end of the eighteenth century his techniques were resurrected by the German Paul Philidor. Their popularity spread throughout Europe, eventually feeding into the spiritualist movement of the nineteenth century.

*A flattering depiction of Pinetti by L. S. Thiery,
from Pinetti's* Amusements physiques *(1784).*

Joseph Pinetti

Born in Tuscany in 1750, Giovanni Giuseppe Pinetti was the most famous magician of the late eighteenth century, becoming known as the 'Professor of Natural Magic'. In fact, he started out as a mathematician, teaching in Rome. There, he would perform tricks to amuse students and to demonstrate physics, and eventually he began to give public performances. His well-known tricks included one in which he cut the head off the shadow of a dove – only to reveal that the dove, too, had been decapitated. He also included automata in his performances.

Moving to Paris, Pinetti performed 'experiments' (essentially magic tricks), quickly catching the attention of Louis XIV. In time, he became the court magician, bringing tricks from the street into the palace and the theatres. This was to be his greatest legacy, an achievement set against the backdrop of a waning belief – at least from the authorities – in witchcraft.

Pinetti, however, also had his detractors. In 1784 the French magician Henri Decremps published *La Magie blanche dévoilée* (White Magic Unveiled), which explained how the tricks were performed. Pinetti responded in the same year with his own book, *Amusements physiques* (Physical Amusements). He then moved to London, where, with a new set of tricks, he won the attention of the English king, George III. After returning to Paris, he moved first to Prussia and then to Russia, where he died in around 1803.

Pinetti had many rivals in the world of stage magic. The German Philip Breslaw and the Prussian Gustavus Katterfelto, for example, were also instrumental in establishing magic in the theatres, again with an appeal to the occult.

Professeur et Démonstrateur de Physique amusante, qui après avoir réduit en cendres une Carte choisie au hazard, jette le Jeu en l'air pour la faire reparaître en la clouant au mur d'un coup de Pistolet.

Queverdo   Hémery

Pinetti performing one of his well-known tricks, from Decremps' La Magie blanche dévoilée.

ROSICRUCIANISM

The legend of Christian Rosenkreuz, who was supposedly born in Germany in 1378, dates back to the early seventeenth century and the publication of three manifestos between 1614 and 1616. According to the first of these manifestos, *Fama Fraternitatis*, Rosenkreuz went on pilgrimage to the Holy Land, where he learnt the occult secrets of the universe. On returning to Germany, he founded the Fraternity of the Rosy Cross. After his death at the age of 106, his seven-sided tomb was forgotten about — until, that is, it was apparently rediscovered 120 years later, in 1604, by followers of the fraternity. His body was uncorrupted, while lying beside it in the sarcophagus was the mysterious *Book T*.

In the last of the manifestos, *The Chymical Wedding of Christian Rosenkreuz*, the protagonist visits a miraculous castle to witness a wedding. Interestingly, the wedding invitation incorporates John Dee's Monas

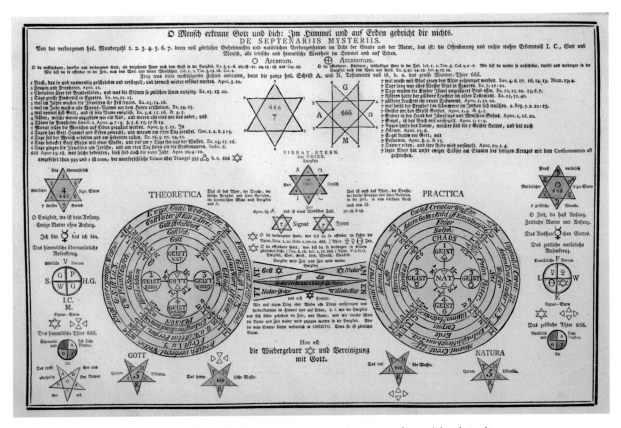

ABOVE *A densely symbolic Rosicrucian engraving exploring numerology and the relationship between the physical and metaphysical realms.* OPPOSITE *An illustration from* Speculum Sophicum Rhodo-Stauroticum *(The Mirror of the Wisdom of the Rosicrucians; 1618), showing the key tenets of the brotherhood. The book is believed to have been written by the alchemist and Rosicrucian Daniel Mögling under the pseudonym Theophilus Schweighardt.*

ABOVE *An engraving containing Rosicrucian symbols, which mix together Christian, pagan and Jewish iconography. The text below it (not shown here) links the symbolism to illustrative biblical quotations.*
OPPOSITE AND PAGES 312–13 *The Rosicrucian movement gave rise to a series of new magical-mystical traditions that endured throughout the 18th and 19th centuries. These diagrams explore the themes of creation, knowledge, spiritual alchemy, the elements and cosmology, as well as drawing on Kabbalistic traditions.*

The three manifestos explain the philosophy and history of Rosicrucianism, telling of an order of philosopher-mystics. The unknown author calls for a moral and spiritual revolution in society, and a deeper understanding of man's role in Creation. Christian Rosenkreuz (referred to as 'Father C.R.C.'), say the manifestos, had learnt Hermetic magic while in the Middle East, but had also been exposed to occult studies in Fez and the Gnostic *alumbrados* (practitioners of a mystical form of Christianity) in Spain. Some scholars have suggested that Father C.R.C.'s journey is actually a veiled reference to the process of transmutation in alchemy.

Rosicrucian philosophy is overwhelmingly Christian, albeit doggedly Protestant and incorporating Hermetic magical thinking. There is evidence, too, of the strong influence of Heinrich Khunrath (*c.* 1560–1605), a Hermetic philosopher from Dresden, Germany, who had met and been influenced by John Dee in 1589.

Some believe that the three Rosicrucian manifestos are hoaxes. However, although the story they tell is certainly difficult to accept unreservedly, they had a huge impact on mystical thinking in Europe, influencing the development of Freemasonry and a raft of Rosicrucian societies in the late nineteenth century.

SCALA PHILOSOPHOPHORIIMCAB·
BALISTICA MAGICA, ATQVE ARBOR AUREA DEMY-
STERYS NUMERY: QVATERNARY, QVINARY ATQVE SEPTENARY.

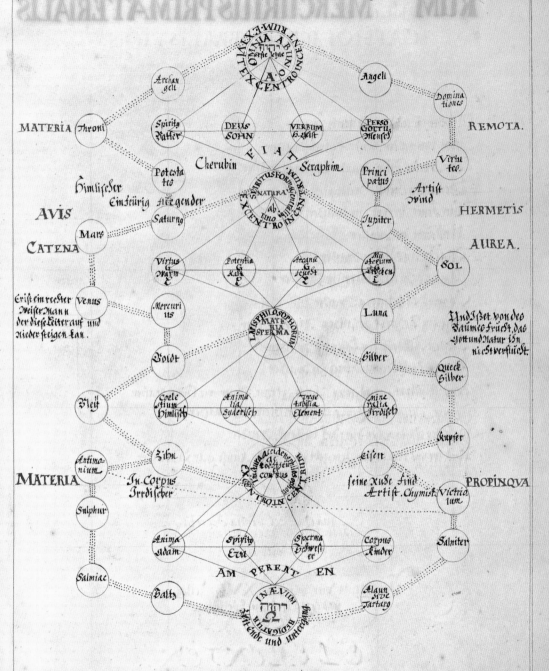

SAPIENTIBUS · SATISEST DICTUM·

Wer Jesum Christum recht erkennt,
Der hat seine Zeit wohl angewendt.

Die geheime Wunder-Zahl. 1. 2. 3. 4. Das rechte Rosen ⊕ Creütz, und die Offenbahrung und die wahre Erkäntnus JEHU CHRISTI,

Gott und Menschen, das ist: Alle himmlische und irrdische Weißheit im Himmel und auf Erden. NB wie der *[mehrere Zeilen in deutscher Kurrentschrift, schwer leserlich]* ... einig Gott ... und ... der Verstand ... ein einiger ewiger Gott, geistlich, himmlisch, unsichtbar, in der Ewigkeit, nach den 3. himmlischen Personen, Geist oder Gott, Wort, Vater, ein Gott, und in der Zeit, irrdisch, sichtbar, leiblich, ein Mensch und Gott; nach dem 3. zeitlichen Personen, Geist, Person, Wort ein Mensch: Dann das Wort ward leiblich h. e. Ewigkeit ward Zeit, Gott ein Mensch h. e. eine Zeit, zwo Zeiten, und eine halbe Zeit, nach dem Alten und Neüen Testament, Propheten und Evangelium der himmlischen und irrdischen Dreyfaltigkeit, gantz im Himmel, und gantz auf Erden,

Sintemahlen in Ihm I. C. wohnet die gantze Fülle der Gottheit leibhaftig. Coloss: 2. Johann 9. 12. et 17.

Es spricht die himmlische Weißheit selber, Ich und der Vater sind Eins, und wer mich sihet, der sihet den Vater; glaubet ja, der Vater in mir, und ich in Ihme, und wer mich siehet, der sihet den Vater der mich gesandt hat, Und wer mich liebet NB: den will ich offenbahren. Und der Vater und ich wollen zu ihm kommen, und Wohnung bey ihm machen. 1. Cor: 6. Eph: 3. 4.

DE SEPTENARY MYSTERYS

Dieses ist aller Neü- und wieder ge- ... himel und Ewiges Leben, und rüde, hier ... -bohrnen kinder Gottes ihr Paradeiß. Seel in der Zeit, und dort in alle Ewigkeit. Joh: 17.

ROSÆ Nach **THEOSOPHIA** und
Das geheime verborgene Rosen kennet, und does viel dar.
1. 2. 3. 4. 5. 6. 7.
TINCTUR.
A. Ω.
Flüss. Flüss.
1. 2. 3. 4. 5. 6. 7.

CRUCIS. Der **THEOLOGIA.**
Creütz, welches die Weld nicht von zu sagen weiß.
1. 2. 3. 4. 5. 6. 7.
TINCTUR.
A. Ω.
gegen wurff.
1. 2. 3. 4. 5. 6. 7.

Die Ewig- keit wird Zeit.

In dieser figur ist begrif 7 fen: Ewigkeit und Zeit, Gott und Mensch, Engel und Teufel, himel und Hölle, das Alte und Neüe Jerusalem, samt allen Geschöpfen und Creaturen, Zeiten und Stunden.

12. Patriarchen	12. Sterne in der Krone. Apoc: 12.
12. Propheten	12. himlische Zeichen
12. Aposteln	12. Monate im Jahre
12. Articul Ihres glaubens	12. Stunden des Tages
12. Stadt Thore im Neüen Jerusalem. Apoc: 21.	12. Stunden der Nacht

A. Ω.

Gott ist ein Ewiger-Unerschaffener
Un-Endlicher-Uber-Natürlicher-
Selbständiger-himlisch-und wesen-
tlicher Geist, und ist in der Natur
und zeit, Ein sichtbarer und Leib-
hafftiger-Sterblicher Mensch worden.

Oculus Divinus, per quem Deus
vivit et Creavit Omnia.

Ein Jeden dings ein außgang,
verkündiget sein Anfang.

Lumen Gratiæ Ergon
sunt Duo

Himlische Eva die
Neüe Geburt.
O! Mensch O! Mensch betracht,
wie Gott das ewige wort ist
Mensch worden.

Einfältig habt ihrs empfangen
wers nicht glaübt der ist verdamt.

Tinctura Coelestis. SS.
Sacramenta.

ROSÆ CRUCIS
VENITE.
Videte, Videte, Videte,
Wer augen hat zu sehen,
der kan und wird wol
recht sehen.
N.B.
Züese Freündschafft
bey dem Archæo
dem betrauten
Thürhüter.

VIDEAMINI COLLEGIUM

Der Stern
aus Mor
Die Son
tig keit
gen Lande.
ne de er gerech-
Mal. am 4.

Jüngfrau   Sophia.

Natur ist ein Erschaffen-Natürlich-
Zeitlich-Endlich-Geistlich-Wesen-
ließ-und Corporalischer Geist,
Ein Gleichnüs bild u desselben
nachdem un-erschaffenen
un-Endlichen-Ewigen geiste
verborgen, und auch sichtbar.

Oculus Naturæ, seu Coeli, per quem
Natura visitat, regit Terrena
Omnia

Lebendig-Tödlich-verderblich,
und wieder neuig ebährlich.

Lumen Naturæ Par Ergon
Fratres

Irrdische Eva die
Alte Geburth.
O! Mensch O! Mensch bedencke
wie die Natur ist eine große
Weld und ein Mensch worden.

Einfältig geht ihrs wieder, ver-
achte das nicht dir selbst zur Schand.
Tinctura Physica Jungfer milch
und Sonnen Schwitz, 6. Kinder
Mütter, u doch eine reine Jungfrau.

PHILOSOPHICA
VENITE.
Arrige, Arrige, Arrige,
AURES.
Wer Ohren hat zu hören
dem darff mann nicht
überlaut rüffen.
N.B.
Er ist der Natur
Vollendiger ver-
schwiegener La-
borant und ge-
heimer Cam-
merdiener.

AD SPIRITUM SANCTUM.

Sub umbra
Alarum
Tuarum
P. F.
Consumatum
est.
Besuster
Schwartz.

INSTRUMENTUM DIVINUM
ZIAT NATURA

Ignis   Aer   Aqua   Terra

CHAOS

THEORIA

Lapis   SYLEX   sive
Tin   ctura
Philoso phorum et
ELIXIER.   Pauci vero electi.

O! Harpocrates
Dominus Providebit.

Exitus Acta probabit.

FREEMASONRY

The exact origins of Freemasonry are obscure. According to legend, however, the order traces its roots to the construction of the Temple of Solomon: it was, it is said, the Freemasons who oversaw the building of the mystical structure, led by Hiram Abiff. In reality, Freemasonry emerged in its 'speculative' (philosophical) form in the seventeenth century, being another manifestation of the interest in the occult that led to Rosicrucianism.

While Freemasonry does not deal directly with magic, it touches on it closely. King Solomon is a figure frequently associated with magic, while much of the Freemasons' philosophy – the building of a new order based on mutual understanding, religious toleration and self-improvement – comes from Hermeticism and the concept of spiritual alchemy. Indeed, the famous Masonic initiation rituals recreate the cycle of birth and death found in alchemy.

ABOVE *Two Masonic tracing boards, painted or printed depictions of the various emblems and symbols of Freemasonry. Such boards are used in the instruction of new members wishing to attain the three degrees of Freemasonry; the boards shown here illustrate the main themes of the first and third degrees.*
OPPOSITE *An engraving exploring the history of the Freemasons and their founding beliefs. In the background is the Temple of Solomon and the All-Seeing Eye.*

A masonic initiation ritual from the 19th century, in which the initiate is struck with a mallet.
Such rituals, which vary from country to country, can have a strong magical element.

A lodge meeting, with the Master on the left. Masons meet to discuss philosophical and spiritual matters, and the process of learning has been compared to a form of internal alchemy.

Freemasonry, like Rosicrucianism, alchemy and ritual magic, is a highly visual tradition, rich in symbols. Indeed, like alchemy, it relies on the gradual revelation of secrets through symbolism. Much of the symbolism comes from Solomon's Temple itself, but is also borrowed from the Knights Templar, alchemy, the Hermetic tradition, Christianity and the classical world.

Freemasonry developed differently in different countries. In Britain and the United States, for example, the focus was typically on the social or the charitable; in France and Latin America, by contrast, the more occult and esoteric side was emphasized. In some countries, such as France and the United States, elaborate systems of 'grades' were created, each with their own associated rites and rituals – many of which appear magical in nature, building on arcane stories involving the Knights Templar.

ABOVE *In this illustration from* La Très Sainte Trinosophie, *a book allegedly written by Alessandro Cagliostro, an adept or initiate looks into the 'Magic Mirror', which reveals its secrets.* OPPOSITE *A portrait of the enigmatic and mysterious Cagliostro.*

Alessandro Cagliostro

In the eighteenth century, a time of great credulity, the line between fact and fiction was often blurred. In the case of Alessandro Cagliostro, much about his life is shrouded in secrecy. Claiming to have been of noble birth, he more likely came from a poor family in Palermo, his real name being Giuseppe Balsamo. Sent to a seminary, he became interested in the occult, and from a young age used his interest in the subject to play tricks on those around him. Later in life he claimed that he had been abandoned as an orphan on Malta, where he had learnt about Kabbalah, alchemy and magic.

Cagliostro is perhaps best known for two things: founding the Egyptian form of Freemasonry, and being the alleged author of *La Très Sainte Trinosophie* (The Most Holy Trinosophia). He claimed to have discovered the Egyptian Masonic rite in a book he bought in London, although it is more likely that he created it himself. It was nevertheless an important departure, introducing an exotic note to magical debate, and putting Egypt at the centre of nineteenth-century occultism. Its rituals are filled with alchemical and occult references.

La Très Sainte Trinosophie, meanwhile, is an illustrated manuscript with little writing and enigmatic illustrations. Composed in a mixture of languages, including Chaldean Hebrew, Ionic Greek and Arabic, as well as French, it brings together occult thinking from across Europe and beyond. It is arranged into twelve sections, each corresponding to a different sign of the zodiac.

Cagliostro lived a complex life, and in 1789 was sentenced to death in Rome for being a Freemason. The sentence was commuted to life imprisonment, however, and he died a few years later. More than a century after the Italian's death, Aleister Crowley would claim that he was a reincarnation of Cagliostro.

OPPOSITE *A female patient being 'Mesmerized' by projected magnetism.*
ABOVE *Anton Mesmer himself hypnotizing a monk using a wand.*

MESMERISM

In the late eighteenth century, the German physician Anton Mesmer (1734–1815) proposed a radical new theory: animals, he claimed, exude an invisible force called 'animal magnetism' ('animal' in this case standing in opposition to 'mineral', and including humans). Capable of being used for healing, this 'magnetism' relied on the concept of a 'vital fluid' that filled all space. In effect, Mesmer was putting forward a solution to the oldest question in magic: how to achieve action at a distance without physical involvement.

In fact, Paracelsus had attempted to use magnets for medical purposes more than two hundred years earlier, while the Persian philosopher and scientist Avicenna had written about hypnosis in the eleventh century. However, Mesmer's high profile and large number of followers ensured that, by the nineteenth century, hypnosis was widespread, also becoming associated with spiritualism and stage magic. It is said that Antoine Court de Gébelin, a disciple of Mesmerism, was discovered dead in his bath after receiving electrical therapy.

ABOVE *Nostradamus, crouching inside a magic circle, uses a mirror to show Catherine de' Medici her children, the future kings of France.* OPPOSITE *The Empress Josephine, consort of Napoleon, consulted astrologers. Here, she is pictured receiving a prophecy from Marie Anne Adelaide Lenormand, a professional fortune-teller during the Napoleonic era.*

MAGIC AT COURT

From the fifteenth century onwards, occult studies began to find favour in the royal courts of Europe, starting with Marsilio Ficino and the Medici family, then continuing with Nostradamus in France and John Dee in England and Prussia. In the seventeenth and eighteenth centuries, especially the latter, monarchs remained keen patrons of intellectual pursuits but also sought diversions. As a result, by 1800 many courts were harbouring visionaries, magicians and sorcerers.

In Sweden, the German fortune-teller Höffern grew famous among the aristocracy in the first half of the eighteenth century for her (occasionally) accurate predictions; some years later, the Swedish fortune-teller Mamsell Arfvidsson (1734–1801) was consulted by Gustav III. Meanwhile, the Swedish mystic and necromancer Henrik Gustaf Ulfvenklou (1756–1819) enjoyed influence in the court of Charles XIII – himself a student of the occult and a Freemason. Antoine Court de Gébelin, that key popularizer of Tarot, counted Louis XVI of France among his most loyal subscribers, while the court of Charles II in England was known to welcome alchemists.

VIII.
The Magic Revival

*The 19th century saw the growth
of a romanticized and Gothic view of magic.*

The Magus
or Celestial Intelligencer
Being a compleat System of

Occult Philosophy.
In Two Books.

Containing the ancient and modern practise of the Cabalistic art, Natural & Celestial Magic &c. Shewing the wonderful effects that may be perform'd by a knowledge of the Celestial influences, the occult properties of ~~Metals~~ & the application of active to passive principles. (Metals, Herbs, & Stones.—

Book 1.st Part 1.st
comprehends the Sciences of

Natural Magic, Alchemy, or Hermetic Philosophy.

Shewing the Nature Creation & fall of Man, ~~Nature of Metals Herbs Stones &c.~~ magical powers inherent in the Soul &c with his natural & supernatural gifts the with a great variety of rare experiments in Nat. Magic.

Part ~~Book~~ 2.d
Contains the Constellatory Practise, or Talismanic Magic

The nature of the Element, stars, Planet, Signs &c. The construction & composition of all sorts of Magic Seals, Images, Rings Glasses &c; the virtue & efficacy of numbers, Characters & figures of good & evil Spirits.

Book 2.

Magnetism, & ~~Caba~~ Cabalistical or Ceremonial Magic.

In which the secret mysteries of the Cabala are explained; Operations by good & evil Spirits, all kinds of Cabalistic figures, tables, Seals, & names, with their use &c. Likewise shewing the times, bonds, offices & conjurations of Spirits.

~~Containing also~~ Book. III. ~~a compleat~~

Biographia Antiqua

The lives of the or most eminent Philosophers Magi &. the whole Magical & Cabalistical Illustrated with a great variety of curious engravings, figures &c.

By Francis Barrett FRC & Professor of
Chemistry, Natural & Occult Philosophy, the Cabala &c.
London 1801

By the close of the eighteenth century, the rationalism of the Enlightenment, together with the advent of industrialization, should have left superstition, magic and perhaps even religion increasingly marginalized. However, as so often happens in human history, events took an unexpected turn.

The late 1700s saw, in Europe at least, a growing interest in the macabre, the Gothic and the supernatural. This movement, which became known as Romanticism, also took a strong interest in esoteric knowledge from other parts of the world, especially the East. In addition, there was a growing curiosity about mysticism, perhaps most obviously in the work of the theologian Emanuel Swedenborg and the physician Anton Mesmer, who, as we have seen, pioneered the study of trance as cure. These men suggested that there remained in the world many inexplicable forces, and both triggered the imaginations of intellectual circles.

The mid-nineteenth century brought with it a new type of popular fascination with the occult. In 1848 the Fox sisters – two teenage girls living in Hydesville, New York – heard some strange noises, which they believed were coming from the spirit world. Adults who witnessed their seances reported that the sisters could communicate with the dead by means of a rapping noise. The reports caused a national sensation. Jumping on the bandwagon, another medium, Edward Wyllie (1848–1911), produced 'spirit photographs' – ghostly apparitions of a kind never before seen. Like the Fox sisters, Wyllie's photographs were later exposed as fakes, manipulations of the photographic process.

In terms of ritual magic, the key publication of the nine-teenth century was Francis Barrett's *The Magus* (1801). A compilation of earlier works attributed to the likes of Hermes Trismegistus, John Dee and Agrippa, it had an enormous influence on Éliphas Lévi and, later, Aleister Crowley. Lévi was a pivotal figure in occult and magical studies in the mid-nineteenth century, synthesizing much of the thinking from the Renaissance and before. Among other things, Lévi believed that the universe as we know it is only a small

OPPOSITE *The title page from the manuscript of* The Magus, *published by Francis Barrett in 1801. The book had a huge influence on later occult and magic studies.*
ABOVE *A suitably symbolic poster advertising an exhibition at the Salon Rose + Croix.*

fraction of the total order of things, that human willpower is a concrete force that can achieve remarkable things, and that man is a microcosm of the macrocosm, with the two being closely connected. He also popularized the use of Tarot cards.

During the latter part of the nineteenth century, more and more esoteric societies were formed, leading inevitably to factions and rivalries. One of the most famous of these rivalries was between two Frenchmen: Joseph-Antoine Boullan, an unorthodox Catholic priest, and the Marquis Stanislas de Guaita, a Rosicrucian. Each accused the other of using magic to harm them. The French writer J. K. Huysmans took Boullan's side, documenting the feud in the novel *Là-Bas* (1891). Huysmans's book also tackles the rise of Satanism in France in the late nineteenth century, ending with a description of a black mass. In fact, France at this time was a hotbed of occultism and magical thinking.

Another esoteric organization to emerge at the end of the nineteenth century was the Mystic Order of the Rose+Croix, which, among other things, held a series of salons exhibiting artworks by the symbolist painters Arnold Böcklin and Fernand Khnopff. In German-speaking countries, the so-called German Occult Revival of around 1890–1910 saw a rising national pride fuse with curiosity about the occult and a fascination with the distant, pagan past. The main exponent of this movement was Guido von List, who, influenced by the Theosophical Society, 'rediscovered' the lost magical language of runes.

The theosophy movement, spurred on by the creation of the Theosophical Society in New York in 1875 by Madame Blavatsky and others, had a powerful influence on many early twentieth-century magical and mystical societies, also fusing Eastern occult thinking with that of the West. One related organization – with an even greater emphasis on practical magic – was the Hermetic Order of the Golden Dawn, founded in 1888. Indeed, Hermetic and Rosicrucian orders multiplied in the final decade of the nineteenth century, among them the Kabbalistic Order of the Rose-Cross, founded by 'Papus' (Gérard Encausse). These organizations vied with one another over the holding of secrets. The most famous member of the Hermetic Order of the Golden Dawn was Aleister Crowley (1875–1947), who, in the early twentieth century, would establish several influential magical organizations single-handedly.

Crowley's feel for the theatrical would not have been out of place on the stage. In fact, it was in the nineteenth century that the professional performing magician, as we might recognize him today, first appeared. Perhaps most famous among such performers was Jean Eugène Robert-Houdin, from Blois in central France. Conjurors at the time were happy to blur the line between their increasingly sophisticated equipment and the spirit world, as can be seen in publicity from the period.

OPPOSITE The 19th century saw a rebirth of interest in national mythologies. In northern Europe, the Finnish artist Akseli Gallen-Kallela became fascinated by the Kalevala, Finland's national epic. Here, he depicts the defence of the Sampo from the evil witch Louhi, who has taken the form of a giant bird. ABOVE Druidism became popular again in the 19th century, as can be seen in this portrait of a somewhat unlikely latter-day Druid.

GOTHIC MAGIC

The late eighteenth century saw a new interest in the macabre, one framed by a revival of Gothic architecture and medieval sensibilities. In poetry and literature, this interest characterized itself as a fascination with the dark, the fantastical and the strange. These and other preoccupations are readily apparent in the publication of such stories as John William Polidori's *The Vampyre* (1819), E. T. A. Hoffmann's 'Der Sandmann' (1817)

and even the folk tales collected by the Brothers Grimm (1812).

Johann Wolfgang von Goethe's poem 'Der Zauberlehrling' (The Sorcerer's Apprentice; 1797) tells of a young sorcerer who attempts to use magic before he is fully ready, with disastrous consequences. A similar theme – of the dangers of playing with unknown or little-understood forces – runs through Mary Shelley's *Frankenstein* (1818).

OPPOSITE *The central theme of the story of Frankenstein is that of man playing God, and the consequences of such hubris.* ABOVE *The Gothic genre put the macabre and supernatural at the centre of culture in the 19th century, with stories of ghosts, demons and attempts at magic gone wrong.*

OPPOSITE *One of the masterpieces of supernatural Gothic art: Henry Fuseli's* Nightmare. *An incubus sits on a woman's chest, while the titular mare stares with shining eyes. The painting's popularity led to Fuseli creating a number of versions; this one dates from 1790–91.* ABOVE, LEFT *An illustration from* Der Geisterseher *(The Ghost-Seer) by Friedrich Schiller. Schiller's unfinished novel deals with necromancy and the supernatural, and inspired further Gothic stories.* ABOVE, RIGHT *Baudelaire's* Les Fleurs du mal *(1857). The foreword equates Satan with Hermes Trismegistus.*

The English writer Edward Bulwer-Lytton – most famous, perhaps, for the opening line 'It was a dark and stormy night' – wrote a series of novels dealing with the occult, including *Zanoni* (1842). The titular character is a Rosicrucian brother who cannot fall in love without sacrificing his immortality. Bulwer-Lytton was fascinated by Kabbalah and mysticism.

Friedrich Schiller's unfinished novel *Der Geisterseher* (The Ghost-Seer; 1787–9) deals with the subjects of necromancy and spiritualism. It is believed that the inspiration for the novel was the German illusionist Johann Georg Schröpfer (see page 304). A century later, the English writer Algernon Blackwood (1869–1951) was producing ghost stories as spooky as anything by his literary forebears. Blackwood, a member of the Hermetic Order of the Golden Dawn, combined Kabbalistic themes with stories of horror and mysticism.

*This score for a popular song, 'Spirit Rappings' (1853), reflects
the widespread fascination with the supernatural during the 19th century.*

The Fox sisters make a table levitate – although this illustration seems to exaggerate somewhat.

SPIRITUALISM

Although the belief that the dead can communicate with the living almost certainly dates back to prehistory, it was not until the mid-nineteenth century that it became widespread across Europe and North America. Principally, this belief took the form of seances, in which people gathered with a spiritual medium to receive messages from spirits, even attempting to interact with the spiritual plane.

The spiritualist movement grew out of a heady concoction: the ideas of Emanuel Swedenborg combined with the theories of Anton Mesmer and some of the beliefs of the 'new' religion of Mormonism. However, it really took off with the Fox sisters – Kate and Margaret – who in 1848 claimed to be able to communicate with the dead through rapping noises. Many years later the sisters confessed to having created the noises themselves, by clicking their joints; by that point, however, spiritualism had established itself across the United States and in Europe, as well as in Brazil.

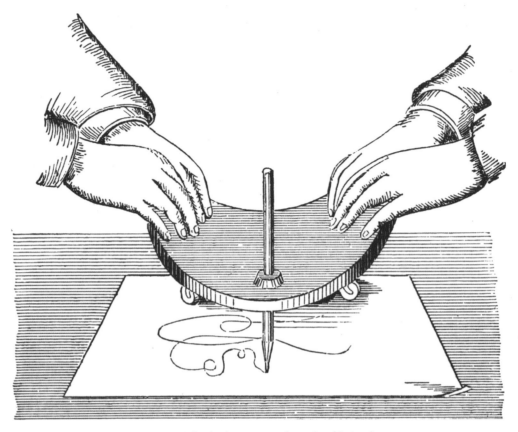

ABOVE *The planchette was one of a number of devices that became popular as a tool for communicating with the 'other side'.* OPPOSITE *The Italian medium Eusapia Palladino holding a seance, complete with the standard levitating table.*

Among the tools used to contact spirits were the Ouija board (from the 1880s onwards) and 'spirit slates', pieces of slate on which, it was believed, spirits could write. It was also said that they could communicate through raps and knocks. In some cases, spirits would apparently manifest themselves as ectoplasm, which would exude from the mouth of the medium.

By the 1920s, in spite of strong support from such respected figures as Sir Arthur Conan Doyle, spiritualism was largely discredited, with Harry Houdini, among others, actively disproving spiritualist theories and attacking fraudulent mediums.

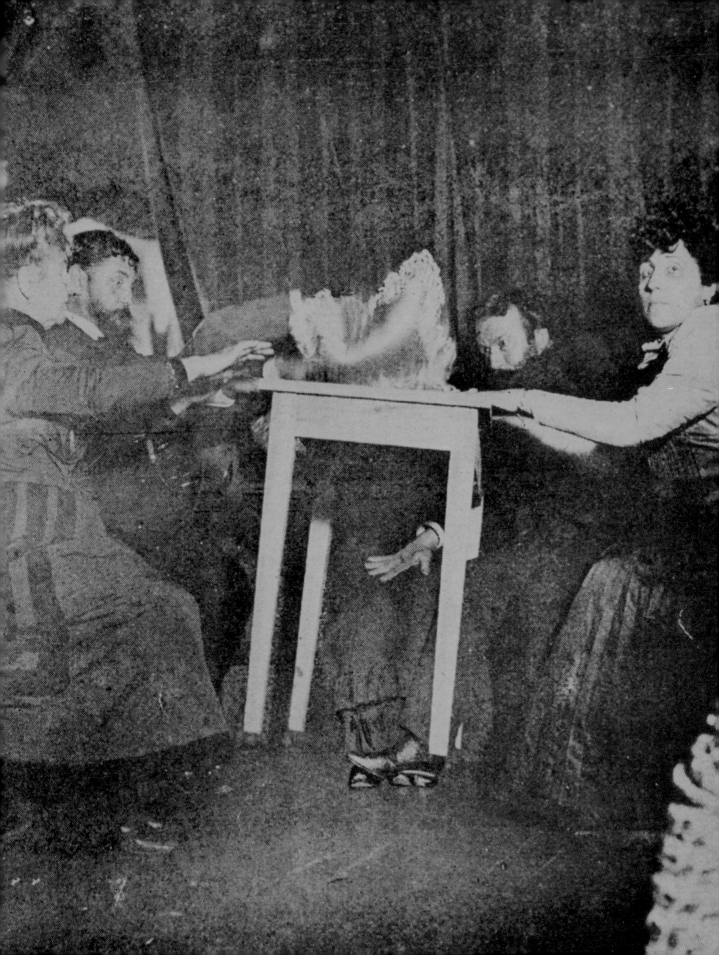

M. Robert-Houdin.

ABOVE *Robert-Houdin performing his famous Orange Tree trick, in which the tree would grow as if by magic. A piece of jewelry borrowed from an audience member would then appear inside one of the oranges.* OPPOSITE *A poster for the Egyptian Hall in London, advertising magic shows and automata. From the late 18th century onwards, new discoveries unleashed a wave of European interest in ancient Egypt.*

STAGE MAGIC
IN THE 19th CENTURY

If stage magic originated in the late eighteenth century, then it was in the nineteenth that it really took off. Often, however, these performances – and those who performed them – retained an air of the occult and the supernatural, tinged with the exoticism of far-away lands (one of the most important venues for magical performances in London was called the Egyptian Hall).

Perhaps the most famous stage magician of the nineteenth century was the Frenchman Jean Eugène Robert-Houdin (1805–1871), sometimes referred to as the father of modern magic. Trained as a watchmaker (he would later put his watchmaking skills to good use in the creation of automata), he became interested in magic after accidentally receiving a manual on the subject. Robert-Houdin brought elegance to stage magic, but also introduced supernatural elements – for example, the psychic trick 'Second Sight'. In one of the strangest episodes of his life, Robert-Houdin was sent by Louis-Napoléon Bonaparte to North Africa to demonstrate that French magic was more powerful than the traditional Marabout sorcery. He succeeded.

EGYPTIAN HALL.

ENTIRE CHANGE OF PERFORMANCE.

M. ROBIN

THE FRENCH WIZARD,

EVERY EVENING AT EIGHT (Saturday Excepted)

GRAND MORNING PERFORMANCES

Wednesday and Saturday At Half-past Two.

" Five Minutes with the Spirits, or the Medium of Inkerman."

Monsieur ROBIN will add to his usual Attractive and Extraordinary

SOIRÉES FANTASTIQUES

DURING LENT,

BY A NEW MODE OF ILLUSTRATION, WITH NOVEL EFFECTS,

VIEWS OF THE TOUR OF
H.R.H. THE PRINCE OF WALES
THROUGH
THE EAST AND THE HOLY LAND

Embracing also the principal Cities which offer interest in this truly marvellous and classic ground.

ADMISSION, 1s. & 2s.   RESERVED STALL CHAIRS, 3s.

CHILDREN UNDER TEN, STALLS, 2s.   AREA, 1s.

Places may be secured, without any extra charge, at the Hall, and at Mr. MITCHELL's Royal Library, 33, Old Bond Street.

Printed by J. MILES & Co., 105 Wardour Street, Oxford Street,—W.

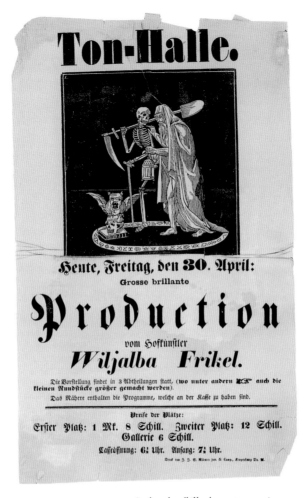

OPPOSITE AND ABOVE *As these handbills show, stage magic in the 19th century continued to play up the supernatural angle, with ghosts, devils, skeletons and magic circles.*

Over the course of the nineteenth century, the acts became more and more sophisticated, and the props increasingly complex. Electricity – still poorly understood by the general public – was used for many different effects, while such magicians as the Dutchman Henri Robin performed scientific experiments alongside more conventional tricks. Indeed, Josef Vanek (1818–1889), one of Hungary's leading magicians, was originally a physics professor. Just as alchemists, in a sense, had been proto-scientists, so too were the magicians of the nineteenth century.

The increasing reliance on elaborate props and stagecraft – as opposed to sleight of hand – was criticized by the Prussian magician Wiljalba Frikell (1816/17–1903). Frikell's attitude towards props did not mean, of course, that he was not an entertainer himself: supposedly, he was the first magician to perform while wearing evening clothes, rather than the traditional 'sorcerer's robes'.

CHIROMANCY

Chiromancy, or palmistry, is the art of predicting a person's future by reading the lines in their hands; it is also used to assess character. Believed to have originated in India several thousand years ago, the practice spread throughout Asia and was known to the ancient Greeks (Alexander the Great was said to read his generals' palms). Underpinning chiromancy is the microcosm–macrocosm principle, but also the idea that all hands are unique and must be so for a reason.

As is common in magic, hand shapes are interpreted according to the four elements. In addition, the different areas of the palm are seen as representing different Greek gods and goddesses. Beyond that, the lines are believed to relate to the heart, the head, the Sun and Mercury.

ABOVE *A soldier has his palm read by a male fortune-teller.*
OPPOSITE *A wise woman reading a palm; on the table in front of her are other divinatory devices, including Tarot cards.*

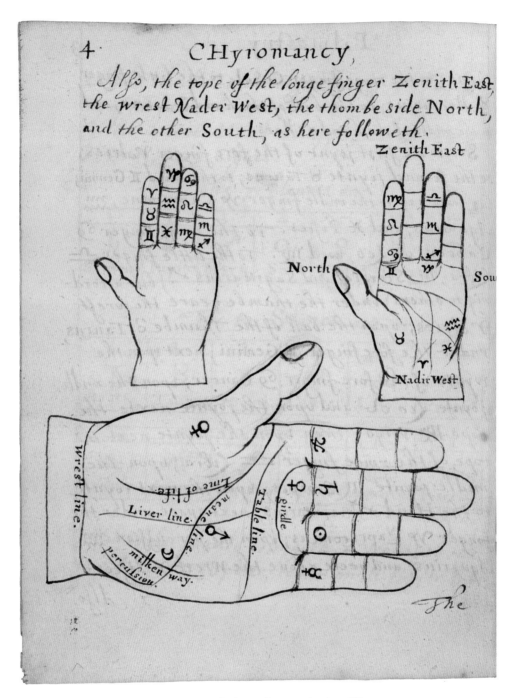

ABOVE AND OPPOSITE *In these 17th-century drawings, different parts of the hand are related to specific planets, gods, organs and the four cardinal directions.*

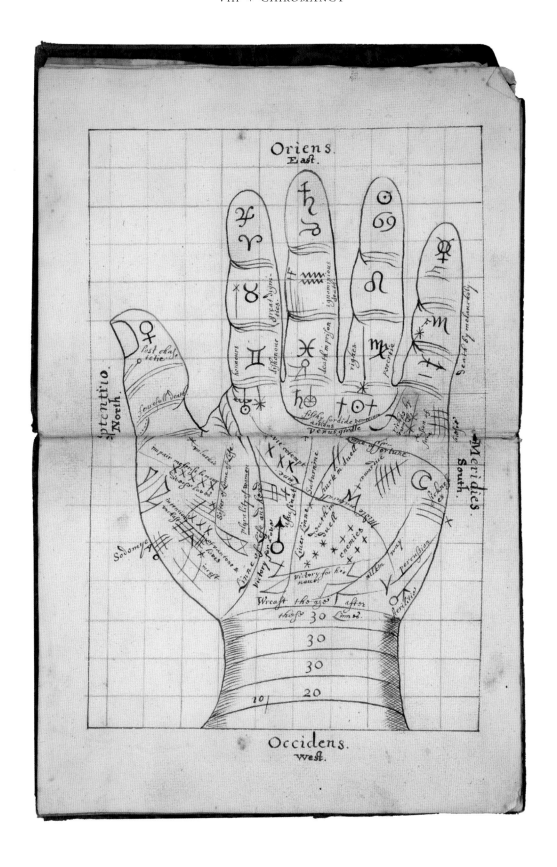

Éliphas Lévi

Arguably the most influential magician of the nineteenth century, Éliphas Lévi was born Alphonse Louis Constant in Paris in 1810. Having decided at an early age to enter the priesthood, he left the seminary before completing his studies. In the mid-1830s Lévi encountered an old man called 'Ganneau', a practitioner of witchcraft, sparking his interest in magic. Lévi was also influenced by Anton Mesmer's concept of animal magnetism.

A pivotal moment in Lévi's life came in England in 1853, when he was introduced to Rosicrucianism through the conduit of Edward Bulwer-Lytton. It was also in England, in London in 1854, that Lévi first practised magic himself, attempting to conjure the spirit of the ancient Greek philosopher Apollonius of Tyre – having prepared for the ritual by fasting and meditating. It was around this time,

too, that he started using the pen name Éliphas Lévi, an attempt to translate his French name into Hebrew.

Essentially, Lévi believed that human willpower could be used to perform miracles. He also revived interest in the microcosm–macrocosm principle, and popularized the concept of 'astral light', a development of animal magnetism.

Lévi's real importance lies in the publication of *Dogme et rituel de la haute magie* (Dogma and Ritual of High Magic), issued in two volumes between 1854 and 1856. These books synthesize earlier magical traditions – alchemy, Hermetic magic, Kabbalah, Tarot – into a single tradition that Lévi believed had always existed. In particular, Lévi's magic system popularized the use of Tarot cards, leading to their widespread use in the twentieth century.

DOGME ET RITUEL

DE LA

HAUTE MAGIE

PAR

ÉLIPHAS LÉVI

Auteur de l'*Histoire de la magie* et de la *Clef des grands mystères*

———

DEUXIÈME ÉDITION TRÈS AUGMENTÉE

Avec 24 Figures

———

TOME SECOND

Rituel

———❖———

PARIS

GERMER BAILLIÈRE, LIBRAIRE-ÉDITEUR

RUE DE L'ÉCOLE-DE-MÉDECINE, 17

LONDRES	**NEW-YORK**
Hippolyte Baillière, Regent street, 219.	Hipp. Baillière brothers, 440, Broadway.

MADRID, C. BAILLY-BAILLIÈRE, PLAZA DEL PRINCIPE ALFONSO, 16.

1861

OPPOSITE *Éliphas Lévi's Tetragrammaton pentagram, believed by the magician to be a symbol of the microcosm or human being.* ABOVE *The illustrations in Lévi's books have achieved great fame in themselves — none more so than his depiction of the pagan deity Baphomet, which has since become the archetypal image of the Devil.*

ABOVE *A witch casts a spell over a cauldron as she prepares a potion.*
In the background is a skeleton, while a young woman kneels within a magic circle.
OPPOSITE *A scorpion is added – carefully – to a magic potion.*

MAGICAL POTIONS

Witchcraft in particular has long been associated with the brewing of magical potions – leading to the archetypal image of a witch bent over a cauldron. Such potions can take the form of philtres (love potions), poisons, or elixirs that either give or prolong life. The ingredients of these potions, especially herbs, are often highly symbolic, but can also be wilfully strange, the most extreme including human bones.

Abramelin oil is used in ceremonial or ritual magic, the recipe having been taken from a medieval grimoire known as *The Book of Abramelin the Mage*. Based on a recipe for holy anointing oil, Abramelin contains a mixture of myrrh, calamus (sweet flag), cinnamon and olive oil. Aleister Crowley had his own recipe for the substance, which is still used in the Thelema religion for anointing the heads of magicians.

ABOVE *This strange image of an unknown ritual contains all the classic elements:*
a three-legged table, fire, a wand, nudity, and ceremonial dress featuring occult symbols.
OPPOSITE *Depictions of ceremonial wands and daggers from a version of* The Key of Solomon.

RITUAL & MAGIC

In the Western occult tradition, a distinction is often made between ceremonial magic, which seeks to elicit change through ritual (often relying on grimoires), and natural magic, such as astrology and alchemy, which builds on the study of nature. The former type of magic, practised by witches and high magicians, was frequently seen as incompatible with mainstream religion.

One of the reasons for this incompatibility is that ceremonial magic relies heavily on ritual, thereby invading the space traditionally occupied by organized religion. In fact, in the nineteenth century, ritual in ceremonial magic became more important, perhaps as a result of the birth of magical and occult fraternities that sought to formalize their proceedings, just as the Freemasons had done before them.

TABLEAU DES INSTRUMENS.

L'Epée.

Le Stilet

Couteau pour les Victimes.

Couteau pour le Bois.

Le Burin.

Le Canif.

Bâton pour toutes les Opérations.

Bâton pour les Opérations de Venus.

La Tasse. L'Ecritoire. Le Réchaud.

C ij.

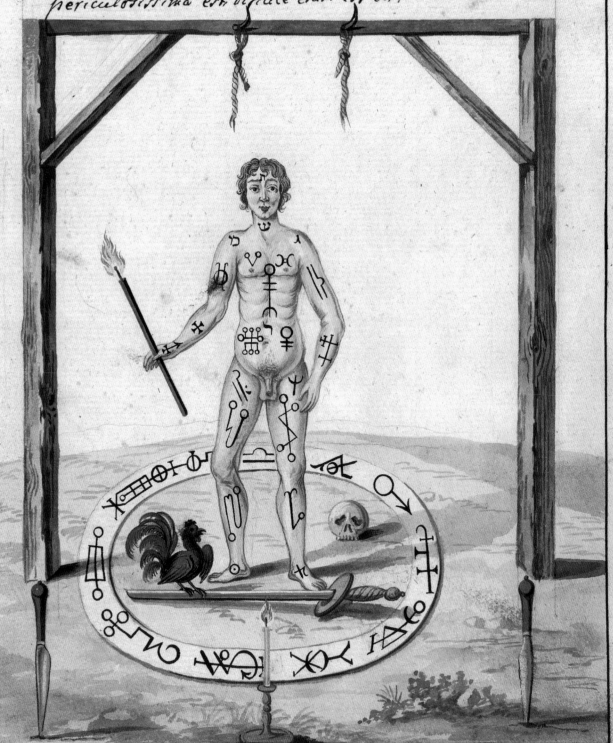

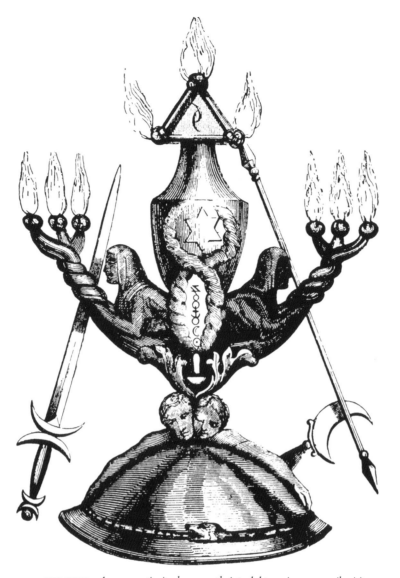

OPPOSITE *A necromantic ritual, apparently intended to conjure up an evil spirit. Daggers, a candle, a sword and even a cockerel are carefully positioned. The gallows suggest that a human body might also be required.* ABOVE *An illustration of magical implements, from the English translation of Lévi's* Dogme et rituel de la haute magie.

Éliphas Lévi's *Dogme et rituel de la haute magie* was instrumental in determining how magic should be performed. Costume, implements, symbols and types of incense to be used were all explained, providing the basis for further development by such organizations as the Hermetic Order of the Golden Dawn and,

eventually, the master of ceremonial magic himself, Aleister Crowley.

The importance of ritual continued to grow in the first half of the twentieth century, up until the rise of Chaos Magic in the 1970s. At that point, rituals were broken down to become more personal and less dogmatic.

ABOVE *The seal of the Theosophical Society incorporates the Star of David, the ankh, the Aum, the swastika and the ouroboros.*
OPPOSITE *A portrait of the Russian occultist and co-founder of the Theosophical Society, Helena Blavatsky.*

THEOSOPHY

The word 'theosophy', meaning 'God's wisdom', refers to the revelation of occult or esoteric knowledge about the mysteries of existence and creation. The term was first used in this context in the thirteenth century, but it was not until the final decades of the nineteenth century that its use became more widespread.

The Theosophical Society, established in New York City in 1875, had three founders: Henry Steel Olcott, William Quan Judge and,

most famously, Helena Petrovna Blavatsky. All three were heavily influenced by Western esotericism, but also by Indian esoteric thought. Blavatsky was a spiritualist, clairvoyant and psychic, who from a young age had been fascinated by the Hermetic tradition, travelling the world in search of hidden wisdom. In 1888 she published *The Secret Doctrine*, which postulated the existence of 'secret masters' — a group of shadowy individuals who controlled human destiny.

ABOVE *Samuel Liddell MacGregor Mathers, one of the order's founders, in magical regalia.*
OPPOSITE *The symbol of the Rosy Cross, also called the Rose Croix. Each adept*
of the order had to paint their own version of this important symbol.

HERMETIC ORDER
OF THE GOLDEN DAWN

Founded in England on 12 February 1888, the Hermetic Order of the Golden Dawn was the most influential magical society of its time. Created by Freemasons and theosophists, it was open to men and women, and grew by word of mouth. Its goal, according to the historian Israel Regardie, was to teach 'the principles of Occult Science and the Magic of Hermes'. The foundational documents, known as the Cipher Manuscripts, dictated the order's rituals and structure. While the precise origins of the documents remain a mystery, they eventually came into the possession of one of the order's founders,

William Wynn Westcott, who then showed them to fellow founding member Samuel Liddell MacGregor Mathers.

According to Westcott, the Cipher Manuscripts contained the address of Anna Sprengel, a German countess and, apparently, a surviving Rosicrucian. It was Sprengel, again according to Westcott, who granted the order permission to found its first lodge: the Temple of Isis-Urania, in London. In all likelihood, both the manuscripts and Sprengel were inventions, but the order had what it saw as a legitimate link to the original Rosicrucians and the history of magic.

One of the order's hand-painted symbols, from the late 19th century.
It features a human figure in the pose of a cross, the Star of David,
the Sun, the Moon, and other occult signs.

Hierarchically, the order was divided into three levels, each containing a number of 'grades' – a structure not unlike that of Freemasonry (the grades, of which there were eleven in total, were linked to the Kabbalistic Tree of Life). The first level of the order was known as the 'Golden Dawn' (with rituals around the metaphysical meanings of the four elements), the second the 'Red Rose and Cross of Gold', and the third the 'Secret Chiefs'. Practical magic began with the second grade. The rituals reflected a strong Egyptian influence, as well as that of Kabbalah, Freemasonry, theurgy, alchemy, Tarot, Rosicrucianism and Enochian magic.

The order grew to have more than a hundred members, the best known among them being Aleister Crowley and the Irish poet W. B. Yeats. In the early years of the twentieth century, however, internal feuding led to the order splintering into many smaller bodies, including Crowley's highly magical A∴A∴. The remaining 'Rectified Rite' abandoned the order's magical elements altogether.

Leila Waddell taking part in a 'ceremony to invoke Artemis', organized by Aleister Crowley after the dissolution of the Hermetic Order of the Golden Dawn. Crowley's muse, Waddell was also a magician in her own right – as well as an accomplished musician.

ABOVE *Aleister Crowley in 1902, aged twenty-seven.*
OPPOSITE *Crowley as a teenager, testing his magic.*

Aleister Crowley

Aleister Crowley, one of the most notorious occultists of the modern era, was born in 1875 to a devoutly religious family. In 1898, following a rebellious youth, he joined the Hermetic Order of the Golden Dawn. He clashed with some of its other members, however, and it was only through the intervention of co-founder Mathers that he was able to pass to the second grade.

A keen traveller and mountaineer, Crowley was forever seeking the most extreme and obscure forms of magic. In around 1900 he attempted the Abramelin ritual, for which he needed very specific conditions; indeed, in order to perform the ritual successfully, he bought Boleskine House in Scotland because of its orientation. The ritual, which would take six months to complete, would give the magician control over the Twelve Lords of Hell. However, Crowley abandoned the ritual before finishing it, and later sold the house.

In 1904, in Egypt, Crowley performed magic in the Great Pyramid of Giza. It was in Egypt, he said, that his guardian angel, Aiwass, had revealed to him *The Book of the Law*. This text would form the basis of Crowley's Thelema religion. Crowley was also a member of the Ordo Templi Orientis, and co-founder of the A∴A∴.

Crowley believed deeply in the existence of magic, although he chose to call it Magick (with a 'k') to differentiate it from simple conjuring. In particular, he performed Enochian magic, and claimed to be able to make himself invisible. He also said he had been attacked by a vampire.

Crowley loved theatricality, and saw costume, location and drugs — as well as sex — as being central to the magical experience. His life remained dogged by controversy and sensationalism. Much to his annoyance, a thinly veiled version of Crowley appeared in Somerset Maugham's *The Magician* (1908).

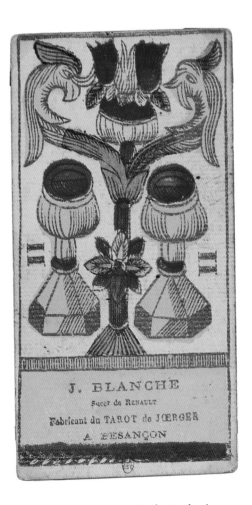

ABOVE AND OPPOSITE *A selection of cards from a 19th-century French Tarot.*

TAROT

Although the cards that make up the Tarot have been used for playing games since the fifteenth century (they are said to have originated in northern Italy), their occult use dates back only to the eighteenth. Today, the Tarot is commonly used as a divination tool.

How, then, did this particular deck of cards become associated with the supernatural? Regular playing cards have been used in divination rituals since the sixteenth century, but the use of the Tarot for this purpose began in the 1700s with Antoine Court de Gébelin (see page 293), who claimed that the Tarot was the summation of the theology of ancient Egypt. In the decades that followed, Éliphas Lévi associated the Tarot with the Kabbalah, while the Marquis Stanislas de Guaita related the trump cards to a person's spiritual evolution; others have claimed that the Tarot is effectively the Book of Hermes Trismegistus. Etteilla (see page 293), who popularized the Tarot in the late eighteenth century, also viewed it as having ancient Egyptian origins.

LE BATELEUR

LE BATELEVR

IL BAGATTO

IL BAGATTO

1 Diritto: IL RE THOT

Aleph

Aleph

1

EL CAOS

LA NADA

1 Rovescio: IL CONSULTANTE

THE MAGICIAN

THE MAGICIAN.

OPPOSITE *Seven cards, most of them different versions of the Magician trump card, from a variety of Tarot decks.* ABOVE *Two women read their fortunes using cards in a painting from 1911 — a time when Tarot and divination were growing in popularity.*

The seventy-two cards of the Tarot are divided into Major Arcana and Minor Arcana – the minor being the four suits (today called Pentacles, Swords, Cups and Wands), the major being the twenty-two trump cards (the Fool, the Magician, Death, and so on). Originally, some cards had less occult names; the Magician, for example, was previously known as the Juggler.

Today, the Tarot comes in a variety of designs. The Marseilles deck dates to the seventeenth century or earlier, while the Oswald Wirth deck (1889) was commissioned by de Guaita. The other main designs are the Rider-Waite deck (1907, still widely used), the Golden Dawn deck, and the deck designed by Aleister Crowley and Lady Frieda Harris, known as the Thoth deck (first issued in 1969).

IX.

Modern Magic

A woman who believes herself to be possessed by spirits lies in a ring of fire during an unofficial exorcism ritual.

The history of magic since the mid-twentieth century has been one of gradual acceptance, curiosity and pluralism, if not of startling originality. Large-scale changes in society – the spread of universal suffrage, the gradual lessening of the authority of established religion, the democratization of access to information – have given rise to a public that is at once curious and capable of informing itself. And while practitioners of magic may still have been considered eccentric in the twentieth century, the social stigma and persecution seen in earlier times have long since lessened.

Without doubt, Aleister Crowley cast a long shadow over twentieth-century magic, inspiring and alienating in equal measure. At the same time, however, he provoked intense interest in the subject, including among the press. His particular brand of ceremonial magic also influenced the codification of, for example, Wicca under Gerald Gardner in the 1940s and 1950s, as well as the development of the Church of Satan under Anton LaVey. The latter organization endeavoured to take Crowley's command – 'Do what thou wilt' – to its logical conclusion, throwing off the last fetters of conventional society.

Some were troubled by what they saw as the manipulation of a gullible public. The stage magician and escapologist Harry Houdini sought constantly to expose fraud, acting as part of the *Scientific American* committee offering a prize to anyone who could demonstrate genuine supernatural ability. Elsewhere, however, the relationship between magic and science began to be better understood, and the past century has also seen widespread theorizing around magic as a topic worthy of sociological, anthropological and psychological study.

This more academic approach to magic is exemplified by the work of the Polish anthropologist Bronisław Malinowski (1884–1942), author of 'Magic, Science and Religion' (1925). With a central thesis suggesting that religion and magic are closely

White witches at the stone circle at Avebury in Wiltshire, England. The witches have just performed a ritual to produce a 'psychic photofit' (bottom, centre) of the person guilty of defacing the stone behind them.

Druids at Stonehenge celebrating the winter solstice.

related, the essay is based on many in-depth, first-hand observations of how magic was being used in everyday life in Australasia and Papua (now Papua New Guinea). The world got smaller, and understanding grew. Malinowski's essay was followed by such publications as Carlos Castaneda's *The Teachings of Don Juan* (1968), which explored the traditional wisdom of a Mexican shaman – and sold hundreds of thousands of copies. Ancient magical techniques were being studied and taken seriously.

In 1921 Margaret Murray (1863–1963) published the influential *Witch-Cult in Western Europe*. Seeking to redefine the history of witchcraft, the book suggested that the persecuted of the sixteenth and seventeenth centuries were actually practitioners of an ancient fertility cult that could trace its roots back to ancient times. The book was also influential in the formulation of modern-day Wicca, even if Murray's thesis has since

ABOVE *A New Orleans police officer holds a cross that has been studded
with nails and decorated with special charms. Found on the doorstep of a woman's house, and bearing
the name of her fiancée, it was assumed to be a voodoo cross intended to split them up.*
OPPOSITE *A modern magical banner and ceremonial sword.*

been questioned. Another important book in making magic a popular subject was *The Morning of the Magicians* (1960) by Louis Pauwels and Jacques Bergier, a detailed investigation into the occult and conspiracy theories (the book also highlighted the interest in occultism on the part of the Nazis, especially Heinrich Himmler).

The 1960s and 1970s offered a favourable climate for magic. Popular culture – iconoclastic and loud – was breaking society's taboos, allowing the new role models, such as the Rolling Stones, actively to engage with magic, just as the Beatles were dabbling in Eastern traditions. The growing availability of psychoactive drugs contributed to the birth of a New Age philosophy that placed a premium on mystical experiences and the interconnectedness of all things. This was the beginning of a genuinely pluralistic world view, one that could imagine many different beliefs being compatible and complementary.

In the realm of the occult, this more anarchic way of thinking eventually led to the formation of a new discipline. Chaos Magic taps into the deep, supernatural roots of the subject. Turning the traditional idea of magic on its head, it no longer relies on arcane, secret knowledge, but instead asks its practitioners to create their own rituals. The well-known British practitioner Phil Hine has defined Chaos Magic as 'a doorway through which we step into mystery, wildness and immanence'. Where magic started as a way of influencing the environment out of necessity, it is now – in the West at least – something that is seen as more recreational, more focused on the development of the individual, as well as a way of finding connections with our environment.

Where does magic go from here? Just as religion continues to thrive in a world of science, it seems unlikely that magic will ever fully disappear. Indeed, today's hyperconnected world offers ever more opportunities for those of a like mind to come together in a way that, historically, they would have been persecuted for. And the things that drive humankind to seek out magic – a desire to control the environment, understand our place in the universe, ensure that our lives turn out well, protect ourselves from chance – are simply part of the human condition. No amount of failed attempts to turn base metal into gold, thwart our enemies or predict the future is about to change that.

OPPOSITE *Eleanor 'Ray' Bone, an influential member of the Wicca movement, performs a ritual at her home. Behind her is a painting of Isis.* ABOVE *Doreen Valiente's ritual altar. On the right is a copy of Gerald Gardner's* Book of Shadows *(see page 376).*

WICCA

Wicca is regarded as a modern, pagan, duotheistic religion that exalts nature but also incorporates elements of ceremonial high magic. It was introduced to the wider world in the 1950s by Gerald Gardner (see page 376), although some believe that its roots go back centuries or even millennia. The teachings of Gardner were built on by two of his followers, Doreen Valiente and Alex Sanders, and the movement rapidly spread beyond the British Isles. Today, it is estimated that there are more than half a million practitioners worldwide.

The name 'Wicca' derives from the Old English word for witch. The movement itself is largely decentralized – a fact that has led to some debate as to what Wicca actually is. All Wiccans celebrate the lunar and solar cycles, with four major witches' sabbaths (the equinoxes and solstices).

ABOVE *A selection of items used in Wiccan ceremonies,
including an athame (knife), a pentacle and a crystal sphere.*
OPPOSITE *Wiccans gather in a circle to perform a ritual
in a deconsecrated church near Amsterdam.*

The Wiccan Rede (law), as expressed by Valiente in 1964, is simple: 'Eight words the Wiccan Rede fulfill, An it harm none do what ye will.' Also central to Wicca is the belief in two gods or forces: the Horned God and the Moon Goddess, representations, respectively, of the Sacred Masculine and the Sacred Feminine.

Most Wiccans practise magic as part of the religion, although it has often been referred to as 'white magic' or 'right-hand path', to avoid association with Satanism ('left-hand path'). Wiccan celebrations are typically performed in a sacred circle, cast with a wand or sword, with candles at the cardinal points.

Wiccan rituals involve an altar, which sometimes supports representations of the four elements. The other key objects are a pentacle, a chalice and an athame (a ceremonial knife). These last two items stand for the feminine and the masculine respectively.

Gerald Gardner in 1951. He is holding a stick once owned by Aleister Crowley.

Gerald Gardner

Although born in the United Kingdom in 1884, Gerald Gardner had all his formative experiences in Asia. Raised in Madeira, Gardner moved to Ceylon (Sri Lanka) at age sixteen, and to Malaya (now part of Malaysia) eleven years later. There, he became fascinated by Malay magic and sorcery, making a study of ceremonial and magical weapons while working mostly on rubber plantations.

To a large extent, Gardner's magical journey began only when he retired from the civil service in 1936 and moved back to the UK with his wife. An earlier trip to Britain in 1927 had introduced Gardner to spiritualism (he had attended a seance), while a later trip in 1932 had brought him into contact with paganism. However, it was the looming war with Germany and a fear of being bombed that led Gardner to seek out the relative peace of Highcliffe, a small town to the south of the New Forest.

In Highcliffe, Gardner encountered the Rosicrucian Order Crotona Fellowship, the members of which staged mystically themed plays. It was through this fellowship that Gardner was introduced to the New Forest Coven, a group of witches who met to perform magic. Gardner was admitted to the coven in September 1939. According to Gardner's testimony, the coven, which continued to exist until 1944, performed a ritual in 1940 to prevent Hitler and his forces from crossing the English Channel. As part of the ritual, the coven raised a 'cone of power' directed towards Germany.

Gardner also became involved with Druidism, and in 1947 was introduced to Aleister Crowley, shortly before the occultist's death. It is said that Crowley initiated Gardner into the Ordo Templi Orientis. In 1948, while staying in the United States, Gardner visited New Orleans, hoping to learn about voodoo.

In the 1950s Gardner worked to define his modern version of witchcraft, which he called 'Wicca'. As part of this endeavour he set about compiling a grimoire of spells and ritual, the *Book of Shadows*. He also wrote *Witchcraft Today* (1954), and engaged openly with the press to promote the Wiccan religion. He died in 1964.

Gardner at work at the Witches' Mill on the Isle of Man. Note the broomstick on the left.

MAGIC IN MODERN CULTURE

The American author H. P. Lovecraft (1890–1937) was a pioneer of fantasy fiction. In particular, he was the founder of the Cthulhu Mythos, a fictional universe named after a demonic deity. Lovecraft's creation would influence Chaos Magic, while Anton LaVey would incorporate elements of Lovecraft's work into the rituals of the Church of Satan. Curiously, Lovecraft was also hired by Harry Houdini to write *The Cancer of Superstition*, a book debunking magic, but the project was never completed.

The mid-twentieth-century fantasy boom received much impetus from the work of J. R. R. Tolkien and C. S. Lewis. Tolkien's works – including *The Hobbit* (1937) and *The Lord of the Rings* (1954–5) – rely heavily on northern European mythology and magic, with fantastical creatures and unfathomable dark spirits. Among the protagonists are wizards who engage in magical battles; more subtly, Gandalf the wizard goes through an alchemical process, changing from grey to white.

More recently, J. K. Rowling's Harry Potter series (1997–2007) has sparked considerable interest in practical magic. Interestingly, it incorporates many elements from the history of magic – the philosopher's stone, Nicolas Flamel – as well as reinventing old tropes on witchcraft.

OPPOSITE *The leader of the Church of Satan, Anton LaVey.* ABOVE *Magic has become a staple of cinema in recent decades. Here, in a still from* The Lord of the Rings: The Return of the King *(2003), the wizard Gandalf rides towards the city of Minas Tirith.*

The opening page of the score for 'Sonneries de la Rose + Croix',
composed by Erik Satie in 1891 while he was working as the official composer for
the Ordre de la Rose-Croix Catholique, du Temple et du Graal.

'The Crossroads', where Robert Johnson was said to have sold his
soul to the Devil in exchange for mastery of the blues.

The link between magic and music is an old one. Both Erik Satie and Claude Debussy were Rosicrucians, while in the early twentieth century the blues singer Tommy Johnson claimed to have sold his soul to Papa Legba, a voodoo god, in return for the ability to play guitar; likewise, Robert Johnson's 'Cross Road Blues' (1937) has been seen as a reference to a tradition that dates back to Hecate (see page 70). In Europe, the rise of folk music went hand in hand with the rediscovery of ancient pagan traditions – and a more widespread use of psychoactive drugs.

The 1960s saw both the advent of rock music and the birth of the New Age movement and satanism. David Bowie returned to occult imagery at the very end of his life, notably in the video for '★' ('Blackstar', 2015). Jimmy Page, founder of Led Zeppelin, bought the house in which Crowley had tried the Abramelin ritual.

In the 1970s the English musician and performance artist Genesis P-Orridge became involved with such countercultural figures as Brion Gysin and William S. Burroughs. He was also heavily influenced by the work of the English artist and occultist Austin Osman Spare (see page 386). In America, the New Orleans-born singer Dr John devoted the whole of his debut album, *Gris-Gris* (1968), to voodoo.

A rare, early photograph of Dion Fortune.

Dion Fortune

Born in Wales in 1890, Dion Fortune was one of the twentieth century's best-known magicians and mediums. Her first visions – of Atlantis – were reported at the age of four, and by twenty she had developed psychic abilities.

A member of the Theosophical Society, Fortune also belonged to Alpha et Omega, another offshoot of the Hermetic Order of the Golden Dawn. However, she came under what she called 'psychic attack' – claiming to have been the victim of black magic – and so left for the Stella Matutina order. Today, she is remembered for founding the Society of the Inner Light (SIL).

Like many magicians, Fortune was a creative person, and in 1919 began to publish fiction – mostly on the themes of magic and mysticism.

Her key written works include *The Sea Priestess* (1935), which would have great influence on the Wicca and Goddess movements, and *The Mystical Qabalah* (also 1935), which did much to re-popularize the Hermetic Kabbalah.

The onset of the Second World War led to one of the most curious episodes in the recent history of magic. Throughout the war, Fortune wrote regularly to the SIL, giving tips on how it could aid the war effort through 'psychic resistance'.

For a time, Fortune lived at the base of Glastonbury Tor – a place deeply associated with magic. It was there, she claimed, that she had received the knowledge that would later become the 'Arthurian Formula', the basis of the workings of the SIL. Fortune died in 1946, but the society she founded survives.

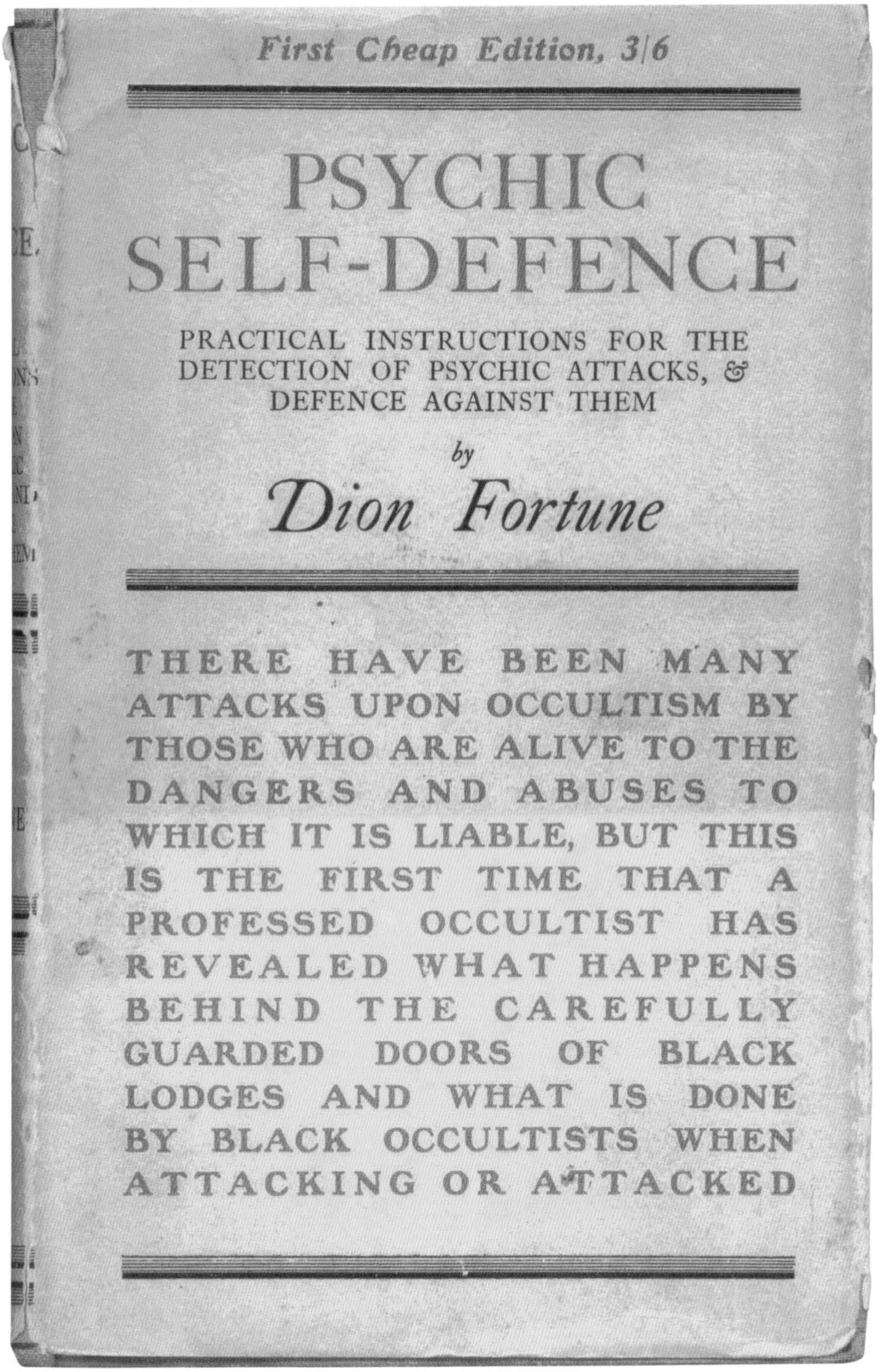

First Cheap Edition, 3/6

PSYCHIC SELF-DEFENCE

PRACTICAL INSTRUCTIONS FOR THE DETECTION OF PSYCHIC ATTACKS, & DEFENCE AGAINST THEM

by

Dion Fortune

THERE HAVE BEEN MANY ATTACKS UPON OCCULTISM BY THOSE WHO ARE ALIVE TO THE DANGERS AND ABUSES TO WHICH IT IS LIABLE, BUT THIS IS THE FIRST TIME THAT A PROFESSED OCCULTIST HAS REVEALED WHAT HAPPENS BEHIND THE CAREFULLY GUARDED DOORS OF BLACK LODGES AND WHAT IS DONE BY BLACK OCCULTISTS WHEN ATTACKING OR ATTACKED

Fortune's books were largely successful, focusing on practical magic.

ABOVE *The primordial state of Chaos, as imagined in the 16th century by Lorenzo Lotto.*
OPPOSITE *A painting by Austin Osman Spare showing a woman praying in front of a makeshift altar. One of the items on the altar appears to relate to Spare's magical philosophy known as Zos Kia Cultus (see page 386).*

CHAOS MAGIC

By the final decades of the twentieth century, with the number of potential sources of magic on the rise, it had become increasingly hard for a practitioner to know which was the right path to take. While its name may suggest destructive anarchy, Chaos Magic recognized that the universe is pluralistic, and that there could be many paths to effective magic.

The concept of Chaos Magic comes from two main sources: the work of Austin Osman Spare on the one hand, and the writings of Peter J. Carroll on the other. Carroll's *Liber Null* (1978) and *Psychonaut* (1982) are the two key texts of Chaos Magic. Carroll's own definition of the practice is as follows: 'Chaosists usually accept the meta-belief that belief itself is only a tool for achieving effects; it is not an end in itself.' Belief, in other words, is simply a state of mind: it is for each practitioner to create their own reality – and their own rules for how to influence that reality.

Austin Osman Spare, and cat, in 1953.

Austin Osman Spare

Born in London in 1886, Austin Osman Spare has had more influence on contemporary magic than almost anyone else. Trained as an artist, he found success at a very young age with art nouveau-style works. However, he also dabbled in automatic writing and drawing – displaying a leaning towards the subversion of surrealism – and was drawn to the works of Agrippa, Madame Blavatsky and Éliphas Lévi. Over time, this interest in the occult fed into his art.

One of Spare's earliest published works is *The Book of Pleasure* (1913), a grimoire originally conceived with only pictures and no words. In 'writing' the book, Spare employed a technique whereby words expressing a desired outcome were compressed and abstracted into a series of sigils – what has been called an 'alphabet of desire'. The process had four stages. First, a desired outcome was expressed in words, after which all the repeated letters were removed. Next, the expression was 'charged' through a process of meditation or ecstatic dancing before finally being forgotten and allowed to disappear into the subconscious. It was at this point that the magic could become effective.

Spare claimed to have been educated in magic in his teens by a mysterious woman he called his 'witch mother'. Most probably, however, this story formed part of his self-mythologizing. What *is* known for certain is that Spare met Aleister Crowley around 1908, and went on to become a member of the A.∴A.∴, until 1912. Spare, though, was not impressed by the hierarchy and formality of ceremonial magic, and soon fell out with Crowley. Years later, in the 1950s, he was introduced to Gerald Gardner, for whom he created a talisman using his sigils.

Within contemporary magical circles, Spare is best known for his idiosyncratic philosophy known as Zos Kia Cultus, where 'Zos' stands for the human mind, and 'Kia' for the universal. Spare's philosophy is in many ways a retelling of the microcosm–macrocosm principle, and is close to the Chinese concept of Tao. In common with the surrealist artists, Spare believed in the power of the unconscious mind, maintaining that magical ability could come from repressed desires.

A self-portrait by a young Austin Osman Spare, in which he depicts himself as a magician.

CONTEMPORARY MAGIC

It is perhaps inevitable that in an age driven by technology, paganism should be making something of a comeback. Indeed, an inevitable reaction to the digitization and secularization of life may well be to look for something more essential and closer to nature.

Neopaganism is an umbrella term used to describe a raft of New Age belief systems based in a distant, pre-Christian past. Arguably dating back to the Renaissance, neopaganism was boosted by the Romantic revival of indigenous folk tales and magic at the end of the eighteenth century. A more recent impetus has been the emergence of such groups as the ecology movement, which seeks to reconnect with the land.

Containing elements of animism, neoshamanism – a branch of neopaganism – is an attempt to return to a more immediate bond with the world. Practitioners use drumming, ritual dance and psychoactive substances to access other levels of consciousness. They also embrace 'power animals', the equivalent of familiar spirits in European witchcraft.

An altar bearing votive offerings at a spring blót (a sacrificial ceremony in honour of the Norse gods) held by the Swedish Ásatrú Society. Placed among the offerings, which include barley, mead and oranges, is an image of Freya, the Norse god of fertility.

A witch from Melbourne, Australia, performs rituals at home after the overturning of a 200-year-old act prohibiting the 'use of any kind of witchcraft, sorcery, enchantment or conjuration'.

The rediscovery of witchcraft can be linked directly to the feminist movement that burgeoned over the course of the twentieth century. Goddesses of the past – Diana, Ceres, Artemis, Freya – are seen as manifestations of a single 'sacred feminine'. At the heart of this renewed interest in witchcraft is the ancient preoccupation with fertility, especially of the land. Indeed, as the American mythologist Joseph Campbell put it, 'woman magic and earth magic are the same'.

The Internet has created many more opportunities for members of the occult community to meet one another, even allowing them to celebrate rituals virtually. Of course, not everything runs smoothly: in 2012, a library in Salem, Massachusetts, prevented its users from accessing 'occult' websites – including those about Wicca – leading to the American Civil Liberties Union bringing a case against it. The ACLU was victorious.

FURTHER READING & LIST OF QUOTATIONS

FURTHER READING

The following publications are aimed at the general reader, and should be widely available. Recommendations on particular themes, such as astrology, alchemy and so on, can be found under the relevant chapter.

GENERAL

Matilde Battistini, *Astrology, Magic, and Alchemy in Art* (trans. Rosanna M. Giammanco Frongia), Los Angeles: The J. Paul Getty Museum, 2007

David J. Collins (ed.), *The Cambridge History of Magic and Witchcraft in the West: From Antiquity to the Present*, New York and Cambridge: Cambridge University Press, 2015

Brian Copenhaver, *The Book of Magic: From Antiquity to the Enlightenment*, London: Penguin Classics, 2015

Owen Davies, *Magic: A Very Short Introduction*, Oxford: Oxford University Press, 2012

Nevill Drury, *Magic and Witchcraft: From Shamanism to the Technopagans*, London: Thames & Hudson, 2004

Antoine Faivre, *Access to Western Esotericism* (Suny Series in Western Esoteric Traditions), New York: SUNY Press, 1994

Antoine Faivre, *Western Esotericism: A Concise History* (SUNY Series in Western Esoteric Traditions) (trans. Christine Rhone), New York: SUNY Press, 2010

James George Frazer, *The Golden Bough: A Study in Magic and Religion: A New Abridgement from the Second and Third Editions*, Oxford: Oxford University Press, 2009

Fred Gettings, *Encyclopedia of the Occult*, London: Rider & Co., 1986

Fred Gettings, *Visions of the Occult: A Visual Panorama of the Worlds of Magic, Divination and the Occult.* London: Guild Publishing Ltd, 1987

Grillot de Givry, *Witchcraft, Magic and Alchemy* (trans. J. Courtenay Locke), New York: Dover, 2009 [1931]

Joscelyn Godwin, *The Golden Thread: The Ageless Wisdom of the Western Mystery Tradition*, Wheaton, Ill.: Quest Books, 2007

Susan Greenwood, *The Illustrated History of Magic and Witchcraft*, Wigston: Anness Publishing, 2011

Manly P. Hall, *Secret Teachings of All Ages*, New York: Jeremy P. Tarcher, 2004

Francis King, *Magic: The Western Tradition*, London: Thames & Hudson, 1975

Christopher Partridge, *The Occult World*, Abingdon: Routledge, 2015

Alexander Roob, *Alchemy & Mysticism (Hermetic Museum)*, Cologne: Taschen, 2014

I: ANCIENT MAGIC

Tzvi Abusch, *Mesopotamian Witchcraft: Towards a History and Understanding of Babylonian Witchcraft Beliefs and Literature*, Leiden: Brill, 2002

Tzvi Abusch and Karel van der Toorn, *Mesopotamian Magic: Textual, Historical and Interpretative Perspectives*, Leiden: Brill, 2000

Michael Baigent, *Astrology in Ancient Mesopotamia: The Science of Omens and the Knowledge of the Heavens*, New York: Bear & Co., 2015

Jeremy Black and Anthony Green, *Gods, Demons and Symbols of Ancient Mesopotamia*, Austin: University of Texas Press, 1992

Bob Brier, *Ancient Egyptian Magic*, New York: William Morrow Paperbacks, 1998

Nicholas Campion, *A History of Western Astrology*, 2 vols, New York: Continuum, 2006–2009

Walter Farber, 'Witchcraft, Magic, and Divination in Ancient Mesopotamia', in Jack M. Sasson *et al.* (eds), *Civilizations of the Ancient Near East, Volume 3*, New York: Charles Scribner's Sons, 1995

Geraldine Pinch, *Magic in Ancient Egypt*, University of Texas Press, 2010

Kasia Szpakowska (ed.), *Through a Glass Darkly: Magic, Dreams, and Prophecy in Ancient Egypt*, Swansea: Classical Press of Wales, 2006

Richard Wilhelm and Cary F. Baynes (trans.), *I Ching or Book of Changes*, New York: Arkana, 1989

II: GREEK & ROMAN MAGIC

Gideon Bohak, *Ancient Jewish Magic: A History*, Cambridge: Cambridge University Press, 2008

Derek Collins, *Magic in the Ancient Greek World*, Hoboken, N.J.: Wiley Blackwell, 2008

Brian Copenhaver, *Hermetica: The Greek Corpus Hermeticum and the Latin Asclepius in a New English Translation: With Notes and Introduction*, Cambridge: Cambridge University Press, 2008

Christopher A. Faraone, *Talismans and Trojan Horses: Guardian Statues in Ancient Greek Myth and Ritual*, Oxford: Oxford University Press, 1992

Christopher A. Faraone, *Ancient Greek Love Magic*, Cambridge, Mass.: Harvard University Press, 1999

Christopher A. Faraone and Dirk Obbink (eds), *Magika Hiera: Ancient Greek Magic and Religion*, New York: Oxford University Press, 1991

John G. Gager, *Curse Tablets and Binding Spells from the Ancient World*, Oxford: Oxford University Press, 1992

Fritz Graf, *Magic in the Ancient World* (trans. Franklin Philip), Cambridge, Mass.: Harvard University Press, 1997

Gary Lachman, *The Quest for Hermes Trismegistus: From Ancient Egypt to the Modern World*, Edinburgh: Floris, 2011

Georg Luck, *Arcana Mundi: Magic and the Occult in the Greek and Roman Worlds – A Collection of Ancient Texts*, Baltimore: John Hopkins Universtiy Press, 2006

Daniel Chanan Matt, *The Essential Kabbalah: The Heart of Jewish Mysticism*, New York: HarperOne, 1995

Marvin W. Meyer and Richard Smith, *Ancient Christian Magic*, Princeton: Princeton University Press, 1999

Daniel Ogden, *Night's Black Agents: Witches, Wizards and the Dead in the Ancient World*, London: Bloomsbury Academic, 2008

Roelof Van Den Broek and Wouter J. Hanegraaff (eds), *Gnosis & Hermeticism from Antiquity to Modern Time* (SUNY Series in Western Esoteric Traditions), New York: SUNY Press, 1997

III: NORTHERN MAGIC

Sioned Davies (trans.), *The Mabinogion*, Oxford: Oxford World's Classics, 2008

Jeffrey Gantz, *Early Irish Myths and Sagas*, London: Penguin Classics, 2000

Richard Heygate and Philip Carr-Gomm, *The Book of English Magic*, London: Hodder Paperbacks, 2010

Ronald Hutton, *Blood and Mistletoe: The History of the Druids in Britain*, New Haven: Yale University Press, 2011

Carolyne Larrington (trans.), *The Poetic Edda*, Oxford: Oxford World's Classics, 2014

Thomas Malory, *Le Morte d'Arthur* (trans. Janet Cowen), London: Penguin, 2004

Stephen A. Mitchell, *Witchcraft and Magic in the Nordic Middle Ages* (The Middle Ages Series), Philadelphia: University of Pennsylvania Press, 2013

Nigel Pennick, *Pagan Magic of the Northern Tradition: Customs, Rites, and Ceremonies*, New York: Destiny Books, 2015

Snorri Sturlson, *The Prose Edda: Norse Mythology* (trans. Jesse L. Byock), London: Penguin Classics, 2005

Edred Thorsson, *Runelore: The Magic, History, and Hidden Codes of the Runes*, Newburyport, Mass.: Weiser, 1987

IV: MEDIEVAL MAGIC

Robert Bartlett, *The Natural and the Supernatural in the Middle Ages* (The Wiles Lectures), Cambridge: Cambridge University Press, 2008

Owen Davies, *Grimoires: A History of Magic Books*, Basingstoke: Palgrave Macmillan, 2010

Valerie Irene Jane Flint, *The Rise of Magic in Early Medieval Europe*, Princeton: Princeton University Press, 1994

K. Jolly, C. Raudvere and E. Peters (eds), *The Athlone History of Witchcraft and Magic in Europe, Volume 3: The Middle Ages*, London: Athlone, 2002

Richard Kieckhefer, *Magic in the Middle Ages*, Cambridge: Cambridge University Press, 2000

Stanislas Klossowski de Rola, *Alchemy: The Secret Art* (Art and Imagination Series), London: Thames & Hudson, 2013

Anne Lawrence-Mathers and Carolina Escobar-Vargas, *Magic and Medieval Society*, New York: Routledge, 2014

P. G. Maxwell-Stuart (ed.), *The Occult in Medieval Europe, 500–1500*, Basingstoke: Palgrave Macmillan, 2005

Catherine Rider, *Magic and Religion in Medieval England*, London: Reaktion, 2013

V: RENAISSANCE MAGIC

Heinrich Cornelius Agrippa von Nettesheim, *The Three Books of Occult Philosophy: A Complete Edition* (ed. Donald Tyson), Woodbury, Minn.: Llewellyn, 1993

Stuart Clark, *Thinking with Demons: The Idea of Witchcraft in Early Modern Europe*, Oxford: Oxford University Press, 1997

Ioan P. Culianu, *Eros and Magic in the Renaissance*, Chicago: University of Chicago Press, 1987

A. Debus and I. Merkel (eds), *Hermeticism and the Renaissance: Intellectual History and the Occult in Early Modern Europe*, Washington, D.C.: Folger Shakespeare Library, 1988

Stanislas Klossowski de Rola, *The Golden Game: Alchemical Engravings of the Seventeenth Century*, London: Thames & Hudson, 1988

Christopher S. Mackay (trans.), *The Hammer of Witches: A Complete Translation of the Malleus Maleficarum*, Cambridge: Cambridge University Press, 2009

John S. Mebane, *Renaissance Magic and the Return of the Golden Age: The Occult Tradition and Marlowe, Jonson, and Shakespeare*, Lincoln, Nebr.: University of Nebraska Press, 1992

Edward Peters and Alan Charles Kors (eds), *Witchcraft in Europe, 400–1700: A Documentary History*, Philadelphia: University of Pennsylvania Press, 2000

Liana Saif, *The Arabic Influences on Early Modern Occult Philosophy* (Palgrave Historical Studies in Witchcraft and Magic), Basingstoke: Palgrave Macmillan, 2015

D. P. Walker, *Spiritual and Demonic Magic: From Ficino to Campanella* (Magic in History Series), Philadelphia: Pennsylvania State University Press, 2000

Benjamin Woolley, *The Queen's Conjuror: The Science and Magic of Dr Dee*, London: Flamingo, 2002

Frances A. Yates, *Giordano Bruno and the Hermetic Tradition*, Chicago: University of Chicago Press, 1991

Frances A. Yates, *The Occult Philosophy in the Elizabethan Age*, New York: Routledge, 2001

VI: WORLD OF MAGIC

Alexandra David-Neel, *Magic and Mystery in Tibet*, New York: Dover, 1971

Thomas A. DuBois, *An Introduction to Shamanism*, Cambridge: Cambridge University Press, 2009

Mircea Eliade, *Shamanism: Archaic Techniques of Ecstasy* (Bollingen Series), Princeton: Princeton University Press, 2004

Tong Enzheng, 'Magicians, Magic, and Shamanism in Ancient China', in *Journal of East Asian Archaeology*, vol. 4, no. 1, pp. 27–73, 2002

Graham Harvey, *Shamanism: A Reader*, New York: Routledge, 2002

Philip A. Kuhn, *Soulstealers: The Chinese Sorcery Scare of 1768*, Cambridge, Mass.: Harvard University Press, 2006

Ireneus Laszlo Legeza, *Tao Magic: The Chinese Art of the Occult*, New York: Pantheon Books, 1975

VII: ENLIGHTENMENT MAGIC

Owen Davies and Willem de Blécourt, *Beyond the Witch Trials: Witchcraft and Magic in Enlightenment Europe*, Manchester: Manchester University Press, 2004

John V. Fleming, *The Dark Side of the Enlightenment: Wizards, Alchemists and Spiritual Seekers in the Age of Reason*, New York: W. W. Norton, 2013

Wouter J. Hanegraaff, *Esotericism and the Academy: Rejected Knowledge in Western Culture*, Cambridge: Cambridge University Press, 2014

Paul Kléber Monod, *Solomon's Secret Arts: The Occult in the Age of Enlightenment*, New Haven: Yale University Press, 2013

Lynn Picknett and Clive Prince, *The Forbidden Universe: The Occult Origins of Science and the Search for the Mind of God*, London: Constable, 2011

Frances Yates, *The Rosicrucian Enlightenment*, New York: Routledge Classics, 2001

VIII: THE MAGIC REVIVAL

Francis Barrett, *The Magus: A Complete System of Occult Philosophy*, San Francisco: Red Wheel/Weiser, 2000

H. P. Blavatsky, *Secret Doctrine*, New York: Jeremy P. Tarcher, 2009

Aleister Crowley, *Magick: Liber ABA, Book 4*, San Francisco: Red Wheel/Weiser, 1994

Éliphas Lévi, *Transcendental Magic: Its Doctrine and Ritual* (trans. Arthur Edward Waite), London: Bracken, 1995

S. L. MacGregor Mathers (trans.), *The Book of the Sacred Magic of Abramelin the Mage*, New York: Dover, 1975

Israel Regardie, with John Michael Greer, *The Golden Dawn: The Original Account of the Teachings, Rites, and Ceremonies of the Hermetic Order*, Woodbury, Minn.: Llewellyn, 2016

Arthur Edward Waite, *The Book of Ceremonial Magic*, New York: Citadel Press, 1986

IX: MODERN MAGIC

Margot Adler, *Drawing Down the Moon: Witches, Druids, Goddess-Worshippers, and Other Pagans in America*, London: Penguin, 1997

Franz Bardon, *Initiation into Hermetics*, Holladay: Merkur Publishing Company, 2015

Raymond Buckland, *Buckland's Complete Book of Witchcraft* (Llewellyn's Practical Magick), Woodbury, Minn.: Llewellyn, 2002

Peter J. Carroll, *Liber Null & Psychonaut: An Introduction to Chaos Magic*, San Francisco: Red Wheel/Weiser, 1987

Julius Evola and the UR Group, *Introduction to Magic: Rituals and Practical Techniques for the Magus*, New York: Inner Traditions, 2001

Gerald Gardner, *Witchcraft Today*, New York: Citadel Press, 2004

Ronald Hutton, *The Triumph of the Moon: A History of Modern Pagan Witchcraft*, Oxford: Oxford University Press, 2001

C. G. Jung, *Psychology and Alchemy*, New York: Routledge, 1980

Louis Pauwels and Jacques Bergier, *The Morning of the Magicians* (Mysteries of the Universe) (trans. Rollo Mays), London: Souvenir Press, 2011

Robert Place, *The Tarot: History, Symbolism, and Divination*, New York: TarcherPerigee, 2005

Starhawk, *The Spiral Dance: A Rebirth of the Ancient Religion of the Goddess*, New York: HarperOne, 1999

LIST OF QUOTATIONS

Quotations from the Bible are taken from the King James version.

Page 8, Pliny: From Book XXX of *The Natural History of Pliny* (trans. John Bostock and H. T. Riley), London: H. G. Bohn, 1855–7

Page 15, Arthur C. Clarke: From 'Hazards of Prophecy: The Failure of Imagination', in *Profiles of the Future: An Inquiry into the Limits of the Possible*, New York: Harper & Row, 1973

Page 16, Aleister Crowley: From *Magick in Theory and Practice*, London: Dover, 1929

Page 16, James George Frazer: From *The Golden Bough: A Study in Magic and Religion*, New York: Macmillan, 1922

Page 29, *Maqlû* extract: From Walter Farber, 'Witchcraft, Magic, and Divination in Ancient Mesopotamia', in Jack M. Sasson *et al.* (eds), *Civilizations of the Ancient Near East, Volume 3*, New York: Charles Scribner's Sons, 1995, pp. 1896–8

Page 33, Agrippa: From Brian P. Copenhaver, 'Astrology and Magic', in Charles B. Schmitt *et al.* (eds), *The Cambridge History of Renaissance Philosophy*, Cambridge: Cambridge University Press, 1988

Page 37, Pliny: From Book XXX of *The Natural History of Pliny* (trans. Bostock and Riley)

Page 59: From Book 2, Chapter 8 of *The Key of Solomon* (trans. S. L. MacGregor Mathers)

Page 62, Plato: From *The Republic* (trans. Benjamin Jowett), Oxford: Clarendon Press, 1888

Page 66, Plato: From *Euthydemus* (trans. W. R. M. Lamb), Cambridge, Mass.: Harvard University Press, 1924

Page 72, Francis Barrett: From *The Magus, or Celestial Intelligencer*, London: Lackington, Allen, and Co., 1801

Page 86, love spell from Greek Magical Papyri (PGM IV, 1525–31): From Hans Dieter Betz, *The Greek Magical Papyri in Translation, Including the Demotic Spells, Volume 1*, Chicago: University of Chicago Press, 1996

Page 91, on Hermes Trismegistus (PGM VIII, 1–63): From Betz, *The Greek Magical Papyri in Translation*

Page 104, Pliny: From *The Natural History of Pliny* (trans. Bostock and Riley)

Page 107, extract from *Poetic Edda*: From Patricia Terry (trans.), *Poems of the Elder Edda*, Philadelphia: University of Pennsylvania Press, 2014

Page 162, Albertus: From Benedek Láng, *Unlocked Books: Manuscripts of Learned Magic in the Medieval Libraries of Central Europe*, Philadelphia: Pennsylvania State University Press, 2010

Page 169, extract from Lex Cornelia: From Immanuel Kant, *The Philosophy of Law* (trans. W. Hastie), Edinburgh: T. & T. Clark, 1887

Page 170, Thomas Aquinas: From *Summa Theologica*, vol. 3, part II, second section, Q. 96, art. 1

Page 190, Marsilio Ficino: From Members of the Language Department of the School of Economic Science, London (trans.), *The Letters of Marsilio Ficino*, 10 vols, London: Shepheard-Walwyn, 1975–2015

Page 193, Sir Walter Raleigh: From *The Works of Sir Walter Ralegh*, Oxford: Oxford University Press, 1829, p. 381

Page 196, Pico della Mirandola: From *Oration on the Dignity of Man* (trans. A. Robert Caponigri), Chicago: Regnery, 1956

Page 200, James George Frazer: From *The Golden Bough*

Page 275, Gu Yong: From Kenneth J. Dewoskin, *Doctors, Diviners and Magicians of Ancient China: Biographies of Fang-shih*, New York: Columbia University Press, 1983

Page 291, Johannes Kepler: From appendix to *Harmonices Mundi and Apology*, 1622

Page 292, Elias Ashmole: From 'Annotations', in *Theatrum Chemicum Britannicum*, London, 1652, p. 444

Page 371, Phil Hine: From *Condensed Chaos: An Introduction to Chaos Magic*, Tempe, Ariz.: New Falcon, 1995

Page 384, Peter J. Carroll: From a lecture given by Joseph Max at 2nd Pantheacon Convention, San Jose, California, 18 February 1996, available online at www.magma.ca/~yeti/lecture.htm (accessed May 2016)

MAGICAL PLACES TO VISIT

The following is a list of museums, bookshops, markets and libraries that are related to magic, the occult and witchcraft. Details of opening times and entrance fees can be found on each venue's website (where available); some are open by appointment only.

BOLIVIA
Mercado de las Brujas
Melchor Jimenez, La Paz
A well-known 'witches' market', selling medicinal plants and the dried animals used in Bolivian magic.

CZECH REPUBLIC
Museum of Alchemists and Magicians of Old Prague
Jánský Vršek 8, Prague 1
www.muzeumalchymistu.cz

Museum of Alchemy
Haštalská 1, 110 00, Prague 1
www.alchemiae.cz

Two museums dedicated to alchemy in one of the European cities most associated with the history of the subject.

DENMARK
Astrology Museum of Copenhagen
Teglgården (Astrologihuset),
Teglværksgade 37, 2100 Copenhagen
www.asmu.dk

FRANCE
Haxahus: The Witches' House
Place de l'Église, 68750 Bergheim
www.haxahus.org
The site of famous witch trials in the late 16th and 17th centuries.

Maison de la Magie Robert-Houdin
1 Place du Château, 41000 Blois
www.maisondelamagie.fr

Musée de la Sorcellerie
La Jonchère, 18410 Blancafort
www.musee-sorcellerie.fr

GERMANY
Alte Burg Penzlin
Warener Chausee 55a, D-17217 Penzlin
A museum highlighting the persecution of witches in the late Middle Ages and early modern period. Features the only surviving examples of 'witch dungeons'.

Magicum: Berlin Magic Museum
Große Hamburger Str. 17, 10115 Berlin
www.magicum-berlin.de
Covers the subjects of astrology, witchcraft and occult magic, in the context of religion.

Museum Hexenbürgermeisterhaus Lemgo
Breite Str. 17–19, D-32657 Lemgo
www.hexenbuergermeisterhaus.de
The former house of a witch-hunter. Includes displays on the history of witchcraft in the local area.

ICELAND
Museum of Icelandic Sorcery and Witchcraft
www.galdrasyning.is
Dedicated to the history of Icelandic sorcery and magical staves – and home of the famous 'necropants'.

ITALY
Museo dei Tarocchi
Via Arturo Palmieri, 5/1 Riola,
40038 Vergato, Bologna
www.museodeitarocchi.net
A museum dedicated to the history of Tarot since the 15th century.

Museo di Triora: Etnografico e della Stregoneria
Corso Italia 1, 18010 Triora IM
www.museotriora.it
The town of Triora – sometimes referred to as the 'Salem of Italy' – is known for its persecution of witches in the late 16th century. In addition to the museum, it is possible to visit a supposed witches' lair, La Cabotina.

MEXICO
Mercado de Sonora
Mexico City, Mexico
www.mercadosonora.com.mx
A market renowned for the sale of magical items.

NETHERLANDS
Amsterdam Theosophical Library
Tolstraat 154, 1074 VM Amsterdam
www.theosofie.nl
A large collection of esoteric books, accessed by appointment only.

Bibliotheca Philosophica Hermetica
Keizersgracht 123, 1016 KV Amsterdam
www.ritmanlibrary.com
Open to the public, this 'Hermetic library' has a stunning collection of books and prints. It also stages regular Hermetic-themed exhibitions.

Museum de Heksenwaag
Leeuweringerstraat 2,
3421 AC Oudewater
www.heksenwaag.nl
This museum, 'The Witches' Weighhouse', features a display on witch-hunting and scales used to weigh witches.

PORTUGAL
Quinta da Regaleira
2710-567 Sintra
www.regaleira.pt
A stately home with curious grottoes and two 'wells of initiation' used in Tarot rites.

SOUTH KOREA
Gahoe Museum
17 Bukchon-ro 12-gil, Jongno-gu, Seoul
gahoemuseum.org (in Korean)
Contains an array of shamanic art and a large collection of amulets.

Museum of Shamanism
952-13, Jeongneung-3 dong,
Seongbuk-gu, Seoul
shamanismmuseum.org (in Korean)

SPAIN
Museo de Brujería y Supersticiones del Moncayo
Calle Sagrado Corazón de Jesús s/n,
50583 Trasmoz, Aragón
www.turismodezaragoza.es

Museo de la Brujería de Segovia
Daoiz 9, Segovia, Castilla y León

Museo de las Brujas
Calle de Beitikokarrika 22,
31710 Zugarramurdi, Navarra
www.turismozugarramurdi.com
Known as the 'witches' town', Zugarramurdi is home not only to this witchcraft museum but also to a series of caves said to have been used for witches' meetings.

Museo Lara
Calle Armiñán 29, 29400 Ronda,
Andalucia
www.museolara.org
Covers the history of witchcraft and of the Inquisition.

SWITZERLAND
Hexenmuseum Schweiz
Mühliacherweg 10, 5105 Auenstein
www.hexenmuseum.ch

Museum Klösterli, Schloss Wyher
Postfach 71, 6218 Ettiswil
www.historischesmuseum.lu.ch
Traces the history of magic and religion in the northern part of Switzerland.

UNITED KINGDOM
Atlantis Bookshop
49A Museum St, London WC1A 1LY
www.theatlantisbookshop.com
The oldest independent occult bookshop in London, founded in 1922 and frequented by Aleister Crowley and Gerald Gardner. It also puts on events and workshops.

The British Museum
Great Russell St, London WC1B 3DG
www.britishmuseum.org
Home to such magical objects as the *Maqlû* tablets and John Dee's scrying mirror, crystal ball and seals.

The Hellfire Caves
Church Lane, West Wycombe, High Wycombe, Buckinghamshire HP14 3AH
www.hellfirecaves.co.uk
The meeting place of Sir Francis Dashwood's Hellfire Club, rumoured also to be the site of black magic.

Horniman Museum and Gardens
100 London Road, Forest Hill,
London SE23 3PQ
www.horniman.ac.uk
A well-known anthropological collection containing a selection of amulets and a Haitian voodoo shrine.

The Magic Circle Museum
12 Stephenson Way, London NW1 2HD
www.themagiccircle.co.uk
A comprehensive collection of objects from the golden age of stage magic. Admission to the museum is restricted, and visits should be booked well in advance.

Mother Shipton's Cave
Prophecy Lodge, High Bridge,
Knaresborough, North Yorkshire HG5 8DD
www.mothershipton.co.uk
A spectacular cave said to have been inhabited by the witch and oracle Mother Shipton.

Museum of Witchcraft and Magic
Boscastle, Cornwall PL35 0HD
www.museumofwitchcraft.com
Houses one of the largest and most well-established witchcraft collections in the world.

Pitt Rivers Museum
Parks Road, Oxford OX1 3PW
www.prm.ox.ac.uk
Home to the anthropological collections of the University of Oxford, including more than 6,000 charms and amulets.

Treadwell's Bookshop
33 Store St, London WC1E 7BS
www.treadwells-london.com
London's best-known esoteric bookshop. It also sells ceremonial implements and organizes regular events.

UNITED STATES
John G. White Folklore Collection
Cleveland Public Library, 325 Superior Avenue NE, Cleveland, OH 44114
www.cpl.org
A rich collection of occult works.

Livingston Masonic Library
Grand Lodge of the State of New York,
71 W 23rd Street, 14th Floor,
New York, NY 10010
www.nymasoniclibrary.org
A masonic library rich in occult, esoteric and Hermetic publications. Open to the public.

New Orleans Historic Voodoo Museum
724 Dumaine St, New Orleans,
LA 70116

Rosicrucian Park
1660 Park Avenue, San Jose, CA 9519
www.rosicrucianpark.org
Incorporates the Egyptian Museum and the Alchemy Museum.

Salem Witch Museum
19½ Washington Square North, Salem,
MA 01970
www.salemwitchmuseum.com

The Warrens' Occult Museum
466–482 Monroe Turnpike, Monroe,
CT 06468
www.warrens.net
Famous for its large collection of haunted objects, and for being owned by paranormal investigators Ed and Lorraine Warren.

Witch Dungeon Museum
16 Lynde St, Salem, MA 01970
www.witchdungeon.com

LIST OF ILLUSTRATIONS

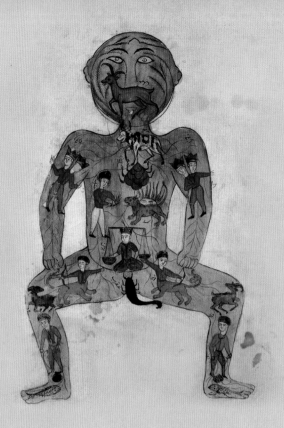

ACKNOWLEDGMENTS

I'd like to thank all of those who supported me while I was working on this book, none more so than my wife Rosa and daughter Alexandra. I'd also like to thank the authors and academics with whom I corresponded, and who gave permission for their works to be reproduced. As ever, the team at Thames & Hudson, led by Philip Watson, have been enthusiastic, supportive and patient. In particular, I'd like to thank my editor, Mark Ralph, the designer, Karin Fremer, and the production controller, Celia Falconer: they have improved this book in countless ways, and prevented all sorts of ridiculous errors slipping through. Needless to say, any faults that remain are mine.

Above: *A Persian version of the 'Zodiac man', showing the connection between the individual and the cosmos.*
Half-title: *The Devil appears to a group of witches, who present him with poppets.*
Frontispiece: *Goya's disturbing image of a witches' sabbath, with a demonic goat controlling proceedings.*

First published in the United Kingdom in 2016 by Thames & Hudson Ltd, 181A High Holborn, London WC1V 7QX

First published in the United States of America in 2016 by Thames & Hudson Inc., 500 Fifth Avenue, New York, New York 10110

Reprinted 2024

The Occult, Witchcraft and Magic © 2016 Christopher Dell

Designed by Karin Fremer

British Library Cataloguing-in-Publication Data
A catalogue record for this book is available from the British Library

Library of Congress Control Number 2015959510

ISBN 978-0-500-51888-5

Printed and bound in China, Lion Productions Ltd

FSC
MIX
Paper | Supporting responsible forestry
FSC® C001701
www.fsc.org

Be the first to know about our new releases, exclusive content and author events by visiting
thamesandhudson.com
thamesandhudsonusa.com
thamesandhudson.com.au